INTERNET OF THINGS AND THE LAW

PLI
PRESS

PLI PRESS is Practising Law Institute's highly regarded publishing division. Our team of dedicated publishing and information professionals is committed to providing you the highest-quality analysis and practice guidance while keeping you updated on current legal developments.

Each year, **PLI PRESS** publishes more than 100 treatises, practice guides, books on lawyering skills, yearbooks, answer books, and journals—written and updated by leading practitioners in their respective practice areas, and edited and managed by our in-house legal editors. We also produce more than 200 Course Handbook titles annually, each corresponding to one of PLI's award-winning CLE programs.

QUESTIONS ABOUT THIS PUBLICATION?

If you have questions about updates to this publication, billing, or shipments, or would like information about our other products, please contact **PLI customer service** at info@pli.edu or at (800) 260-4PLI.

For any other questions or suggestions about this book, please contact the PLI Press **editorial department** at plipress@pli.edu.

For general information about Practising Law Institute, please visit **www.pli.edu**.

To view a full list of PLI Press publications,
visit **www.pli.edu/plipress**.

Practising Law Institute • 1177 Avenue of the Americas • New York, NY 10036

INTERNET OF THINGS AND THE LAW

Thaddeus Hoffmeister

Practising Law Institute
New York City
#267497

This work is designed to provide practical and useful information on the subject matter covered. However, it is sold with the understanding that neither the publisher nor the author is engaged in rendering legal, accounting, or other professional services. If legal advice or other expert assistance is required, the services of a competent professional should be sought.

Legal Editor: Lori Wood

LCCN: 2019934931

ISBN: 978-1-4024-3363-4

This book is dedicated to A and Z.

About the Author

Thaddeus Hoffmeister is a professor at the University of Dayton School of Law where he teaches courses related to criminal law, juries, and technology. He has published a number of books, law review articles, and essays, and has been widely cited in various media outlets ranging from the *New York Times* to CNN to *Wired* magazine. Outside of his work in academia, Professor Hoffmeister teaches legal seminars to attorneys and judges, works as an (acting) Magistrate Judge in Dayton Municipal Court, and serves as a Judge Advocate General in the National Guard.

Table of Chapters

Table of Contents

Chapter 1   What Is IoT?

Chapter 2   Regulatory Framework of the IoT

Chapter 3   Privacy

Chapter 4   Security

Chapter 5   Contracts

Chapter 6   Ownership and Intellectual Property

Chapter 7   Consumer Protection Litigation

Chapter 10   International Law

Preface

This book explores the intersection of the Internet of Things (IoT) and the law. The IoT has been defined as objects or "things" embedded with technology to allow them to interact in real time with the physical environment, people, and other devices. The IoT ranges from everyday household products like a coffee maker and toothbrush to insulin pumps and component parts of machines. Essentially, if the device has an on/off switch there is a very good chance that it is or will become part of the IoT.

While all the ramifications of the IoT are not fully understood today, one thing is very clear: the IoT will impact our legal system. Therefore, law students, attorneys, and judges should devote more time preparing for and considering the legal implications of a world where anything that can be connected, will be connected. This book hopes to serve as a starting point for those seeking a deeper understanding of the IoT's role within the law or those searching for answers to novel legal questions that arise when machines go online to communicate with each other.

Topics covered in this book range from consumer protection to contracts to intellectual property to criminal law/procedure to privacy and security. Two other areas—privacy and security—are the biggest hurdles to universal acceptance of the IoT and are examined in-depth. While many consider privacy and security two sides of the same coin, they are not and should be treated differently. Finally, the last chapter of the book explores how other countries are addressing the challenges of living in an IoT world.

Acknowledgments

This book has been greatly aided by a number of current and former students who are now successful attorneys. First and foremost, I would like to acknowledge the work of Daniel (DJ) Berens, who spent a significant amount of time on the book. He wrote and edited a number of chapters. This book would not be in its current form without the painstaking efforts of DJ, who has a sharp legal mind coupled with a wide breadth of knowledge about all things related to technology.

Next, I would like to thank Alysa Medina, who wrote chapter 10 and edited a number of other chapters. Alysa is quickly developing into an expert in international law and has impressive research and writing skills. Other individuals deserving of acknowledgment are Sana Hussain for her work on chapter 6, Madison Rittley for chapter 7, and Nicolette Trevenen for her overall editing and writing abilities. Finally, I would like to acknowledge Lauren Devine, my current research assistant, who skillfully edited the entire book.

Chapter 1

What Is IoT?

§ 1:1   Definition of IoT

The Internet of Things—IoT—has been defined in different ways.[1] It has been stated that "[t]he term is a catch-all for the proliferation of objects in our homes and workplaces and cities that are acquiring varying degrees of networked intelligence. Devices that sense and communicate are not new, but technological developments have made

---

1.   Roberto Minerva, Abyi Biru & Domenico Rotondi, *Towards a Definition of the Internet of Things*, IEEE INTERNET INITIATIVE (May 27, 2015).

sensing and connectivity inexpensive, unobtrusive and ubiquitous."[2] Others define IoT as objects or things embedded with technology that allows them to interact with the physical environment, people, and other devices in real time.[3] Merriam-Webster's online dictionary defines IoT as the "networking capability that allows information to be sent to and received from objects and devices (such as fixtures and kitchen appliances) using the Internet." Some have even described the IoT as "connecting any device with an on and off switch to the Internet (and/or to each other)."[4]

The National Institute of Standards and Technology has distinguished IoT from the "Network of Things,"[5] concluding that the former refers to a device "tethered to the Internet," while the latter could be a device connected to a local area network as opposed to the Internet. This distinction was made in order to allow technologists a method of talking about the same things when discussing different parts of the IoT.[6]

Another distinction has been drawn between IoT and "the Internet of Devices." Here, a "device" is defined as "technology that collects data or interacts with its environment, and differentiates it from 'things,' which refers to objects about which data is collected."[7] Finally, while computers, smartphones, tablets, and similar devices are used to control or communicate with other devices, they are generally excluded from the definition of "things."

Defining IoT matters for a number of reasons, particularly as it concerns the regulation of the IoT. The broader the definition, the more difficult it is to legislate in this area.[8]

§ 1:2   History of the IoT

If placed on the Internet's historical timeline, the IoT might be viewed as the final stage of Internet development. Stage I occurred

---

2.   *Clearly Opaque Privacy Risks of the Internet of Things*, THE INTERNET OF THINGS PRIVACY FORUM (May 2018).

3.   Irena Bojanova, *Defining the Internet of Things*, COMPUTING NOW (Mar. 16, 2015).

4.   Jacob Morgan, *A Simple Explanation of the 'Internet of Things,'* FORBES (May 13, 2014).

5.   Jeffrey Voas, *Networks of 'Things,'* NIST Special Publication 800-183 (July 2016), https://nvlpubs.nist.gov/nistpubs/SpecialPublications/NIST.SP.800-183.pdf.

6.   Mohana Ravindranath, *Who's in Charge of Regulating the Internet of Things?*, NEXTGOV.COM (2016), www.nextgov.com/emerging-tech/2016/09/internet-things-regulating-charge/131208/ (last visited Jan. 25, 2018).

7.   Tom Glover, *Connected Things, Not Devices*, THOUGHTWORKS (Jan. 1, 2018).

8.   Derek B. Johnson, *Why Is No One Raising a Hand to Regulate the Internet of Things?*, FCW (Mar. 16, 2018).

— monitor products

with the creation of the Internet by ARPANET in the late 1960s.[9] Stage II illustrates the commercialization of the Internet which began with the creation of the World Wide Web in 1989. Stage III marked the proliferation of social media sites in the 2000s, which allowed individuals to communicate and share ideas with each other online. Stage IV is when the IoT emerged; machines are now able to interact and share ideas with each other. Some believe that the IoT will lead to a world where objects and people interact seamlessly and the Internet disappears as a separate entity.

The first recorded use of the phrase "Internet of Things" was by Kevin Ashton in a 1999 presentation to senior executives at Proctor & Gamble in Cincinnati, Ohio.[10] Ashton used the term to describe how Radio Frequency Identification (RFID) tags could be linked to the Internet. The term was then legitimized in 2005 when the International Telecommunications Union published a report entitled "The Internet of Things."[11] The phrase was added to the Oxford English Dictionary in 2013 and defined as follows: "noun—a proposed development of the Internet in which everyday objects have network connections, allowing them to send and receive data."[12]

While the specific terminology might have been novel in 1999, the concept underlying the IoT had been around since at least the 1980s. Common business practices at that time already included placing RFID tags on products in stores to monitor inventory and creating sensor networks to monitor electricity use in hotels.[13] One of the first-ever examples of a consumer product connected to the Internet (at the time ARPANET) occurred in the early 1980s at Carnegie Mellon University.[14] Programmers connected a Coke machine to the ARPANET so that individuals could monitor the availability of products without physically going to the machine.[15]

The subsequent expansion of IoT devices into the domestic or non-commercial market can be attributed to three major factors. First, the price of sensors, a key component of IoT devices, dropped dramatically. In the 1980s, when IoT devices first arrived on the scene, they

9. Thaddeus Hoffmeister, *Effective Social Networking for Lawyers: #KeepingUpWithTheEthics*, 26th Annual PILT Seminar (May 17, 2016).
10. Scott Shackelford et al., *When Toasters Attack: A Polycentric Approach to Enhancing the "Security of Things,"* 2017 U. ILL. L. REV. 415.
11. John Gudgel, *Objects of Concern? Risk, Rewards and Regulation in the "Internet of Things,"* SSRN (Apr. 30, 2014).
12. *Id.*
13. Internet of Things: Privacy & Security in a Connected World, FTC STAFF REPORT (Jan. 2015).
14. Dennis Kennedy, *Webbed World Preparing for the Internet of Things*, 100-JUL A.B.A. J. 29 (July 2014).
15. *Id.*

required Microelectromechanical systems (MEMS).[16] Initially, these sensors cost approximately $25 per unit. Today, those same sensors cost only $1 per unit. The decrease in price allowed manufacturers of IoT devices to add wireless chips to almost any device for a small cost.[17]

The second factor relates to an increased awareness of companies and consumer product manufacturers that basic items could provide them with valuable information about consumers' habits and preferences.[18] The data collected by IoT devices can be stored locally, shared wirelessly, or centrally collected to allow for easy monitoring by third parties. Therefore, this information, especially when combined with offline data, can create very precise consumer profiles.[19]

The third factor influencing the expansion of IoT devices into the mainstream market is the widespread availability of broadband Internet.[20] With high-speed Internet connections, devices are now able to communicate with each other in most parts of the developed world.[21]

Today, IoT devices are commonplace for both consumer-facing and industrial purposes. This in turn has led to greater awareness and appreciation of IoT by society as a whole.

§ 1:3   How the IoT Works

An object becomes part of the IoT because it has a computer chip or similar component attached to or embedded within it.[22] This chip or component then in turn provides the object with a unique identifier and Internet connectivity. With this connectivity, the object can communicate with a network of computers and other smart objects. Connectivity to the Internet can be wired or wireless. Once objects connect to the Internet and interact with other Internet-connected devices they become "smart" objects or devices.[23]

---

16.   Alexander Wolfe, *Little MEMS Sensors Make Big Data Sing*, FORBES (June 10, 2013).

17.   Scott Shackelford et al., *When Toasters Attack: A Polycentric Approach to Enhancing the "Security of Things,"* 2017 U. ILL. L. REV. 415.

18.   Nikole Davenport, *Smart Washers May Clean Your Clothes, But Hacks Can Clean Out Your Privacy, and Underdeveloped Regulations Could Leave You Hanging on a Line*, 32 J. MARSHALL J. INFO. TECH. & PRIVACY L. 259 (2016).

19.   *Id.*

20.   Shackelford et al., *supra* note 17.

21.   *Id.*

22.   Eric A. Fischer, *The Internet of Things: Frequently Asked Questions*, CONG. RESEARCH SERV. (Oct. 13, 2015).

23.   John Gudgel, *Objects of Concern? Risks, Rewards and Regulation in the "Internet of Things,"* unpublished manuscript (Apr. 29, 2014).

The information passed among IoT devices varies by device. For example, a smart thermometer may only pass along ambient temperature readings to a weather center.[24] In contrast, an IoT medical device that uses a number of sensors might transmit information about a person's body temperature, pulse, blood pressure, and other vital signs to a healthcare provider.[25]

cloud

In addition to passing information between machines, IoT devices can upload and store information to a cloud-based computing platform.[26] Once in the cloud, this information may be accessed for analytics, aggregation, assimilation, or utilization. The storage of information in remote computing platforms elevates their importance, in certain instances, to that of the IoT device itself.

On the industrial side, IoT devices can also be part of internal command networks.[27] Here, control systems maintain manufacturing processes through input from IoT devices and human operators. In addition, IoT devices can create systems that allow for the exchange of information and commands among themselves.

1. sensors collect data

Another way to examine the IoT involves dividing it into three parts. One part consists of the sensors that collect data.[28] The second part may be classified as the "smarts" that processes the information collected by the sensors. The third part is comprised of the actuators that impact our environment. If analogized to the human body, Part I is the eyes and ears, Part II is the brain, and Part III is the hands and feet. This analogy closely resembles a robot.

2. smarts

3. actuators impact environmen

Finally, in order for the IoT communication functionality to be exact, the object must be distinguished in some fashion. This occurs via the Internet Protocol (IP) address, a unique number assigned to every Internet-connected device.[29] At present, most devices connect to the Internet via a 32-bit IPv4 address. However, this form of IP address assignment can only handle 4.3 billion numbers which is vastly insufficient for all of the IoT devices coming online—not to mention smartphones. As a result, a new version of IP address assignment was created, IPv6, which will become the preferred method by which devices connect to the Internet. Fortunately, IPv6 can handle over 340 trillion IP addresses.[30]

---

24. Fischer, *supra* note 22.
25. *Id.*
26. Davenport, *supra* note 18.
27. *Id.*
28. Bruce Schneier, *We Need Stronger Cybersecurity Laws for the Internet of Things*, CNN (Nov. 10, 2018).
29. Gudgel, *supra* note 23.
30. Fischer, *supra* note 22.

§ 1:4   Benefits

Since the IoT is still relatively new and constantly evolving, determining the extent of its benefits to society is difficult. At least initially, it appears that the IoT will lead to "enhanced integration, efficiency, and productivity across many sectors of U.S. and global economies."[31] The IoT will also fundamentally change how people and objects interact.[32] Some describe the potential of IoT as enabling humans to construct cities that are more like computers in open air; where residents interact with the city in real time with an ongoing loop of information.[33]

At present, the IoT offers a wide array of benefits to individual users ranging from improving quality of life to reducing energy consumption. For example, IoT insulin pumps and blood-pressure cuffs allow patients to record, track, and monitor their own vital signs without physically going to a doctor's office. These, and similar IoT devices in the health field have "the ability to . . . draw the patients in and engage them in their own care."[34] Other examples include smart meters that can analyze consumer usage and identify problems with home appliances.[35] This in turn allows homeowners to make better choices about their use of electricity. Other sensors within the house, like "water bugs" can alert consumers about problems with pipes or water leaks. Additional benefits derived from the IoT are discussed later in this chapter.

§ 1:5   Drawbacks

Like with most advancements in technology, the IoT also raises a number of concerns. The problem areas cited most often are privacy and security. While many consider privacy and security to be two sides of the same coin, in reality, they are not, and should therefore be treated differently.[36] "Privacy" concerns safeguarding an individual's *confidential information* whereas "security" is the *method* by which that information is kept safe.[37]

With respect to privacy, the primary challenge lies within the type of information collected by the IoT device and how that information

---

31.   *Id.*
32.   *Id.*
33.   *Id.*
34.   Internet of Things Privacy & Security in a Connected World, FTC Staff Report (Jan. 2015).
35.   *Id.*
36.   Davenport, *supra* note 18.
37.   *Id.*

might be used.[38] For example, IoT devices both directly and indirectly create large amounts of data on consumers. This information then allows companies and the government to sort individuals more precisely than ever before.[39] This sorting could have data points that include the user's race, employment status, health history, and more.[40] When used individually, these data points may not reveal much relevant information; however, when combined in unexpected ways, they can tell a lot about an individual consumer.[41] This information, depending on how it is used, could have both positive and negative consequences for consumers. For example, employers, insurers, and lenders could use this information to engage in economic discrimination.[42] Another area of concern is whether consumers will have any real choice about what is revealed to a third party.[43]

As for security, hackers have been able to access a wide range of IoT devices ranging from refrigerators to thermostats to garage doors.[44] These types of hacks can, in certain instances, be more harmful to society than those involving traditional computers because IoT devices sense "the world around us, and affect that world in a direct physical manner."[45] Some also consider security to be an arms race between the attacker and defender where the former has numerous advantages over the latter.[46] Both privacy and security will be discussed in depth in chapters 3 and 4, respectively.

§ 1:6   Challenges

In addition to the drawbacks previously mentioned, there are other challenges currently confronting the world of IoT; the first and foremost of which is interoperability. The European Research Cluster on the Internet of Things defines "interoperability" as "the ability of two or more systems or components to exchange data and use information." Interoperability among IoT devices spurs innovation, creates efficiencies, and facilitates security.[47]

---

38.   Scott R. Peppet, *Regulating the Internet of Things: First Steps Toward Managing Discrimination, Privacy, Security, and Consent*, 93 TEX. L. REV. 85 (2014).
39.   *Id.*
40.   Davenport, *supra* note 18.
41.   Peppet, *supra* note 38.
42.   *Id.*
43.   *Id.*
44.   Fed. Bureau of Investigation, Internet of Things Poses Opportunities for Cyber Crime (Sept. 10, 2015).
45.   Schneier, *supra* note 28.
46.   *Id.*
47.   Stephanie Lynn Sharon & Nikita A. Tuckett, *The Internet of Things: Interoperability, Industry Standards & Related IP Licensing Approaches*,

At present, there is no consensus among standards organizations and industry stakeholders on the method by which IoT devices will communicate with each other.[48] While most favor uniform standards and acknowledge the benefits of such uniformity, few are willing to agree on one universally accepted method.[49] As a result, there is currently a hodgepodge of different standard-setting organizations, ranging from Open Connectivity Foundation (OCF) to Thread Group to ZigBee Alliance to Z-Wave Alliance, promoting their own method of communication.[50]

diff ways to communicate

The OCF consists of a group of technology companies including Samsung, Cisco, and GE Software. OCF sponsors IoTivity specification which is "an open source software framework enabling seamless device-to-device connectivity to address the emerging needs of the IoT."[51] The goal of IoTivity "is to create a new standard by which billions of wired and wireless devices will connect to each other and the Internet."[52]

The Thread Group consists of cutting-edge companies like Silicon Labs, Google's Nest Labs, and Samsung Electronics.[53] The Thread specification uses low-powered radio protocol called IPv6 over Low Power Wireless Personal Area Networks, while most other specifications rely on Wi-Fi. According to Thread Group, its specification goes to networking.[54] Thus, other specifications, like AllJoyn and IoTivity which rely on Wi-Fi or Bluetooth networks, could be used with Thread-enabled products.

The Zigbee Alliance, founded in 2002, consists of members including AT&T, Emerson, and Cisco Systems.[55] According to Zigbee Alliance, "Zigbee is the only complete IoT solution—from mesh network to the universal language that allows smart objects to work together."[56] At present, there are millions of ZigBee-enabled IoT devices in use today.

Morrison & Foerster, SOCIALLY AWARE BLOG: THE LAW AND BUSINESS OF SOCIAL MEDIA (Feb. 2, 2016), www.sociallyawareblog.com/2016/02/02/the-internet-of-things-evaluating-the-interplay-of-interoperability-industry-standards-and-related-ip-licensing-approaches/.

48. *Id.*
49. *Id.*
50. *Id.*
51. Wikipedia: IoTivity. *See also* www.iotivity.org.
52. *Id.*
53. Sharon & Tuckett, *supra* note 47.
54. *Id.*
55. *Id.*
56. *See* https://zigbeealliance.org/solution/zigbee/ (last visited June 28, 2020).

The Z-Wave Alliance was established in 2005 by a group of home control product manufacturers.[57] The Z-Wave Alliance consists of 700 companies and over 2,400 products.[58] The Z-Wave Alliance defines Z-Wave as, "a low powered radio frequency communication[ ] that supports full mesh networks without the need for a coordinator node."

At present, it is unclear which standard will gain world-wide acceptance. Thus, the major players in the IoT world are hedging their bets and joining various standards organizations instead of just picking one.[59]

There are a number of reasons why companies have not agreed upon uniform standards to govern the communication method of IoT devices. First and foremost is the "perceived competitive and economic advantages of building proprietary systems for market domination in the IoT."[60] Not surprisingly, these so-called "walled gardens" are seen as impediments by those who support interoperability. This lack of agreement has resulted in a virtual smorgasbord of IoT standards. If interoperability standards are patented, they will most likely create a barrier to entry, especially if the third-party users are required to pay an exorbitant licensing fee.

Certain organizations such as OCF rely on RAND-Z or FRAND. Under this model, member companies of OCF "offer a zero-royalty, reasonable and non-discriminatory license to their code for member organizations."[61] This model also requires members to provide OCF with a license to the member's contributions, and members must agree not to enforce IP rights against other members if "reasonable and non-discriminatory compensation for practice of IP rights can otherwise be obtained."[62]

Another potential issue with intellectual property is data ownership. This topic will be explored in depth in chapter 4. In short, there is no set answer for all IoT devices. Rather, it will most likely depend on the contract agreed to by the parties involved.[63]

§ 1:7   Net Neutrality

At its core, net neutrality stands for two principles: (1) Internet service providers should treat all data on the Internet equally; and

---

57.   *See* https://z-wavealliance.org/z-wave_alliance_history/ (last visited June 28, 2020).

58.   *Id.*

59.   Sharon & Tuckett, *supra* note 47.

60.   *Id.*

61.   *Id.*

62.   *Id.*

63.   Robert S. Berezin, *The Next Big Thing: 'Internet of Things' Litigation and Regulatory Risk*, N.Y.L.J. (Nov. 2, 2015).

net neutrality rules

(2) Internet service providers should not discriminate against users by charging them different rates depending upon the content, website, platform, application type of attached equipment, or method of communication they view or use. By way of example, Internet service providers under net neutrality would not be allowed to block, slow down, impede, or charge higher rates for specific websites and online content.[64]

In 2015, the Federal Communications Center (FCC) affirmed net neutrality principles by issuing its Open Internet Order, which reclassified Internet access as a common carrier telecommunications service.[65] Internet access had previously been classified as an information service. In 2017, the FCC, under a new administration, voted to repeal portions of the Open Internet Order, which in turn reclassified Internet access as an information service. In 2019, the U.S. Court of Appeals for the District of Columbia Circuit upheld the FCC's 2017 decision repealing net neutrality.[66] Thus, the battle has now turned to the states where several have taken it upon themselves to pass state-specific laws to maintain net neutrality.[67]

up to the states

One of the great unknowns with IoT is the impact of net neutrality on the industry. This is primarily due to two factors. First, there has not been a consistent policy by the federal government on net neutrality. Various administrations have taken contrasting views on the advantages and disadvantages of net neutrality. Second, since IoT is such a nascent industry, it is difficult to know the myriad ways in which net neutrality may influence it in the long term.

Some view net neutrality as an overall positive measure for the IoT industry, arguing that the rule ensures openness and non-discriminatory practices by Internet service providers, which in turn spurs industry growth and consumer demand.[68] Others argue that net neutrality will limit investment and innovation to the detriment of greater Internet deployment of services.[69]

---

64.   Katharine Trendacosta, *Real Net Neutrality Is More Than a Ban on Blocking, Throttling, and Paid Prioritization*, ELEC. FRONTIER FOUND. (Feb. 7, 2019), www.eff.org/deeplinks/2019/02/real-net-neutrality-more-ban-blocking-throttling-and-paid-prioritization.

65.   Fed. Commc'ns Comm'n, *In re* Protecting and Promoting the Open Internet, Report and Order on Remand, Declaratory Ruling, and Order (Feb. 26, 2015), https://transition.fcc.gov/Daily_Releases/Daily_Business/2015/db0312/FCC-15-24A1.pdf.

66.   Mozilla Corp. v. Fed. Commc'ns Comm'n, 940 F.3d 1 (D.C. Cir. 2019).

67.   Heather Morton, *Net Neutrality Legislation in States*, NCSL.ORG (Jan. 23, 2019).

68.   Fischer, *supra* note 22.

69.   *Id.*

§ 1:8   IoT in the World

As one commentator has stated, "From inside the home to right across society, the IoT is a rebellion that guarantees to change people's lives."[70] Already, IoT is playing a major role in everyone's day-to-day lives, ranging anywhere from the management of an airport's passenger flow to heating buildings to caring for the elderly to finding someone's lost keys.[71] Thanks to the invention of low-cost computational devices, Internet-based home automation can become a reality. Historically, IoT sensors had to be connected to a local computer system in order to be controlled by an embedded module. Today, affordable wireless technology enables IoT sensors to transmit data directly to the cloud rather than requiring a local system to send the information out. At present, IoT allows people to build flexible and cost-effective systems that can easily be connected to, and accessed from, the home, workplace, and most anywhere else.[72]

The best way to understand IoT technology is to examine the different industries/areas where IoT has had its greatest influence. The eight industries/areas that have seen the biggest impact from the IoT are: home and office, cities, manufacturing, vehicles, transportation, health care, energy, and agriculture. In the near future, as billions of devices come online, it is expected that in addition to the eight industries/areas previously mentioned others will quickly adopt IoT technology.[73]

§ 1:8.1   *Home and Office*

For years, consumers have been promised appliances that could be controlled from bed or alert them when something needed to be replaced. One of the biggest success stories for the home that has emerged is the Nest Learning Thermostat owned by Google. The Nest thermostat provides homeowners with data-driven tools to better control their energy usage in the home.[74] The ability for homeowners to control energy consumption while maintaining a comfortable

---

70. Teksun, *Importance of Internet of Things (IoT) in Our Live*, MEDIUM (Sept. 2, 2017), https://medium.com/@TeksunGroup/importance-of-internet-of-things-iot-in-our-live-b71e53d50a44.
71. *Id.*
72. *Id.*
73. Alec Scott, *Eight Ways the Internet of Things Will Change the Way We Live and Work*, THE GLOBE AND MAIL (2017), www.theglobeandmail.com/report-on-business/rob-magazine/the-future-is-smart/article24586994/.
74. *Id.*

environment and lowering their utility bills is a basic but effective way for an IoT device to integrate into one's home.[75]

Another manufacturer of smart home products is Crestron, which has developed a number of IoT products related to control systems, audio/visual distribution, lighting control, collaborative technology, motorized shades, home security systems, and speakers, to name a few.[76] One of the control systems that Crestron has on the market is called Crestron's 4-Series Processors, which serves as the central processor and interface for every audio, video, and environmental element of the home, boardroom, classroom, or command center.[77]

Apple also jumped into the home IoT products market with the release of HomeKit, a platform that allows developers to create device-controlling apps.[78] The goal of HomeKit was to provide a gateway into the IoT industry. Thus, when a user gets the HomeKit app, she can control all the HomeKit accessories such as lights, front door locks, temperature, stereo, and more from an iPhone, iPad, Mac, Apple TV, or even the HomePod.

In the workplace, companies like Cisco are stepping forward in order to increase bottom-line efficiency and worker convenience. Cisco controls the core functions of all of its worldwide buildings from four different locations. These four locations can control the climate, electricity usage, and the security of the many buildings that Cisco owns.

It has also become increasingly common for office buildings to have a sophisticated internal climate control system. A brand new skyscraper in Winnipeg, Canada, designed for Manitoba Hydro, contains a massive natural humidifier, which is a steamy room several stories high filled with tropical plants and a water feature. This room is connected to pipes that allow for moist air to be pumped throughout the building. Further, the building's system knows when to open and close blinds, to allow sunshine in, as a way of benefitting from the free solar heat, or to keep the sunlight out.

Integrating IoT technology into the workplace is predicted to create significant change to include: improved efficiency and productivity; cheaper, greener technology; new and expanded roles for data; expedited

---

75.   Forbes Tech. Council, *Best Smart Home Devices and How IoT Is Changing the Way We Live*, FORBES (June 6, 2017), www.forbes.com/sites/forbestechcouncil/2017/06/06/best-smart-home-devices-and-how-iot-is-changing-the-way-we-live/#72d046aa43bd.

76.   About Crestron, www.crestron.com/about/company-overview-information (last visited May 28, 2020).

77.   *Crestron Control Systems*, Crestron Control Systems–Design Integration, www.crestron.com/Products/Control-Hardware-Software/Hardware/Control-Systems/MC4 (last visited June 28, 2020).

78.   Scott, *supra* note 73.

movement of people and goods; completely remote device management; increased device management complexity; and expanded workloads caused by disruptions in almost every industry.[79]

A business entity will be able to follow every aspect of its operations, from managing inventory to supervising field service employees. By allowing the entity to connect every tool and device within a centralized system, their ability to control everything is increased. This in turn improves data analysis and management results while improving the ability of owners to expand.

Additionally, the use of IoT will allow the average commercial building to reduce its energy consumption by switching off when no one is around. Further, by placing functions into a standby mode, they can automatically start up at the beginning of the business day or whenever someone walks into the room. This technology is currently available in the marketplace and continues to evolve, undergoing developments and enhancements with each new release or update.

Greater collaboration is another way IoT enhances the workplace. Despite fears that the IoT would create an isolated workplace experience, in practice, it has, in many instances, improved interactions among employees. According to a survey conducted by the *Harvard Business Review*, companies employing IoT-based initiatives derive important benefits from them and approximately 58% of respondents saw increased collaboration within the business.[80] One example is remote workers creating a real presence inside the company from anywhere in the world.[81] Video conferencing becomes more useful with the migration from fixed devices, such as a computer or smartphone, to any part of an enterprise base. One major factor hindering widespread adoption of IoT technology into internal business processes is office connectivity, which involves more than just printers and computers; rather, it is a complex and constantly evolving ecosystem with the potential of transforming everyday equipment into smart equipment.

While some home and office IoT devices are large scale, IoT devices need not be large nor perform a major function. Some IoT devices can be useful for just one small thing—such as the smart refrigerator,

---

79. Sara Angeles, *8 Ways the Internet of Things Will Change the Way We Work*, BUS. NEWS DAILY (Jan. 18, 2019), www.businessnewsdaily.com/4858-internet-of-things-will-change-work.html#text=%22IoT%20has%20the%20potential%20to,tracking%20much%20simpler%20and%20seamless (last visited June 28, 2020).

80. *Id. See also Internet of Things: Science Fiction or Business Fact?*, HARV. BUS. REV. (2014), https://hbr.org/resources/pdfs/comm/verizon/18980_HBR_Verizon_IoT_Nov_14.pdf (last visited Sept. 24, 2018).

81. Angeles, *supra* note 79.

smart sprinkler controller, and the Wink and Philips Hue devices for controlling a home's lights, power, and security.[82] Then there are practical IoT devices, such as Tagg, a device that allows an owner to remotely track the location and vitals of their cat or dog.[83] Amazon has also released a line of buttons that a consumer can stick around the house programmed to order an item at the "click of a button." And, of course, there are other IoT devices whose usefulness some might question, such as "Brad," the smart but needy toaster that checks the activity of other connected toasters and will wiggle its toggle if it feels neglected based on inadequate usage.

§ 1:8.2   Cities

Currently, more than 50% of the world's populace lives in urban environments. Further, it is predicted that by 2050, approximately two-thirds of all people will live as city-dwellers,[84] which equates to approximately 2.5 billion individuals that urban centers will need to house, employ, and transport. This is an issue because today's cities are already plagued by traffic, smog, crime, overflowing trash bins, and inefficient lighting, which can consume approximately one-quarter to one-half of a municipal city's electricity budget. Thus, technology that impacts any one of these big-ticket issues can drastically change cities.

One of the biggest problem areas for cities is traffic, and one measure that can help ease congestion is ride-sharing. In the IoT world, car-sharing involves connected cars and smartphones. Using GPS data, users can find the nearest available vehicle and the operator can bill based on the actual use. The goal would be to reduce the number of cars on the street and the amount of emissions coming from the cars.

Another innovation is the smart parking space search. A study done by the German Association of the Automotive Industry found that German drivers waste 560 million hours simply looking for available parking spaces per year.[85] This wastes millions of liters of fuel and results in excessive amounts of exhaust in the air. To combat these issues and others, Spain embedded approximately four hundred

---

82.   Forbes Tech. Council, *Best Smart Home Devices and How IoT Is Changing the Way We Live*, FORBES (June 6, 2017), www.forbes.com/sites/forbestechcouncil/2017/06/06/best-smart-home-devices-and-how-iot-is-changing-the-way-we-live/#380b4b5543bd.

83.   Scott, *supra* note 73.

84.   *Id.*

85.   *See Welcome to the Connected City*, T-SYS. INT'L, www.t-systems.com/en/perspectives/internet-of-things/iot5/smart-city-402770 (last visited May 28, 2020).

spain parking solution

sensors around the city center.[86] These sensors are designed to trans-mit information about parking availability to a connected lighting system which in turn alerts motorists about available parking spaces. Further, these embedded sensors can also relay real-time information on empty spots to an app for drivers to use.[87] Approximately 30% of traffic congestion occurs due to drivers searching for a place to park.[88]

The Israeli city of Tel Aviv is also tackling heavy traffic by reserving a lane for buses, shuttles, taxis, and carpoolers. This reserved lane is also available to normal commuters, but it comes at a cost. Sensors in the asphalt will pick up the license plate number and charge the credit card of the car's owner for driving in this lane. The rate for the charge varies depending on how busy the road currently is, which is also detected through sensors in the road.[89]

Another big use for IoT technology in reducing traffic is to embed stoplights with video sensors. The embedded video sensors adjust green, yellow, and red lights according to the cars and the time of day. Not only does this feature reduce traffic congestion, it also reduces smog because vehicles idling at red lights burn up to 17% of the fuel consumed in urban areas.[90]

San Diego's use of IoT lighting devices in 3,000 streetlamps saves an estimated $250,000 a year. The purpose of the devices in the streetlamps is to turn on only when a pedestrian or a vehicle approaches. Additionally, these streetlamps have the capability of pointing out vacant parking spots to drivers and alerting traffic enforcement to illegally parked cars.[91] Researchers also hope to use the sensor data to learn which intersections are the most dangerous and require a redesign based upon pedestrian near-misses with cars as opposed to just solely basing re-design on recorded accidents.[92]

Further, it is possible to connect the new smart streetlights to the existing ShotSpotter network, which locates the source of gunfire.[93] This greatly expands the traditional coverage of ShotSpotter. The sensing lights could also detect sounds and alert police to dangerous situations by recognizing broken glass, a gunshot, or car crash.

---

86. *Id.*
87. Scott, *supra* note 73.
88. *Id.*
89. *Id.*
90. *Id.*
91. Tekla S. Perry, *San Diego Installs Smart Streetlights to Monitor the Metropolis*, IEEE SPECTRUM: TECH., ENG'G, AND SCI. NEWS (Jan. 1, 2018), https://spectrum.ieee.org/computing/it/san-diego-installs-smart-streetlights-to-monitor-the-metropolis.
92. *Id.*
93. *Id.*

Another area enhanced by IoT is garbage collection. Philadelphia has created Big Bellies, a $4,000 solar-powered garbage can capable of crushing waste and sending an alert to dispatch requesting pickup when full.[94] Already, these garbage cans reduced the number of times that trash has to be collected in a week from seventeen to just three. By reducing the frequency of trash collections by fourteen in a week, Philadelphia saved $1 million a year on fuel, maintenance, and labor costs. Similarly, in Amsterdam, the city equipped over 2,000 waste bins with sensors.[95] These sensors register the current level of trash in the receptacle and report that information to a central system. Now, waste disposal companies in Amsterdam know exactly when a bin needs to be emptied. This has created a system of collecting waste on demand instead of at regular intervals, thus cutting down on time emptying half-full bins. With this new process, the city has become cleaner as overflowing bins are emptied in a timely and efficient manner.

Similar to the home and office IoT devices, city IoT devices and apps do not always impact large groups of people but nonetheless make a difference to individual residents. For instance, an app has emerged that identifies walking routes considered to be the quietest on the way toward a destination. These routes are perfect for those who wish to talk while strolling.[96] Another app, "Digital Cane," is designed around traffic and location data in order to assist the visually impaired in crossing the street. A third app has been developed to assist food truck drivers find ideal locations with parking spaces that correlate with high pedestrian traffic. Another app attempts to identify interesting events as they occur by tracking where pedestrians go or congregate.

§ 1:8.3 *Manufacturing*

A third area that IoT will improve is manufacturing. For example, the Harley-Davidson motorcycle plant was a typical assembly-line operation prior to the integration of IoT into its processes.[97] The factory added a slew of sensors in order to collect data on the factory floor to detect any bottlenecks in the assembly process. After doing this, managers shifted the layout of one of the processes when they discovered that something was holding up the line. In another part of the factory, sensors are used to detect whether or not the conditions of the room, such as the air flow and moisture, is optimal for painting,

---

94.   Scott, *supra* note 73.
95.   *Welcome to the Connected City, supra* note 85.
96.   Perry, *supra* note 91.
97.   Scott, *supra* note 73.

and if they are not, the system automatically makes the necessary changes. This type of manufacturing system is not cheap; it can run around $500,000 to $1 million for a single factory. Despite the cost, the factory now turns out 25% more bikes with 30% less workers. Instead of a twenty-one-day delivery time, the factory has a six-hour delivery time.

In Germany, IoT has also been used in a Siemens plant to assist in churning out around 12 million PLCs a year (a PLC is a switchboard that can control systems). Siemens uses the microsensors in the manufacturing and assembly process in order to eliminate any and all defects. They have claimed that their PLCs are perfect 99.99885% of the time.[98]

One big advantage for manufacturers who employ IoT devices is managers will have greater visibility through their smartphones and tablets of real-time information on the manufacturing floor. A positive side effect of this visibility is a significant decrease in machine downtime. Accenture reported that IoT technology has the capability of reducing average repair costs by 12%, maintenance by 30%, and downtime by as much as 70%.[99]

As shown above, the greatest impact IoT will have on manufacturing is the speed of production and associated costs. While up-front expenditures can be expensive, the benefits realized outweigh the costs.

§ 1:8.4   Vehicles

"The rise of self-driving cars, controlled through Wi-Fi, smartphones, and technology smartly crafted by the manufacturers, is close at hand."[100] It has been estimated that by 2021, self-driving cars will be a $42 billion dollar industry.[101] Autonomous cars offer numerous benefits. First, they will free up humans to do other things besides sit behind a wheel. The estimated time that individuals will be able to recoup amounts to approximately an extra fifty minutes a day for other activities, such as work, recreation, and family time. Self-driving cars will also transfer potentially dangerous tasks to machines. However, in order for autonomous cars to become mainstream, manufacturers will need to get self-driving IoT technology to the point of near perfection.

---

98.   *Id.*
99.   *Id.*
100. *Smart Car of the Future*, HiQ (July 12, 2017), https://hiq.ai/smart-car-2/smart-car-of-the-future (last visited June 28, 2020).
101. Melinda Sacks, *In Two Years, There Could Be 10 Million Self-Driving Cars on the Roads*, STANFORD MAG. (Mar. 2018).

A new Tesla S electric sedan comes with Autopilot, which uses a combination of camera, radar, and 360-degree sonar sensors to drive on open roads and in stop-and-go traffic.[102] The car even has the ability to pull into a parallel parking spot on its own. Additionally, the camera reads posted speed limits and warns drivers when their speed exceeds the posted limit, and the car seat will even vibrate should the driver veer out of their lane.

With all the IoT components enabled in the car, the engineers behind the technology receive streams of data from the vehicle. Programmers use the data to craft updates for the software and send it back to the car in order to boost the range of the IoT devices and add additional features. With integrated IoT, car functionality will constantly expand, such that the functions present when the car is driven off the lot will not be the same the following year or even ninety days later.

At present, researchers want to create a model car that can interact with the driver's smartphone in order to gather information about appointments and then propose routes to navigate there while also displaying real-time traffic information. Freightliner has received a Nevada license for a robo-truck, the world's first, which has already steered itself through hundreds of miles of testing on the state's roads, with a human operator supervising.

Some believe that smart car technology will be most disruptive around the middle of the century.[103] Therefore, the perfect self-driving technology will take some time to achieve.[104] Nonetheless, car companies and their suppliers around the world are making steady progress.

Every year there are approximately 8 million traffic accidents and 1.3 million deaths from crashes world-wide.[105] Cisco's Smart Connected Vehicles division claims that the use of autonomous cars would eliminate up to 85% of head-on collisions. Further, autonomous cars decrease traffic because of their ability to communicate with other vehicles. With enhanced communication, cars can drive much closer together. This type of driving, also referred to as "platooning" by traffic experts, would save drivers and passengers some 90 billion hours now spent in traffic jams each year, which generates 220 million metric tonnes of carbon-equivalent and wastes around $1 trillion in fuel costs and lost productivity.[106]

---

102.   Scott, *supra* note 73.
103.   Sacks, *supra* note 101.
104.   *Id.*
105.   Scott, *supra* note 73.
106.   *Id.*

§ 1:8.5   *Transportation*

Cars are not the only modes of transportation benefiting from IoT. Planes, trains, and the maritime industry will all undergo major changes because of IoT innovations.

[A]   Aviation

As an industry, aviation has been slow to adopt new technology. For example, the nation-wide air traffic control system still runs on computer infrastructure built in the 1970s. One reason for the hesitancy to incorporate cutting-edge technology is the risk of a potential glitch on a newer system that must communicate with aircraft thousands of feet in the air, especially if the current system works fine.

While sensors and IoT are new concepts for most industries and areas, they are not for aviation. Airplanes have been equipped with sensors for some time in order to collect data on fuel efficiency, altitude, location, and maintenance issues. The main difference between other industries and the aviation sector is that the data from airplanes are only processed after the airplane has landed, whereas other industries process data immediately. However, with the advances in connectivity and data processing software, there are fewer disadvantages to the aviation industry sending off data mid-flight.

Sensors, nowadays, have the ability to detect and isolate developing problems in aircraft engines. Sensors can communicate those problems to both pilot and ground crews while the plane is still in the air. Additionally, sensors provide more efficiency by measuring fuel use during flight and moving wing flaps, and performing other functions that reduce unnecessary drag on the plane. This has helped reduce fuel consumption by 1% in a year, and in an industry where fuel spending can be around $30 billion annually, even 1% adds up quickly.[107]

In practice, every single component of Virgin Atlantic's Boeing 787 is attached to a wireless airplane network, which provides real-time IoT data.[108] The information produced per flight, approximately one-third of a terabyte of data, has proven to be quite useful. If a jet engine has been performing poorly during the flight, upon landing, a team of engineers is ready to immediately locate and remedy the problem.

The London City Airport has also adopted IoT in order to better understand and track passenger flow and behavior in the airport. An interconnected sensor network and data hub allows airport officials

---

107.   *Id.*
108.   Doug Drinkwater, *10 Stellar Real-Life Examples of IoT Taking Flight in Aviation*, INTERNET OF BUS., https://internetofbusiness.com/10-real-life-examples-iot-aviation/ (last visited May 28, 2020).

to measure passenger journeys in the airport. The IoT also allows for the airport to track assets moving through the airport via GPS, 3G, and Wi-Fi devices. Additionally, the airport can deliver location-based services to customers.[109]

The foregoing indicates that IoT implementation within the aviation sector goes beyond the aircraft itself. In addition to offering airports ways to manage its fliers, IoT offers new ways of providing services and advertising to people inside airports. With the versatility of what IoT can offer, the aviation industry can leverage these technological advancements in many different areas to expand into as well as build upon in order to increase efficiency of the aircraft and keep track of individuals inside the airport.

[B] Rail

The rail business has also experienced some beneficial changes based on the adoption of the IoT. Britain's Network Rail Telecom has been installing sensors in and along railroad tracks.[110] These sensors will form a centralized hub that alerts officials to the need for track maintenance or some danger that threatens the rails, such as a landslide or flooding. The use of these sensors has the possibility of reducing approximately 1.3 million hours currently spent on rail inspections.[111]

IoT benefits not only railroads, but also subways. New York City's Canarsie subway line has installed "smart tracks" that provides a more precise location pinpointing system. With the "smart tracks" precise location data, the time between trains can be reduced, thus allowing more trains on a busy route. It is estimated that "smart tracks" will increase the number of subway trains to twenty-six per hour, up from fifteen an hour.

[C] Maritime

Finally, the maritime industry has also benefited from the IoT. In Germany, the main port of Hamburg has teamed up with Cisco and SAP to allow the 10,000 ships that unload at this port each year and a majority of the 9 million containers that move through the port to transmit and constantly update their precise arrival times. With more accurate times, the 550 trucks that arrive every day can arrange to pick up and drop off cargo right at the moment of arrival, thus reducing traffic congestion and aimless driving of truck drivers looking for a parking spot.[112]

---

109.   *Id.*
110.   Scott, *supra* note 73.
111.   *Id.*
112.   *Id.*

§ 1:8.6 Healthcare

Another field with a significant uptick in IoT usage is healthcare. IoT has many different applications in healthcare, ranging from remote monitoring to smart sensors and medical device integration.[113] The IoT potential is virtually limitless and goes well beyond just keeping patients safe and healthy. For example, IoT improves the manner by which physicians deliver care.

One of the more popular methods of employing IoT in healthcare is remote monitoring (also known as telehealth).[114] Telehealth minimizes the cost of patient visitation and eliminates the need for some in-person visitations with physicians. By reducing in-person visitations, telehealth improves quality of living for patients with limited mobility and for those unable to drive.

The health field also relies on sensors to monitor patients like premature babies.[115] Normal sensors can't be used on certain infants because they must to be placed directly on the skin. A premature baby's skin is delicate and could be harmed if a sensor is placed directly on it. Instead, sensors now feature high-definition cameras that monitor the skin color, breathing, and temperature of the baby and alert nurses of any changes to the conditions. In the future, similar devices will assist doctors and nurses in the care and monitoring of patients, either at home or in the hospital. Smart beds are already in use at New York–Presbyterian Hospital; they immediately alert the nursing station when a patient gets up.

Another example of how the IoT assists the healthcare field is by tracking of staff, patients, and inventory throughout the hospital.[116] Generally, in a smaller facility, keeping track of everything is not an issue. But larger facilities with multiple structures and campuses, hundreds of staff, and thousands of patients are in dire need of these IoT tracking devices. The IoT method of real-time location systems is an inexpensive method of monitoring day-to-day activities in a hospital setting that is unobtrusive, effective, and cutting-edge.

IoT tracking is also an option for those who want to monitor friends and family both during and immediately after surgery.[117] In

---

113. *A Guide to Healthcare IoT Possibilities and Obstacles*, SEARCHHEALTHIT, https://searchhealthit.techtarget.com/essentialguide/A-guide-to-healthcare-IoT-possibilities-and-obstacles (last visited May 28, 2020).

114. Kayla Matthews, *6 Exciting IoT Use Cases in Healthcare*, IOT FOR ALL (Jan. 16, 2020), www.iotforall.com/exciting-iot-use-cases-in-healthcare/.

115. Scott, *supra* note 73.

116. Matthews, *supra* note 114.

117. Mildred Segura, Christopher Butler & Farah Tabibkoei, *The Internet of Medical Things Raises Novel Compliance Challenges*, MED DEVICE ONLINE (Jan. 3, 2018).

some hospitals, patients are outfitted with a real-time location system prior to surgery. This in turn allows others to follow the process of the operation all the way to the recovery room by watching screens that display anonymized ID codes in waiting rooms throughout the hospital.[118]

A fourth way IoT improves the healthcare industry is by enhancing drug management.[119] Some prescription pills now contain microscopic sensors the size of a grain of rice that send a signal to an external device. These devices, generally worn as a patch, ensure proper dosage and usage. The information generated by the sensors helps patients remember to take their prescriptions, if they forget to take them, as well as helps in prescribing future medications. Further, patients access the information through a smartphone app in order to track personal performance and improve their habits.

Not all healthcare IoT innovations involve hospitals or medical devices. There is also a booming market for IoT fitness trackers. This market, which includes FitBit, Apple Watch, and others, has surpassed $2 billion and over 84 million devices sold.[120] IoT fitness trackers monitor heart rate, sleep patterns, diet, exercise, and other data and share that information with mobile apps. These devices also have the potential of sharing health information with medical care providers and insurers. Some insurers, such as John Hancock, now require all life insurance policy holders to use a FitBit or similar device.[121]

Another benefit arises in the treatment of chronic disease through the combination of wearable IoT tech, mobile connectivity, and analytics.[122] With devices like Fitbit that utilize the IoT to monitor personal health, individuals can share information generated with their doctor in order to resolve any recurring issues. Companies like Health Net Connect pool all this data in order to improve clinical treatment as well as reduce medical costs for patients.[123]

Despite all the positives, IoT does carry some risk for the healthcare industry. For example, the number of connected devices and the sheer volume of data generated and collected creates a logistical challenge for hospital IT staff. This is especially true at smaller facilities. Additionally, the data generated and collected is confidential, and the ability to keep it all secure even when exchanged amongst devices

---

118.   *Id.*
119.   Matthews, *supra* note 114.
120.   Scott, *supra* note 73.
121.   Suzanne Barlyn, *Strap on the Fitbit: John Hancock to Sell Only Interactive Life Insurance*, ASSOCIATED PRESS (Sept. 19, 2018).
122.   Matthews, *supra* note 114.
123.   *Id.*

nurse lawsuit
overide
system

will be a challenge.[124] Despite these risks, most view the medical industry's adoption of the IoT as an overall positive.

§ 1:8.7   *Energy*

When originally created, the energy grid was designed to deliver power on an as-needed basis.[125] The original idea was to create a delicate balance of supply and demand, which was a challenge since demand varies by the time of day, the weather, and the season. However, a smart grid provides an easier way to deliver power. The basic theory is that power is priced on demand and that price is trans-mitted to smart meters, thermostats, and appliances so that they can draw the power needed during off-peak times when energy is cheap-est. This system attempts to balance the system loads to make power networks less susceptible to black- and brown-outs.

Pilot programs show the real-world possibility of smart grids. In fact, the United States has set 2030 as an informal deadline to finish most of the components of the smart grid. Florida Power and Light's employment of a smart grid yielded $3.4 million in productivity savings and a 99.98% service reliability.[126] Additionally, companies that install smart energy grids are expected to save collectively up to $160 billion.[127] Ontario replaced many of their old meters with smart ones.[128] These smart meters currently only transmit time-of-day usage directly to the utility; however, they can also receive pricing information and govern themselves.[129]

Texas grid

Another innovation for the energy sector involves Zero-Net Buildings (ZNE).[130] In a Zero-Net building, the amount of energy used by the building within a year is equal to the amount of renew-able energy generated by the building. Zero-Net buildings are created through the use of a combination of IoT, Artificial Intelligence, solar energy, batteries, and LED light systems. These buildings, gaining in popularity, boast lower electric bills, reduced emissions, and zero-net carbon footprint.

---

124.   *Id.*
125.   Scott, *supra* note 73.
126.   *Renewable Energy and the IoT,* http://cdn.pes.eu.com/v/20180916/ wp-content/uploads/2019/06/PES-W-2-19-Gabriel-Comment-1.pdf (last visited June 28, 2020).
127.   *Id.*
128.   Scott, *supra* note 73.
129.   *Id.*
130.   *Renewable Energy and the IoT, supra* note 126.

§ 1:8.8   Agriculture

Despite many preconceived notions, farmers are generally the early adopters of technology.[131] With farms becoming increasingly larger and the average size doubling in the last twenty-five years, farmers quickly deploy data-gathering, Internet-linked devices in order to assist them in keeping track of the land. For instance, new John Deere machines do more than just plow, sow, and reap a field. These machines collect a plethora of data, such as air and soil temperatures, moisture, wind speed, humidity, solar radiation, and even rainfall.[132]

To feed a global population expected to hit 9.6 billion by 2050, agriculture must adopt the IoT.[133] Between the demand for more food from a rising population and the challenges of extreme weather, rising climate change, and environmental impacts, the use of technology to assist farmers in growing food has become more important.

The increased demand for food has led to "smart farming," defined as a "capital-intensive and hi-tech system of growing food cleanly and sustainable for the masses." Smart farming incorporates information and communication technology (ICT) directly into agriculture. Once integrated, the system allows a farmer to monitor their crops through sensors to check light, humidity, temperature, soil moisture, and more. The system also allows the irrigation system to be automated.

Giving farmers more control over their fields through data collecting via sensors and constant monitoring via mobile device allows for more crops to thrive. Further, smart farming assists in other areas outside of just the conventional large farms. Organic farms and family farms can also benefit by allowing easier expansion. Additionally, smart farming helps the environment through more efficient usage of water and by optimizing treatment of the fields.

§ 1:9   Conclusion

IoT has revolutionized the way machines interact with other machines, humans, and the environment. The possibilities of what IoT and its integration capabilities can do is endless; however, there is a finite number of ways that IoT intersects with the law. The rest of the book will cover those various areas.

---

131.   Scott, *supra* note 73.
132.   *Id.*
133.   *IoT Applications in Agriculture*, IOT FOR ALL (Jan. 3, 2020), www. iotforall.com/iot-applications-in-agriculture/.

Chapter 2

Regulatory
Framework of the IoT

§ 2:1   Overview

A number of federal regulatory agencies exercise jurisdiction over aspects of the IoT and several federal laws play a critical role in regulating the industry. This chapter explores these agencies and laws, as well as more recent IoT-specific legislation. The focus of this chapter is primarily *proposed* IoT legislation, since very few IoT-specific laws have yet to be enacted. IoT legislation that governs areas like privacy and security will be covered in the respective chapters that follow.

§ 2:2   Regulatory Agencies

Every industry must adhere to its own applicable regulations and governing bodies. The medical field, for example, must follow HIPAA (Health Insurance Portability and Accountability Act) and HHS (Health and Human Services) requirements, both of which govern the medical industry in order to protect patients and consumers. But what agencies or regulations govern the IoT?[1] Is there an agency or group of agencies that dictate regulations for the IoT? Is there an entity that ensures that a self-driving car does not put passengers in danger? Is there an agency that makes sure IoT cameras do not send the videos they collect to unauthorized third parties? Is there a commission or body that regulates data collected from devices to prevent usage in a way that compromises personal data? At present, the answer to these questions is unclear.[2]

While no single federal agency has complete regulatory authority over the IoT, a number of agencies, including the following, provide some regulatory oversight in various contexts:

- The Consumer Financial Protection Bureau: provides consumer protection in the financial sector;

- The Department of Defense: governs foundational technology for the IoT;

- The Department of Energy: oversees "green" buildings and "smart" electrical grids;

- The Department of Homeland Security: coordinates security for sixteen critical infrastructure sectors;

---

1.   Mohana Ravindranath, *Who's in Charge of Regulating the Internet of Things?*, NEXTGOV.COM (Sept. 1, 2016), www.nextgov.com/emerging-tech/2016/09/internet-things-regulating-charge/131208/.

2.   Bruce Schneier, *Click Here to Kill Everyone*, NYMAG.COM (Jan. 27, 2017). Some have argued that in order to ensure security and to safeguard privacy in the IoT age, a new governmental regulatory agency, similar to those that arose with the advent of cars, trains, airplanes, the radio, and nuclear power, is needed.

- The Department of Justice: adjudicates criminal acts related to the IoT;

- The Department of Transportation: regulates "smart" cars;

- The Federal Aviation Administration: regulates unmanned aerial vehicles;

- The Federal Communications Commission: manages and assigns spectrum for non-federal entities;

- The Federal Trade Commission: enforces consumer protection policies for IoT users;

- The Food & Drug Administration: monitors cybersecurity of Internet-connected medical devices;

- The National Institute of Standards and Technology: creates regulatory and performance standards for IoT devices; and

- The National Telecommunications and Information Administration: provides spectrum management for federal entities.[3]

Oftentimes, regulatory and legal issues raised by the IoT span the oversight of multiple agencies or otherwise do not fall completely under the jurisdiction of one specific agency.

The IoT differs from other fields in that it primarily relies on pre-existing regulations and legal frameworks in order to patch together its own regulatory guidelines and standards of operation. In contrast, most other industries are specifically governed by laws and regulations that directly relate to that particular field. For example, in the medical industry, specific laws and regulations were created and implemented as an acknowledgment of their need and importance.[4] By relying on regulations enacted for other industries, the many nuanced areas of the IoT, especially those impacting consumers, are often either underregulated or completely unregulated, creating "grey areas" for the industry. Furthermore, this piecemeal—rather than comprehensive—approach, merely corrects problems reactively as they appear and does little to proactively address future issues likely to arise.

---

3.   Eric A. Fischer, *The Internet of Things: Frequently Asked Questions*, CONG. RESEARCH SERV. (Oct. 13, 2015).

4.   Robert Field, *Why Is Healthcare Regulation So Complex?*, NAT'L CTR. FOR BIOTECHNOLOGY INFO., www.ncbi.nlm.nih.gov/pmc/articles/PMC 2730786/ (last visited May 28, 2020).

§ 2:2.1   The Consumer Financial Protection Bureau (CFPB)

The CFPB was established by the Dodd-Frank Wall Street Reform and Consumer Protection Act, which was passed in direct response to the financial crisis of 2007.[5] The CFPB is responsible for consumer protections in the financial sector; this includes stringent oversight of financial institutions to prevent their engagement in deceptive practices.[6] Presently, the CFPB has yet to take action with respect to regulating information and data gathered from an IoT device. However, the CFPB recently brought a $100,000 civil fine against Dwolla, an online payment platform, for the company's deceptive practices involving securing customers' sensitive personal information.[7] Much of the information collected by Dwolla, such as customers' names, addresses, dates of birth, Social Security numbers, and bank account information, is also collected by other IoT providers and processed by IoT devices.[8] Thus, few would be surprised to see the CFPB file similar suits against manufacturers of IoT devices that also process consumers' financial data in order to protect consumers and maintain integrity within industry operations.[9]

§ 2:2.2   The Department of Defense (DOD)

In 1941, during the battle waged between Allied merchant ships and German U-boats over the North Atlantic seas, victory was dependent upon either side's ability to obtain and effectively synthesize the greatest amount of information. In those days, whomever could generate and analyze information the quickest—and in turn adjust tactical posture, logistical supply lines, intelligence groups, and support facilities—would emerge as the victor. Information was gathered by codebreaking and sensors on aircraft that relayed information to centralized command centers.[10]

---

5.   About Us, CONSUMER FIN. PROT. BUREAU, www.consumerfinance.gov/about-us/ (last visited May 28, 2020).

6.   Nikole Davenport, *Smart Washers May Clean Your Clothes, But Hacks Can Clean Out Your Privacy, and Underdeveloped Regulations Could Leave You Hanging on a Line*, 32 J. MARSHALL J. INFO. TECH. & PRIVACY L. 259 (2016).

7.   CFPB Press Release, CFPB Takes Action Against Dwolla for Misrepresenting Data Security Practices (Mar. 2, 2016).

8.   Davenport, *supra* note 6.

9.   *Id.*

10. Brett Loubert, *How the Internet of Things Can Drive Value for the U.S. Military*, CIOReview, https://aerospace-defense.cioreview.com/cxoinsight/how-the-internet-of-things-can-drive-value-for-the-us-military-nid-18352-cid-5.html (last visited May 28, 2020).

Within the military, the flow of information is at the heart of logistics and intelligence. In some cases, data processing is classified in the same category as artillery because of the great impact it can have. Because of the importance that the military places on information, it is constantly exploring new technology and developing tools to improve communication, routing, and data processing. To this point, in recent years, the IoT has become a vital component of military technology with its advanced communication, routing, and data processing capabilities. New IoT technology has also in turn transformed the role of Chief Information Officer (CIO) into a more mission-focused position rather than solely encompassing Information and Technology (IT) management responsibilities. The CIO is now typically in charge of teaching active duty service members how to use various IoT technologies and demonstrating how each device or process factors into the broader mission and enhances the decision-making process.[11]

In addition to its range in functionality, using the IoT in the military can also reduce the cost of asset tracking. For example, instead of requiring individuals to fill out delivery receipts or conduct equipment inventory audits by hand, simply placing a sensor on individual assets and connecting the sensors to a centralized reporting network effectively saves time and resources and provides more accurate accountability results. Additionally, the DOD can leverage the IoT to save money on facilities management. One pilot study in this particular area found that implementing IoT solutions in a Naval Station would reduce energy usage by 20–30%, translating to an annual savings of approximately $500 million for that single Naval Station, alone.[12]

The military will certainly explore numerous avenues to most effectively implement IoT technology. Most importantly, it must investigate different uses of the IoT to improve its methods of obtaining and analyzing information faster while also saving money.

§ 2:2.3   *The Department of Energy (DOE)*

The DOE is charged with orchestrating the wholesale modernization of our nation's electrical grid.[13] Section 1302 of the Energy Independence and Security Act of 2007, 42 U.S.C. § 17382, directs the Secretary of Energy to "report to Congress concerning the status of the smart grid deployments nationwide and any regulatory or government barriers to continued deployment. The report shall provide the current status and prospects of smart grid development, including

---

11.   *Id.*
12.   *Id.*
13.   *The Smart Grid: An Introduction*, ENERGY.GOV, www.energy.gov/sites/prod/files/oeprod/DocumentsandMedia/DOE_SG_Book_Single_Pages.pdf.

information on technology penetration, communications network capabilities, costs, and obstacles. It may include recommendations for State and Federal policies or actions helpful to facilitate the transition to a smart grid."[14]

Currently, IoT devices, vehicles, buildings, and other items that can send and receive data offer the promise of new, advanced services by forging connections between the virtual and physical world while improving communication and control technologies. This two-way communication is a key component of progress in DOE's grid modernization efforts from previous Smart Grid work to today's Grid Modernization Initiative.[15] Further, the IoT offers new opportunities for consumers to engage with the power sector as it simultaneously improves efficiency and performance across the power grid.[16] Through the IoT, advanced sensors can gather new data from grid assets to provide grid operators with better insight into infrastructure performance. The DOE and private companies have thus been working across the electrical system to research, develop, and apply advanced communications and controls technologies to improve reliability, efficiency, and security of the U.S. grid.[17]

Integrating the IoT with the existing electrical grid changes all aspects of grid planning and operations by introducing new requirements for interoperability and cybersecurity, and by managing new troves of big data such as advanced meters and sensors.[18] This enhanced integration of distributed energy resources, green-buildings, smart vehicles, and energy storage into the grid allows the DOE to adapt more quickly to fast-changing conditions and allows for improved access to reliable, safe, and affordable energy.[19]

§ 2:2.4   The Department of Homeland Security (DHS)

There are sixteen critical infrastructure sectors whose assets, systems, and networks, whether physical or virtual, are considered so vital to the United States that their incapacitation or destruction would have a debilitating effect on the country's physical security, economic security, public health and safety, or any combination thereof.[20] Founded in 2002, the DHS is charged with strengthening and

---

14.   42 U.S.C. § 17382.
15.   *Grid Modernization Initiative*, DEP'T OF ENERGY, www.energy.gov/grid-modernization-initiative (last visited May 28, 2020).
16.   *Id.*
17.   *Id.*
18.   *The Smart Grid: An Introduction*, *supra* note 13.
19.   *Grid Modernization Initiative*, *supra* note 15.
20.   *Critical Infrastructure Sectors*, DEP'T OF HOMELAND SEC. (2018), www.cisa.gov/critical-infrastructure-sectors (last visited May 28, 2020).

maintaining the security, functionality, and resiliency of these infra-structures.[21] As network connections increasingly integrate and auto-mate into our nation's critical infrastructure, important processes that were once performed manually are now vulnerable to cyber threats.[22] Our ever-increasing national dependence on network-connected tech-nologies has expanded faster than our means to effectively secure it.[23] While the benefits of the IoT are undeniable, the harsh reality is that security is not keeping up with the pace of innovation.[24] To combat this problem, the DHS created *Strategic Principles for Securing the Internet of Things* with the purpose of improving the security of the IoT across its full range of design, manufacturing, and deployment of activities.[25] Widespread adoption of these strategic principles and the associated suggested best practices would dramatically improve the security posture of the IoT for the DHS.[26]

§ 2:2.5   *The Department of Justice (DOJ)*

In February 2018, the Attorney General announced the creation of a Cyber-Digital Task Force within the DOJ.[27] The Task Force was assigned to assess the many ways that the DOJ combats the global cyber threat, as well as to identify how federal law enforcement can more effectively accomplish its mission in this vital and evolving area.[28] The Task Force was asked to review the mass exploitation of com-puters, along with the weaponization of everyday consumer devices to launch attacks on American citizens and businesses.[29] The report noted that recent staggering growth within the IoT sector has allowed malicious actors to build botnets from under-protected IoT devices to launch attacks.[30] Botnets are a collection of Internet-connected

---

21.   *Id.*
22.   *Strategic Principles for Securing the Internet of Things (IoT)*, DEP'T OF HOMELAND SEC. (Nov. 15, 2016), www.dhs.gov/sites/default/files/ publications/Strategic_Principles_for_Securing_the_Internet_of_Things-2016-1115-FINAL.pdf.
23.   *Critical Infrastructure Sectors*, *supra* note 20.
24.   *Strategic Principles for Securing the Internet of Things (IoT)*, *supra* note 22.
25.   *Id.*
26.   *Id.*
27.   *Report of the Attorney General's Cyber Digital Task Force*, U.S. Dep't of Justice—Office of the Deputy Att'y Gen. (July 2, 2018), www.justice.gov/ ag/page/file/1076696/download.
28.   Michael Diakiwski & Megan Brown, *DOJ's Cyber-Digital Task Force Report Touches IoT, Critical Infrastructure, Supply Chain Risk, and More*, WILEY CONNECT (July 20, 2018), www.wileyconnect.com/home/2018/7/20/ dojs-cyber-digital-task-force-report-touches-iot-critical-infrastructure-supply-chain-risk-and-more.
29.   *Id.*
30.   *Id.*

devices, such as PCs, servers, mobile products, and IoT devices that are infected and controlled by a common type of malware.[31] The report identified the DOJ's difficulty in combating these networks because the criminals who run such botnets often are located abroad, making investigation and prosecution more challenging.[32] However, though the DOJ has had some success in targeting and disabling botnets through arrests and prosecutions, at present, the innovation and security measures surrounding IoT devices still outpaces the enforcement of regulations and advances in law, raising more public safety concerns.[33]

§ 2:2.6   The Federal Aviation Administration (FAA)

While the government has not yet developed a full cross-agency strategy for regulating all IoT developments,[34] the FAA is in the process of creating regulations for drones, also known as unmanned aerial vehicles.[35] Originally used for missions too "dull, dirty or dangerous" for humans, mostly in military applications, drone use is rapidly expanding to commercial, scientific, recreational, agricultural, and other applications.[36] Drones play an important role in the IoT because they are critically dependent on sensors, antennae, and embedded software to provide two-way communications for remote control and monitoring.[37] This expansion of drone usage has led the FAA to implement the FAA Modernization and Reform Act of 2012.[38] The primary goal of this regulation is to regulate commercial drone usage.[39]

§ 2:2.7   The Federal Communications
Commission (FCC)

The FCC, pursuant to section 222 of the Telecommunications Act of 1996, may regulate the privacy of customer information provided to,

---

31.   *See* https://searchsecurity.techtarget.com/definition/botnet?_ga=2.161377 147.796043664.1590685522-1814282500.1590685522 (last visited May 28, 2020).

32.   Diakiwski & Brown, *supra* note 28.

33.   *Report of the Attorney General's Cyber Digital Task Force, supra* note 27.

34.   Andrew Meola, *U.S. Government Asks for Help in Developing IoT Technologies*, BUS. INSIDER (Apr. 13, 2016), www.businessinsider.com/ us-government-asks-for-help-in-developing-iot-technologies-2016-4.

35.   *Id.*

36.   *Id.*

37.   *Drones*, ANSYS ICEPAK, www.ansys.com/Campaigns/internet-of-things/ drones (last visited May 28, 2020).

38.   FAA Modernization and Reform Act, Pub. L. No. 112-095.

39.   *Id.*

and obtained by, telecommunication carriers.[40] The FCC enforces section 222 by limiting the ability of telecommunication carriers to access, use, and disclose Customer Proprietary Network Information (CPNI).[41] Specifically, section 222 limits how CPNI may be disclosed to third parties. However, it remains an open question whether section 222 will apply to IoT data.[42]

§ 2:2.8 The Federal Trade Commission (FTC)

While a number of federal agencies touch upon different areas of the IoT, the FTC, by far, ends up with the lion's share of regulatory responsibility, especially with respect to consumer protection. The FTC primarily enforces IoT privacy and security pursuant to its authority to police unfair and deceptive trade practices through section 5 of the FTC Act.[43] Interestingly, the FTC defines the IoT as "devices or sensors that connect, store or transmit information with or between each other via the internet," but it does not include computers, smartphones, and tablets within this definition.[44]

§ 2:2.9 The Food & Drug Administration (FDA)

In January 2016, the FDA released draft guidelines for IoT devices.[45] The guidelines covered data collection, security concerns, and recommendations related to IoT medical devices.[46] With respect to cybersecurity, the FDA follows the guidelines established by the National Institute of Standards and Technology (NIST).[47] Also, similar to the NIST, the FDA expects those who operate within the IoT industry to self-regulate.[48]

In 2017, the FDA, in its Design Considerations and Pre-Market Submission Recommendations for Interoperable Medical Devices,

---

40. Nikole Davenport, *Smart Washers May Clean Your Clothes, But Hacks Can Clean Out Your Privacy, and Underdeveloped Regulations Could Leave You Hanging on a Line*, 32 J. MARSHALL J. INFO. TECH. & PRIVACY L. 259 (2016).
41. *Id.*
42. *Id.*
43. 15 U.S.C. § 45(a).
44. *Id.*
45. Press Release, FDA Outlines Cybersecurity Recommendations for Medical Device Manufacturers, Food & Drug Admin. (Jan. 15, 2016), www.fda.gov/newsevents/newsroom/pressannouncements/ucm481968.htm.
46. Davenport, *supra* note 40.
47. *Id.*
48. *Id.*

identified six areas that interoperable medical device manufacturers should consider when developing and designing products:

1. the purpose of the electronic interface;

2. the anticipated users;

3. risk management;

4. verifications and validation;

5. labeling considerations; and

6. use of consensus standards.[49]

§ 2:2.10 The National Institute of Standards and Technology (NIST) and The National Telecommunications and Information Administration (NTIA)

Two agencies, the NIST and the NTIA, offer the same advice with regard to how the IoT should be implemented. The NIST is a non-regulatory agency of the Department of Commerce whose mission is to promote innovation and industrial competitiveness. In September 2015, the NIST released its IoT Framework. Among other things, this framework improves security in the IoT realm by "providing a common set of considerations for the design of devices and a common language to allow designers to promote interactions between devices."[50] This NIST Framework assists with regulating the IoT industry by establishing the appropriate level of "cybersecurity care in IoT negligence actions."

The NTIA is an executive branch agency responsible for advising the president on telecommunications and information policy issues.[51] Its programs and policy-making focuses on expanding use of spectrum and broadband Internet access and adoption, and ensuring that the Internet will remain an engine for continued innovation and economic growth.[52] The NTIA is also one of the leaders in research and data on the status of broadband availability and adoption in the United States.[53]

---

49. Mildred Segura, Christopher Butler & Farah Tabikhoei, *The Internet of Medical Things Raise Novel Compliance Challenges*, MED DEVICE ONLINE (Jan. 3, 2018).

50. Scott J. Shackelford, Anjanette Raymond, Danuvasin Charoen, Rakshana Balakrishnan, Prakhar Dixit, Julianna Gjonaj & Rachith Kavi, *When Toasters Attack: A Polycentric Approach to Enhancing the "Security of Things,"* 2017 U. ILL. L. REV. 415.

51. About NTIA, NAT'L TELECOMM. & INFO. ADMIN., www.ntia.doc.gov/about (last visited Dec. 28, 2018).

52. *Id.*

53. *Id.*

Based on the recommendations from the NTIA and the NIST, the Cellular Telecommunications and Internet Association offers cyber-security certificate programs specifically designed for IoT devices to create a more secure foundation for smart cities, grids, connected cars, and other IoT applications.[54] In addition, the NTIA and the NIST were directed by the Department of Commerce to study IoT devices, best practices, and the potential for regulating the industry.[55] Both the NTIA and the NIST are becoming more important players at the municipal level as cities increasingly think about how to pre-vent cyber attacks from the growing number of IoT devices coming online.[56] The preventative ideas generated by both agencies are con-sidered increasingly valuable due to their potential impact in combat-ting the escalation of high-profile ransomware attacks; such attacks recently shut down city functions in Atlanta and Baltimore.[57]

§ 2:3 General Legislation

At present, most of the laws currently applicable to the IoT were originally created for other industries. Nonetheless, they have been mostly effective in providing at least some oversight to the burgeon-ing IoT sector. In this section, the impact of the following federal laws on the IoT will be covered: the Federal Trade Commission Act; the Health Insurance Portability and Accountability Act; the Fair Credit Reporting Act; the Children's Online Privacy Protection Act; and the Electronic Communications Privacy Act.

§ 2:3.1 The Federal Trade Commission Act (FTCA)

Section 5 of the FTCA prohibits unfair or deceptive acts or prac-tices in, or affecting, commerce.[58] The FTC has used both the unfair and deceptive prongs of the Act to regulate in the areas of consumer privacy and security.[59] Enforcement generally comes in the form of consent decrees between the FTC and the offending entity.[60]

---

54. Jason Plautz, *CTIA Announces Cybersecurity Certification for IoT Devices*, SMARTCITIESDIVE (Aug. 22, 2018), www.smartcitiesdive.com/news/ctia-announces-cybersecurity-certification-for-iot-devices/530635/.
55. *Id.*
56. *Id.*
57. *Id.*
58. *A Brief Overview of the Federal Trade Commission's Investigative and Law Enforcement Authority*, FED. TRADE COMM'N (2017), www.ftc.gov/about-ftc/what-we-do/enforcement-authority (last visited May 28, 2020).
59. Scott Peppet, *Regulating the Internet of Things: First Steps Toward Managing Discrimination, Privacy, Security, and Consent*, 93 TEX. L. REV. 85 (2014).
60. *Id.*

Unfair practices include those that "cause or [are] likely to cause substantial injury to consumers which are not reasonably avoidable by consumers themselves and not outweighed by countervailing benefits to consumers or to competition."[61] In unfairness cases, the FTC must demonstrate that the IoT company injured consumers in a way that violates public policy, which may be challenging in the areas of security and privacy.[62] One notable exception is *FTC v. Wyndham Worldwide Corp.*,[63] in which the court determined that data practices could be deemed "unfair" under the FTCA and that section 45(a) provided Wyndham with fair notice that its practices exposed it to liability. The case arose from a hack of one of Wyndham's property management systems that processed consumer information including names, addresses, contact information, and credit card information; the hackers accessed more than 619,000 accounts, resulting in a loss of $10.6 million in fraudulent charges. It has been suggested that the FTC's authority here could be strengthened by legislative action.[64]

In order for an act to be deceptive, there must be: (1) a representation, omission, or practice likely to mislead the consumer; (2) the consumer must have acted reasonably in the circumstance; and (3) the representation, omission, or practice must be a "material" one.[65] The FTC uses the deception prong analysis when a company represents one thing but, in reality, practices something completely different. For instance, if a company's privacy policy states that it never collects user information, but it indeed collected user information, the FTC can charge that company with a section 5 violation based on a deceptive practice. This very broad power has been repeatedly upheld by the courts. In fact, the TRENDNet case discussed in chapter 4 is just one example of an FTC enforcement action in this area.

§ 2:3.2   The Health Insurance Portability and Accountability Act (HIPAA)

HIPAA was passed in 1996 in an effort to "improve the portability and accountability of health insurance coverage" and to create uniform rules regarding electronic health transmissions.[66] In 2003, HIPAA, through the Privacy Rule, defined Protected Health

---

61. *Id.*
62. 15 U.S.C. § 45(n).
63. FTC v. Wyndham Worldwide Corp., 10 F. Supp. 3d 602 (D.N.J. 2014).
64. *See* Peppet, *supra* note 59.
65. Federal Trade Commission Act Section 5: Unfair or Deceptive Acts or Practices (Dec. 2016), www.federalreserve.gov/boarddocs/supmanual/cch/ftca.pdf.
66. *HIPAA History*, HIPAA J., www.hipaajournal.com/hipaa-history/ (last visited May 28, 2020).

Information (PHI) as "any information held by a covered entity which concerns health status, the provision of healthcare, or payment for healthcare that can be linked to an individual."[67] Entities covered by HIPAA include health plans, healthcare clearinghouses, and healthcare providers who transmit health information in electronic form in connection with transactions.[68] Covered entities are the only ones that must comply with the HIPAA privacy regulations.

Health plans are individual or group plans that provide or pay the cost of medical care. These plans include: healthcare, dental, vision, and prescription drug insurers; health maintenance organizations; Medicare; Medicaid; and long-term care insurers. A healthcare provider who electronically transmits health information in connection with certain transactions, regardless of size, is considered a covered entity. These transactions generally include insurance claims, benefit eligibility inquiries, referral authorization requests, or other transactions for which HHS has established standards. Transactions are covered regardless of whether they involve a direct electronic transmission or instead rely on a manual billing service or third party.

Healthcare clearinghouses process nonstandard information received from another entity into a standard format or data content, or vice versa. The clearinghouses generally receive PHI or individually identifiable health information when providing services as a "business associate," which is a person or organization, outside of a covered entity's workforce, "that performs certain functions or activities on behalf of, or provides certain services to, a covered entity that involve the use or disclosure of individually identifiable health information." All individually identifiable health information is PHI, and the privacy rule protects that information held or transmitted by a covered entity or its business associate, in any form or media, whether electronic, paper, or oral. PHI includes either *direct identifiers* or *indirect identifiers*. Direct identifiers are information that could lead someone directly to the individual, such as names, telephone numbers, Social Security numbers, and biometrics. Indirect identifiers are information that can lead an individual to the subject when combined with other pieces of information, for example, geographic subdivisions smaller than a state, all ages over age eighty-nine, medical record numbers, longitude/latitude, and IP addresses.

HIPAA does not restrict the use or disclosure of de-identified health information. De-identified information neither identifies nor

---

67. *Id.*
68. HHS OFFICE OF THE SECRETARY & OFFICE FOR CIVIL RIGHTS (OCR), Summary of the HIPAA Privacy Rule, HHS.GOV, www.hhs.gov/hipaa/for-professionals/privacy/laws-regulations/index.html (last visited May 28, 2020).

provides a reasonable basis to identify an individual. There are two ways for information to be de-identified: (1) a formal determination by a qualified statistician; or (2) the removal of specified identifiers of the individual and of their relatives, family, and employers as required; de-identification is adequate only if the covered entity has no actual knowledge that the remaining information could be used to identify the individual.[69]

Covered entities may use and disclose PHI if the individual consents to the disclosure or falls within one of the six permitted exceptions, where the use or disclosure is:

1. to the individual;

2. for treatment, payment, and healthcare operations;

3. made under circumstances where the individual has the opportunity to agree or object;

4. incident to an otherwise permitted use and disclosure;

5. for public interest and benefit activities; or

6. a limited data set for the purposes of research, public health, or healthcare operations.[70]

In the HIPAA Privacy Rule, specific procedures must be followed by covered entities. Furthermore, the HIPAA Security Rule regulates a subset of the Privacy Rule, called electronic Protected Health Information (ePHI).[71] The HIPPA Security Rule is the codification of information technology standards and best practices.[72] The Security Rule requires the implementation of three types of safeguards: administrative, physical, and technical.

Administrative safeguards can include: policies and procedures; development, implementation, and maintenance of security measures; and administrative actions created to manage and protect ePHI. Administrative safeguards are policies that inform employees of the job functions they can and cannot perform and provide examples of how employees should react in certain situations.

Physical safeguards are measures, policies, and procedures related to buildings and equipment, natural and environmental hazards, and unauthorized intrusion. Physical safeguards can be locked doors, locked file cabinets, etc.

---

69.   *Id.*
70.   *Id.*
71.   *HIPAA Security Rule,* HITECH Act, www.hipaasurvivalguide.com/hipaa-security-rule.php (last visited May 28, 2020).
72.   *Id.*

tech safeguards

Finally, technical safeguards are policies and procedures governing technology in order to protect use, control, and access to ePHIs. Technical safeguards can be seminars on web safety, detecting phishing emails, and even mandatory password length and periodic changes to login procedures.

When an IoT device conveys PHI about an individual to a covered entity, HIPAA governs that data. Not only is the IoT device conveying something to a covered entity, the device, and consequently the company, becomes a covered entity. Because of this relationship, HIPAA applies to the actions of the IoT company when conveying PHI if it fits into the definition. However, if someone simply goes to the store and buys a wearable device like a Fitbit, which maintains health-related information, the Fitbit is not a covered HIPAA entity; therefore, the data the device collects are not bound by, or protected under, HIPAA.[73] In contrast, if a person receives a wearable device through their hospital or doctor, the subsequently collected healthcare data are covered by HIPAA.

§ 2:3.3   *The Fair Credit Reporting Act (FCRA)*

The FCRA provides consumers certain rights with respect to their credit reports.[74] The law regulates how consumer reporting agencies (CRAs) use consumer information. The full definition of a CRA is as follows:

> [A]ny person which, for monetary fees, dues, or on a cooperative nonprofit basis, regularly engages in whole or in part in the practice of assembling or evaluating consumer credit information or other information on consumers for the purpose of furnishing consumer reports to third parties, and which uses any means or facility of interstate commerce for the purpose of preparing or furnishing consumer reports.[75]

A consumer report is defined as follows:

> [A]ny written, oral, or other communication of any information by a CRA bearing on a consumer's credit worthiness, credit

---

73.   While a Fitbit, depending on the context in which it is used, may or may not be covered under HIPAA, the manufacturer maintains that the device itself is HIPAA compliant. Press Release, Fitbit Extends Corporate Wellness Offering with HIPAA Compliant Capabilities (Sept. 15, 2016), https://investor.fitbit.com/press/press-releases/press-release-details/2015/fitbit-extends-corporate-wellness-offering-with-hipaa-compliant-capabilities/default.aspx.

74.   15 U.S.C. § 1681.

75.   *Id.*

standing, credit capacity, character, general reputation, personal characteristics, or mode of living which is used or expected to be used or collected in whole or in part for the purpose of serving as a factor in establishing the consumer's eligibility for (1) credit or insurance to be used primarily for personal, family, or household purposes, or (2) employment purposes, or (3) other purposes authorized under section 604.[76]

The reach of the FCRA with respect to IoT devices is somewhat limited as noted in a 2015 report by the FTC, the entity responsible for enforcing violations of the FCRA. According to the FTC,

> [T]he FCRA excludes most "first parties" that collect consumer information; thus, it would not generally cover IoT device manufacturers that do their own in-house analytics. Nor would the FCRA cover companies that collect data directly from consumers' connected devices and then use that data to make in-house credit, insurance, or other eligibility decisions—something that could become increasingly common as the IoT develops.[77]

no first parties covered

The 2015 FTC Report provided a real-world application of the FCRA to an IoT device: an insurance company offering consumers the option of submitting data from a Fitbit or wellness tracker in exchange for lowering their health insurance premium. According to the FTC Report, the provisions of the FCRA to include those mandating the consumer's right to access information and correct errors may be inapplicable. However, if Fitbit wanted to sell user data to an outside third party, like a prospective employer or insurance company, the FTC might deem Fitbit a CRA under the FCRA. This in turn would give consumers the right to dispute the accuracy of any information provided by Fitbit.

Another FCRA limitation concerns tailored offers made through elaborate marketing techniques. For instance, a company aggregates data and sells consumer profile information to include IoT data to an online shopping store at the exact instance that the consumer goes to the online shopping store. If a profile is then subsequently relied upon to tailor ads to the consumer on the website, the tailored offer does not generate FCRA regulations.

tailored offers not covered.

---

76. The Fair Credit Reporting Act, https://epic.org/privacy/financial/fcra.html (last visited Mar. 19, 2018).

77. Internet of Things: Privacy & Security in a Connected World, FTC STAFF REPORT (Jan. 2015), www.ftc.gov/system/files/documents/reports/federal-trade-commission-staff-report-november-2013-workshop-entitled-internet-things-privacy/150127iotrpt.pdf.

The final FCRA limitation for consumers with respect to data gathered with an IoT device concerns the purpose of the law.[78] The FCRA was created to protect the accuracy of credit reports. Generally speaking, accuracy is not a problem when data is derived from a machine; the concern, from the consumer's view, is the inferences drawn from that data and how that data are subsequently used.[79] The FCRA applies to the inputs, but does not apply to the inferences drawn therefrom.[80] Thus, consumers have little protection against using those inferences to derive a credit score.

§ 2:3.4 The Children's Online Privacy Protection Act (COPPA)

The COPPA was created to protect the privacy of children under the age of thirteen when using the Internet. The purpose of the law, passed in 1998, was to give parents some control over the information their children share online. The relevant aspects of COPPA are:

1. parental consent for the collection or use of a child's personal information;

2. methods for obtaining consent;

3. establishment of a privacy policy; and

4. website operators' responsibilities for marketing.[81]

The actual text of the law "prohibits unfair or deceptive acts or practices in connection with the collection, use, and/or disclosure of personal information from and about children on the Internet."[82] COPPA applies to websites either directed at children under thirteen years of age or that know they are collecting personal information from children under thirteen. For the purposes of the IoT, it is important to note how COPPA defines the "Internet."

"Internet" is defined as: *internet def.*

> [C]ollectively[,] the myriad of computer and telecommunications facilities, including equipment and operating software, which

---

78. Nikole Davenport, *Smart Washers May Clean Your Clothes, But Hacks Can Clean Out Your Privacy, and Underdeveloped Regulations Could Leave You Hanging on a Line*, 32 J. MARSHALL J. INFO. TECH. & PRIVACY L. 259 (2016).

79. *Id.*

80. Scott Peppet, *Regulating the Internet of Things: First Steps Toward Managing Discrimination, Privacy, Security, and Consent*, 93 TEX. L. REV. 85 (2014).

81. Children's Online Privacy Protection Rule, 78 Fed. Reg. 3971 (2013).

82. eCFR—Code of Federal Regulations, tit. 16, § 312.3.

> comprise the interconnected world-wide network of networks
> that employ the transmission Control Protocol/Internet Protocol,
> or any predecessor or successor protocols to such protocol, to
> communicate information of all kinds by wire, radio, or other
> methods of transmission.[83]

This expansive definition will likely capture most IoT devices used by, or directed at, children under thirteen years of age, even those not connected to the Internet.

Another wrinkle within the COPPA applies to IoT companies that do not necessarily produce or manage devices directed at children. Operators of general audience websites or online services that nevertheless have actual knowledge that they are collecting, using, or disclosing information from children under the age of thirteen are still regulated by COPPA.[84] This means that, if there is a website that requires individuals to sign up and provide basic information about themselves (e.g., date of birth in order to enter the site), the operator then has actual knowledge as to the age of the user. Therefore, if an IoT company is sufficiently certain that the device or online service could either be used by children under the age of thirteen or directly targeted to them, then they must comply with COPPA. For instance, Amazon's Alexa devices are not marketed directly to children but, children indeed use the devices. Children can ask Alexa to order things, either purposely or accidentally; they request Alexa to read stories to them; and Alexa may be accidentally or negligently activated while children are around. If Alexa then stores a child's information, including the child's voice inputs, then that engagement triggers COPPA compliance. Finally, an IoT device created and marketed directly to children would also fall within the scope of COPPA.

§ 2:3.5   *The Electronic Communications Privacy Act (ECPA)*

The ECPA was enacted in order to protect "wire, oral, and electronic communications while those communications are being made, are in transit, and when they are stored on computers."[85] The ECPA is made up of three legislative acts: the Wiretap Act, the Stored Communications Act (SCA), and the Pen Register Act. Unlike the foregoing federal laws, the ECPA focuses on protecting data during

---

83.   *Id.* § 312.2.
84.   *Complying with COPPA: Frequently Asked Questions*, FED. TRADE COMM'N, www.ftc.gov/tips-advice/business-center/guidance/complying-coppa-frequently-asked-questions#General%20Questions (last visited May 28, 2020).
85.   Elec. Commc'ns Privacy Act of 1986, 18 U.S.C. §§ 2510–23.

transit

transit and storage processes from being exploited by a malicious third party. When the ECPA is combined with COPPA, the FCRA, HIPPA, and section five of the FTCA, they collectively create powerful privacy protections for conduct that falls within their respective areas.

Wiretap act

The Wiretap Act "prohibits the intentional, actual or attempted interception, use, disclosure, or procure[ment] [of] any other person to intercept or endeavor to intercept any wire, oral, or electronic communication."[86] This legislation applies to email, telephones, and electronically stored data.[87] The Wiretap Act protects against the improper interception of electronic communication while in transit, for example, the use of a "bug" to eavesdrop on a telephone conversation.

The SCA "protects the privacy of the contents of files stored by service providers and of records held about the subscriber by service providers." This includes subscribers' name, billing records, IP addresses, and actual content.[88] The SCA was enacted because the Internet gave rise to a host of privacy breaches that the Fourth Amendment did not adequately address.

pen register act

The Pen Register Act prohibits the installation or use of pen register or a trap and trace device without a court order obtained under section 3123 of the Foreign Intelligence Surveillance Act of 1978.[89] A government agency that is authorized to install such a device must use technology reasonably available to restrict the use of the device so as not to include the contents of any wire or electronic communication.

not include contents wire comm.

§ 2:4 Federal IoT-Specific Legislation

It can be difficult to draft legislation to address technology that evolves as quickly as the IoT. Nonetheless, the federal government has made incremental steps to craft IoT-specific legislation. Most of the proposed bills discussed below involve IoT industry guidance or recommendations rather than the imposition of a government regulation or mandate.[90] However, as the IoT industry matures, many expect increased federal regulation and government oversight.

§ 2:4.1 *Congressional Resolutions*

To date, both houses of Congress have passed resolutions pertaining to the IoT. H.R. 847 and S.R. 110 were both unanimously

---

86. *Id.*
87. *Id.*
88. *Id.*
89. 18 U.S.C. ch. 206.
90. Lloyd McCoy, *Regulation is the Best Hope for IoT Security—Imagine That*, CSO (Mar. 12, 2018), www.csoonline.com/article/3262584/regulation-is-the-best-hope-for-iot-security-imagine-that.html.

adopted in the 114th Congress.[91] These mirror image bills are resolutions that express the sense of Congress and do not require the signature of the president. Both resolutions call for "a national strategy for the Internet of Things to promote economic growth and consumer empowerment."[92] The bills also recommended federal policies that "prioritize accelerating the development and deployment of the Internet of Things in a way that recognizes its benefits, allows for future innovation, and responsibly protects against misuse."[93]

§ 2:4.2   The DIGIT Act

The DIGIT Act (Developing Innovation and Growing of the Internet of Things) was introduced in the U.S. House of Representatives in 2017.[94] The DIGIT Act defines the IoT as "the growing number of connected and interconnected devices."[95] This definition is both broad and narrow at the same time. The definition is broad in the sense that it includes not only Internet-connect devices, but also phone, television, and radio networks.[96] The DIGIT Act is narrow in scope because it defines "the use of the Internet for controlling, monitoring, tracking, and interconnecting everyday objects."[97]

The DIGIT Act estimates that there will be more than 50,000,000,000 devices connected to the Internet in the year 2020.[98] This number most likely encompasses both wireless devices and products connected via cable to the Internet.[99] Congress also projects that the IoT has the potential of generating trillions of dollars in new economic activity worldwide.[100] The IoT has been calculated to be potentially worth $19 trillion in 2020.[101]

The DIGIT Act further proposes the creation of a working group of stakeholders to provide recommendations to Congress regarding how

---

91.   Arlen Gary, *House Urges 'National Strategy' for IoT Development*, MULTICHANNEL.COM (Sept. 20, 2016).

92.   *Id.*

93.   *Id.*

94.   DIGIT Act of 2017, H.R. 686, 115th Congress. The House of Representatives did not take action on the bill and it has yet to be reintroduced in the 116th Congress. However, the Senate passed its version of the DIGIT Act (S. 1611) in the 116th Congress and it awaits action by the House of Representatives.

95.   *Id.*

96.   An Overview of the Proposed DIGIT Act, InfoSec Resources (Feb. 11, 2019), http://resources.infosecinstitute.com/overview-proposed-digit-act/#gref.

97.   *Id.*

98.   DIGIT Act of 2017, H.R. 686, 115th Congress.

99.   An Overview of the Proposed DIGIT Act, *supra* note 96.

100.   DIGIT Act of 2017, *supra* note 98.

101.   An Overview of the Proposed DIGIT Act, *supra* note 96.

to "plan and encourage the proliferation of the Internet of Things."[102] This working group would examine five aspects of the IoT:

1. current and future spectrum needs;

2. regulatory environment;

3. consumer protection;

4. privacy and security; and

5. the current use of this technology by federal agencies.[103]

The DIGIT Act aims to accurately estimate current and future spectrum needs so that the U.S. government can encourage the development of innovative technology that will lead to a more productive use of the spectrum. In examining the regulatory environment of the IoT, the working group would examine sector-specific regulations and general regulations alike, to ensure adherence to corresponding standards—for example, credit and debit card transactions following the payment card industry standards, and consumer-wearable health technology complying with HIPAA regulations.

The group will also examine issues surrounding consumer protections. For example, the group may look at the lack of transparency among IoT devices as well as the difficulty in explaining privacy policies to consumers due to so-called "legalese" within user agreements and other documents. One of the group's primary focus areas is the use of the IoT for unlawful surveillance, active intrusion in private life, and data profiling. The first two aspects are significant because of the potential for hackers to monitor people in disruptive or intrusive ways. The third aspect requires the group to examine the ability of sellers to create detailed consumer profiles of IoT device users.[104]

While the DIGIT Act has not officially been enacted, it illustrates the government's concerns with both consumer protections and unnecessary or burdensome regulations. In the DIGIT Act, Congress acknowledges that regulation can hinder the development of the IoT and indicates that it would prefer to approach the topic slowly, gathering as much information about the field before taking action. Barring some catastrophic event in which the IoT causes massive damage to the U.S. populace, Congress will most likely allow the IoT industry to continue to self-regulate through conformance to pre-existing regulations.

In order for IoT companies to continue to push for only limited regulation, they must create and adhere to industry standards and

---

102.   *Id.*
103.   *Id.*
104.   *Id.*

best practices from other sectors. If they fail to do so, then government regulation is far more likely. By way of example, the movie and video game industries created a rating system that details the content of a movie or game and assigns a predetermined rating based on those criteria. If this rating surpasses a certain threshold, retail stores and theaters must restrict who is permitted to access the content. The movie and video game industries thus saved themselves from government intrusion and potentially poor regulatory schemes by taking it upon themselves to self-impose guidelines to appease the public while still maintaining control of their respective sectors. IoT companies can therefore consider the movie and video game industries as role models to craft their own regulations in order to avoid or limit government intervention.

§ 2:4.3   *The Internet of Medical Things Resilience Partnership Act of 2017*

In an effort to provide greater oversight of IoT medical devices, several members of Congress in 2017 introduced H.R. 3985, the Internet of Medical Things Resilience Partnership Act of 2017.[105] The bill's goal was to "establish a working group of public and private entities led by the Food and Drug Administration to recommend voluntary frameworks and guidelines to increase the security and resilience of the Internet of Medical Things devices, and for other purposes."[106] The proposed working group includes: the FTC, the FDA, the DHHS, the Department of Commerce, medical device manufacturers, cloud computing experts, healthcare providers, insurers, and software and hardware developers.[107]

Specifically, the bill requires the FDA Commissioner to work with NIST in order to create a working group to draft a report to Congress. The report will include the following information:

1.   an identification of existing cybersecurity standards, guidelines, frameworks, and best practices that are applicable to mitigate vulnerabilities in the devices described in subsection (a);

2.   an identification of existing and developing international and domestic cybersecurity standards, guidelines, frameworks, and best practices that mitigate vulnerabilities in such devices;

---

105.   115th Congress, H.R. 3985.
106.   *Id.*
107.   Mildred Segura, Christopher Butler & Farah Tabikhoei, *The Internet of Medical Things Raise Novel Compliance Challenges*, MED DEVICE ONLINE (Jan. 3, 2018).

3. a specification of high-priority gaps for which new or revised standards are needed; and

4. potential action plans by which such gaps can be addressed.[108]

§ 2:4.4 The State of Modern Application, Research, and Trends of IoT Act

The House bill, State of Modern Application, Research, and Trends of IoT Act (SMART IoT Act), requires the Secretary of Commerce to conduct a study on the state of the Internet-connected devices industry.[109] Upon completion, the Secretary will submit the study to Congress. Based on the testimony accompanying this legislation, it appears that the study will lay the groundwork for future regulation of the IoT.[110]

§ 2:5 Conclusion

Since the IoT touches on so many different areas of industry and consumer use, it is regulated by a great number of different federal agencies ranging from the DOD to the CFPB to the FDA. This situation is unlikely to change absent the creation of a new federal agency formed specifically to govern the IoT. Based on this nation's history in creating agencies to regulate new industries and technologies— for example, railroads (Federal Railroad Administration), radio (Federal Communications Commission), automobiles (National Highway Traffic Safety Administration), airplanes (Federal Aviation Administration), and nuclear power (Nuclear Regulatory Commission)—it is possible that such an agency may be created in the near future.

As for legislation targeting the IoT, most legislators focus on bills addressing privacy or security; notable exceptions are the DIGIT Act, the SMART IoT Act, and the Internet of Medical Things Resilience Partnership Act of 2017. However, to date, no laws directly addressing the IoT have been passed at the federal level save for non-binding Resolutions. Thus, it remains to be seen whether Congress will defer to the individual states to regulate the IoT industry.

---

108. 115th Congress, H.R. 3985. The House of Representatives did not take action on the bill and it has yet to be re-introduced in the116th Congress.

109. State of Modern Application, Research, and Trends of IoT Act, H.R. 6032, 115th Cong. (2018). This is not the first medical cybersecurity task force created by the legislative branch. Section 405 of the Cybersecurity Act of 2015 created the Health Care Industry Cybersecurity Task Force.

110. Opening Statement of Chairman Bob Latta: Hearing on Internet of Things Legislation Before the Commerce Subcomm. on Dig. Commerce and Consumer Protection of the H. Comm. on Energy & Commerce, 115th Cong. (2018).

Chapter 3

Privacy

§ 3:1   Overview

Privacy is one of two major issues that threaten widespread adoption of the IoT.[1] The other is security, discussed in chapter 4. This chapter provides an overview of privacy as it relates to the IoT and briefly highlights federal laws targeting IoT privacy matters. However, due to the dearth of federal laws addressing digital privacy, this chapter is primarily focused on state efforts to regulate privacy. Privacy litigation involving the IoT will also be discussed. Finally, chapter 10 examines privacy laws in various countries in connection with the IoT.

§ 3:2   Regulation of Privacy in IoT Arena

Generally, IoT privacy concerns arise *directly* from the collection of information by IoT devices and *indirectly* from the inferences that are subsequently drawn based upon that information—a process sometimes referred to as sensor fusion.[2]

§ 3:2.1   *Sensor Fusion*

"Sensor fusion" is defined as using data from multiple sources to extrapolate and synthesize a more revealing data profile.[3] By combining information from one or more different IoT sensors, unexpected inferences can be drawn. For instance, an accelerometer or gyroscope found in most smartwatches can provide specific details about an individual's physical movement and location. When this information is combined with data from other IoT sensors, reasonable conclusions can be made about the individual wearing the smartwatch, e.g., mood, stress level, personality type, mental health, physical health, sleeping habits, etc. This virtual treasure trove of information is compiled automatically in most instances because of the nature of IoT devices and the need for them to function under specific circumstances. Sensor fusion, the practice of which is rarely disclosed to, or understood by, users, decreases the likelihood that information collected at the source will remain anonymous.

While IoT data collection, whether conducted directly or indirectly, can have numerous positive benefits, including improved credit, insurance, and employment decisions, there are also several downsides. For example, at least one major insurance company only

---

1.   Swaroop Poudel, *Internet of Things: Underlying Technologies, Interoperability, and Threats to Privacy and Security*, 31 BERKELEY TECH. L.J. 996–1022, 1013 (2016).

2.   *Id.*

3.   *Clearly Opaque Privacy Risks of the Internet of Things*, INTERNET OF THINGS PRIVACY FORUM (May 2018), www.iotprivacyforum.org/.

offers "interactive policies that track fitness and health data through wearable devices and smartphones."[4] Privacy advocates worry that the information gleaned from these devices will be used to insure only the healthiest customers, leaving others with no coverage or coverage at a higher cost.[5] Another drawback includes the omnipresence of IoT products and the resulting general lack of privacy. Individuals may be influenced to avoid certain behaviors that could be perceived as anomalous, even when in the comfort of their private homes, because such conduct is likely being captured in some fashion by an IoT device.[6]

§ 3:2.2   *Omnibus vs. Sectoral Approach*

At present, one of the biggest regulatory challenges facing privacy in the IoT arena is the lack of uniform laws. The U.S. federal government, unlike other countries and the European Union, primarily relies upon a sectoral approach to safeguarding privacy. Rather than one omnibus federal privacy law, each industry is governed by its own separate laws that incorporate privacy.[7] For instance, the medical field complies with the Health Insurance Portability and Accountability Act (HIPAA), and the consumer finance field is governed by the Fair Credit Reporting Act (FCRA) and the Gramm-Leach-Bliley Act.[8] In addition, the FTC has authority to regulate data privacy pursuant to the "unfair or deceptive" provision of the Federal Trade Commission Act.[9] These statutes and others, as they relate to the IoT, are discussed in more detail in chapter 2.

Some believe that the IoT thrives best under the U.S. sectoral approach because it is the least restrictive on business; this provides companies with flexibility in how they collect, use, and manage data. However, the sectoral approach often leaves gaps in the regulatory structure which in turn must be filled by best practices from individual states, other countries, and the EU.

---

4. Suzanne Barlton, *Strap on the Fitbit: John Hancock to Sell Only Interactive Life Insurance*, Reuters (Sept. 19, 2018).
5. *Id.*
6. *Id.*
7. One omnibus federal privacy law was passed in the 1970s, the Privacy Act (5 U.S.C. § 552a). However, the Privacy Act concerns the collection, maintenance, use, and dissemination of information about individuals contained in a system of records by the federal government.
8. 44 C.F.R. § 160.103 (HIPAA), 15 U.S.C. § 1681 *et seq.* (FCRA), and 15 U.S.C. §§ 6801–09 (GLBA).
9. 15 U.S.C. §§ 41–58 (FTCA).

§ 3:2.3   *Privacy Policies*

With the exception of the Children Online Privacy Protection Act (COPPA), there are no federal laws that specifically address privacy policy requirements for IoT devices.[10] As a result, some IoT privacy policies are imperfect and suffer from deficiencies that include (1) ambiguous personally identifiable information language, (2) questionable ownership of sensor data, (3) sparse details on the type of data collected and the methods of collection, (4) lack of a clear right to access, modify, or delete information, and (5) few specifics regarding whether collected information is processed on the device or elsewhere.[11] Due to the absence of federal laws relating to IoT privacy policies, a few states have taken it upon themselves to establish guidelines.[12] For example, California's statute provides:

> The privacy policy required by subdivision (a) shall do all of the following:
>
> Identify the categories of personally identifiable information that the operator collects through the Web site or online service about individual consumers who use or visit its commercial Web site or online service and the categories of third-party persons or entities with whom the operator may share that personally identifiable information.
>
> If the operator maintains a process for an individual consumer who uses or visits its commercial Web site or online service to review and request changes to any of his or her personally identifiable information that is collected through the Web site or online service, provide a description of that process.
>
> Describe the process by which the operator notifies consumers who use or visit its commercial Web site or online service of material changes to the operator's privacy policy for that Web site or online service.
>
> Identify its effective date.
>
> Disclose how the operator responds to Web browser "do not track" signals or other mechanisms that provide consumers the ability to exercise choice regarding the collection of personally identifiable information about an individual consumer's online activities over time and across third-party Web sites or online services, if the operator engages in that collection.

---

10.   15 U.S.C. § 6502(b)(1)(A)(1) (COPPA).
11.   Scott Peppet, *Regulating the Internet of Things: First Steps Toward Managing Discrimination, Privacy, Security, and Consent*, 93 TEX. L. REV. 85 (2014).
12.   CAL. BUS. & PROF. CODE § 22575(b)(1)–(7); NEB. REV. STAT. § 87-302(14); 18 PA. CONS. STAT. § 4107(a)(10); and 80 DEL. LAWS, c. 148 § 1.

Disclose whether other parties may collect personally identifiable information about an individual consumer's online activities over time and across different Web sites when a consumer uses the operator's Web site or service.

An operator may satisfy the requirement of paragraph (5) by providing a clear and conspicuous hyperlink in the operator's privacy policy to an online location containing a description, including the effects, of any program or protocol the operator follows that offers the consumer that choice.[13]

A number of challenges arise when applying California's privacy policy law to IoT devices. First, the definition of "personally identifiable information" is generally under inclusive when applied to the various types of information collected by IoT devices. Second, most IoT devices do not have a place for a "clear and conspicuous hyperlink in the operator's privacy policy to an online location" so instead this link is placed on the user's phone or some long forgotten website. Similar to the state laws applying to data breaches discussed in chapter 4 (Security), state laws pertaining to privacy policies were not necessarily drafted with IoT devices in mind.

§ 3:3   Federal Approaches

The federal government has attempted to use both the sectoral and the omnibus approach to regulate privacy as it relates to the IoT, neither of which has proven completely successful to date. However, with the passage of the California Consumer Privacy Act (CCPA) of 2018, which became effective on July 1, 2020, Congress may be spurred into action to pass privacy-related legislation.[14] It should be noted that the federal agency primarily responsible for enforcing IoT privacy, the FTC, has urged Congress to consider "enacting broad-based (as opposed to IoT specific) privacy legislation."[15]

§ 3:3.1   *Executive Branch*

In 2012, the Executive Branch put forward a blueprint of the first privacy bill of rights.[16] Three years later, the president introduced

---

13.   CAL. BUS. & PROF. CODE § 22575(b)(1)–(7).

14.   Emily Cadei, *Californians Have New Privacy Protections. Google Wants Republicans to Weaken Them*, SACBEE.COM (Oct. 11, 2018).

15.   FTC Staff Report, *Data Brokers: A Call for Transparency and Accountability* (May 2014), www.ftc.gov/system/files/documents/reports/data-brokers-call-transparency-accountability-report-federal-trade-commission-may-2014/140527databrokerreport.pdf.

16.   EXEC. OFFICE OF THE PRESIDENT, *Administration Discussion Draft: Consumer Privacy Bill of Rights Act of 2015* (Feb. 27, 2015).

a draft bill entitled the Consumer Privacy Bill of Rights Act of 2015.[17] This proposal, among other things, addressed personal data, transparency/consent, individual control of data, collection and responsible use, security, accountability, and enforcement.[18] The Consumer Privacy Bill of Rights, which has been criticized for both going too far and for not going far enough, was intended "to establish baseline protections for individual privacy in the commercial arena and to foster timely, flexible implementation of these protections through enforceable codes of conduct developed for diverse stakeholders."[19] The proposal was never enacted into law.[20]

§ 3:3.2   Congress

One of the first ever omnibus general data privacy bills, the Personal Data and Privacy Security Act, was introduced in the Senate in 2009.[21] While this bill, like many afterwards, was never passed, the political climate on Capitol Hill now appears to be changing.[22] This can be attributed to two factors: (1) consumers are more interested in their digital privacy, and (2) states are taking it upon themselves to legislate in this area.[23] As discussed, the CCPA recently became effective in 2020[24] and many IoT stakeholders are pushing for new federal legislation in order to supersede the CCPA.[25]

In 2018, there were a number of digital privacy bills introduced in Congress. In the House of Representatives, one member introduced two different pieces of legislation. The first, H.R. 6547, the Application Privacy, Protection and Security Act of 2018, regulates how data is collected and secured on mobile devices. The second, H.R. 6548, Data Broker Accountability and Transparency Act, requires data brokers to establish procedures for accessing and correcting collected information and allows consumers to have their data erased from servers.[26]

In the Senate, the Customer Online Notification for Stopping Edge-Provider Network Transgressions Act (CONSENT Act) was

---

17.   *Id.*
18.   *Id.*
19.   *Tech Industry Response to the President's Discussion Draft Privacy Proposal*, THE INFO. TECH. INDUS. COUNCIL (Feb. 27, 2015).
20.   Natasha Singer, *Why a Push for Online Privacy Is Bogged Down in Washington*, N.Y. TIMES, Feb. 28, 2016.
21.   *Personal Data Privacy* and *Security Act of 2009*, 111th Cong. (2009–2010).
22.   Cadei, *supra* note 14.
23.   *Id.*
24.   *Id.*
25.   *Id.*
26.   Dan Clark, *Federal Data Privacy Legislation Is Likely Next Year, Tech Lawyers Say*, CORP. COUNS. (Nov. 29, 2018).

introduced in an effort to reign in data-hungry businesses and to require the establishment of online privacy protections by the FTC.[27] The CONSENT Act, among other things, mandated:

(1) opt-in consent from users before sharing, selling, or using personal information;

(2) reasonable security measures;

(3) notifications of data breaches; and

(4) notifications about the collection, use, and selling of personal information.[28]

The Data Care Act, also introduced in the Senate in 2018, requires websites, apps, and other online providers to take responsible steps to safeguard personal information and stop the misuse of users' data.[29] It moves away from the traditional "notice and choice" framework and instead places the burden on data collectors to ensure that users know and agree to the method of personal data collection and the use of personal data.

The Data Care Act prescribes three main duties of online providers:

• Duty of Care: Must reasonably secure individual identifying data and promptly inform users of data breaches that involve sensitive information;

• Duty of Loyalty: May not use individual identifying data in ways that harm users; and

• Duty of Confidentiality: Must ensure that the duties of care and loyalty extend to third parties when disclosing, selling, or sharing individual identifying data.

The Data Care Act also strengthens the FTC's enforcement power:

• Federal and State Enforcement: A violation of the duties will be treated as a violation of an FTC [Federal Trade Commission] rule with fine authority. States may also bring civil enforcement actions, but the FTC can intervene; and

• Rulemaking Authority: FTC is granted rulemaking authority to implement the Act.[30]

---

27. Data Care Act of 2018 (S. 3744), 115th Cong. and Consent Act (S. 2639), 115th Cong. *See also* Paul Bischoff, *What Is the Consumer Privacy Bill of Rights?*, COMPARITECH (Nov. 27, 2018).
28. Consent Act (S. 2639), 115th Cong.
29. Data Care Act of 2018 (S. 3744), 115th Cong.
30. *Id.*

Taking the sectoral approach, both the House and Senate have considered legislation to regulate autonomous cars. In 2018, the House passed the Self-Drive Act (H.R. 3388).[31] This bill makes it easier to introduce and test autonomous cars by defining the roles of the state and federal government in the process and offering exemptions to motor vehicle standards.[32] With respect to privacy, the bill requires manufacturers to create a written "privacy plan" concerning the "collection, use sharing, and storage of information about the vehicle owners or occupants."[33] The bill also creates the Highly Automated Vehicles Advisory Council that monitors and advises the National Highway Traffic Safety Administration (NHTSA) on consumer privacy and security.[34]

Like most legislation, H.R. 3388 was not without flaws.[35] Privacy critics complain that the bill does not discuss the deletion of data nor does it give consumers the right to review, challenge, and erase data.[36] Privacy advocates claim that consumers are entitled to know how

---

31.   Self-Drive Act, H.R. 3388, 115th Cong.
32.   *Id.*
33.   *Id.*

    (1)   . . . Such policy shall include the following:

        (A) The practices of the manufacturer with respect to the way that information about vehicle owners or occupants is collected, used, shared, or stored.

        (B) The practices of the manufacturer with respect to the choices offered to vehicle owners or occupants regarding the collection, use, sharing, and storage of such information.

        (C) The practices of the manufacturer with respect to the data minimization, de-identification, and retention of information about vehicle owners or occupants.

        (D) The practices of the manufacturer with respect to extending its privacy plan to the entities it shares such information with.

    (2)   A method for providing notice to vehicle owners or occupants about the privacy policy.

    (3)   If information about vehicle owners or occupants is altered or combined so that the information can no longer reasonably be linked to the highly automated vehicle, vehicle that performs partial driving automation, or automated driving system from which the information is retrieved, the vehicle owner, or occupants, the manufacturer is not required to include the process or practices regarding that information in the privacy policy.

    (4)   If information about an occupant is anonymized or encrypted the manufacturer is not required to include the process or practices regarding that information in the privacy policy.

34.   *Id.*
35.   Brady Dale, *Self-Driving Car Riders' Privacy 'Unsafe at Any Speed' in New House Legislation*, OBSERVER (Sept. 8, 2017).
36.   *Id.*

much of their data is collected, who collects it, and for what purposes.[37] Privacy proponents also want automotive manufacturers to set up a point of contact for consumers with questions.[38]

H.R. 3388 never became law because its Senate counterpart, the AV START Act, failed to make it to the Senate floor despite leaving its respective committee.[39] While the AV START Act (S. 1885) did address some of the privacy criticisms raised by H.R. 3388, e.g., creation of a publicly accessible and searchable online database that "describ[es] the type of information collected about individuals during the operation of a motor vehicle, how that information and the conclusions derived from that information will be handled, measures taken to protect against unauthorized disclosure of personally identifiable information, and manufacturers' privacy policies," it didn't go far enough for those whose main sticking point with the bill was privacy.[40] Other remaining privacy concerns related to the ownership of collected data and the process for removing that data once the car transferred to the possession of another individual.[41]

§ 3:3.3   FIPPs

In the early 1970s, upon the introduction of computers to the workforce, organizations began large-scale collection of personal data.[42] At that time, there were few rules or laws to safeguard the personal information that was collected.[43] In 1974, the federal government passed the Privacy Act, which included the Fair Information Practice Principles (FIPPs).[44] Although not enforceable by law, FIPPs are considered the privacy "gold standard" and are relied upon by government agencies in order to maintain privacy-friendly data collection practices that target consumers.[45] The FIPPs "embody the important

---

37. *Id.*
38. *Id.*
39. Stephanie Akin, *AVs Have Lawmakers Playing Regulatory 'Whack a Mole,'* CQ-ROLL CALL (Dec. 18, 2018).
40. Ballard Spahr, *AV START Act Addresses Privacy and Cybersecurity Issues Associated with the Development of Highly Autonomous Vehicles* (Dec. 15, 2018).
41. *Id.* S. 1885 as amended did create a Data Access Advisory Committee to address issues related to control and access to data generated by autonomous cars. The bill as amended also directed the Comptroller General to study the issue of removing PII once the car is possessed by another via sale or lease.
42. Robert Gellman, *Fair Information Practices: A Basic History* (Oct. 7, 2019), https://bobgellman.com/rg-docs/rg-FIPshistory.pdf.
43. *Id.*
44. *Id.*
45. FTC, *Privacy Online: A Report to Congress* (1998).

underlying concept of transparency, consumer autonomy, and accountability."[46] The influence of FIPPs can be seen in the GDPR and sectoral privacy laws like HIPPA.[47]

The seven FIPPs principles are:

1. Notice;

2. Choice;

3. Access;

4. Accuracy;

5. Security;

6. Accountability; and

7. Data minimization.[48]

In the age of the IoT, some wonder about the continued viability of all seven principles.[49] Specific questions have been raised about *data minimization*, *notice*, and *choice*. As for *data minimization*, which refers to the concept of limiting the scope of collected information and disposing of it once it is no longer needed, some believe that imposing such a rule on the somewhat nascent IoT industry would limit growth and slow development. Furthermore, many believe that the value of information may not be readily apparent when first collected, and thus premature destruction may come back later to "haunt" the collector.

Regarding *notice* and *choice*, some have questioned whether true *notice* and *choice* can occur with IoT devices, some of which lack a screen or other interface with the consumer. Another concern with proper *notice* and *choice* is the vast number of IoT devices and the pervasive and persistent nature of their information collection. Requiring *notice* and *choice* every time data is collected by an IoT device may become burdensome, and could lead some to ignore all notices or refuse to use any device. As the IoT market matures, it remains to be seen whether these challenges to FIPPs can be overcome.[50]

---

46.   FTC, *Protecting Consumer Privacy in an ERA of Rapid Change: A Proposed Framework for Businesses and Policy Makers* (2010).

47.   FTC, *Internet of Things Privacy & Security in a Connected World* (Jan. 2015).

48.   *Id.*

49.   *Id.*

50.   *Id.*

§ 3:4   State Approaches

Similar to the federal government, states have taken both a sectoral and omnibus approach to regulating privacy in the IoT. In addition to creating laws that regulate privacy policies, states have passed laws that target specific IoT devices like Event Data Recorders (EDRs), smart televisions, and smart meters. Also, a few states are either considering passing or have already passed, an omnibus privacy law.

§ 3:4.1   *Event Data Recorders (EDRs)*

Most new automobiles built today are equipped with EDRs (also known as "black boxes") which record a wide range of vehicle information. Pursuant to the requirements imposed by the National Highway Traffic Safety Administration (NHTSA), EDRs must, at a minimum, capture fifteen different types of information including: braking status, vehicle speed, accelerator position, engine revolutions per minute, safety belt usage, air-bag deployment, and number and timing of crash events.[51] NHTSA places no limitations on whether manufacturers may gather other types of car data.[52] Pursuant to the Driver Privacy Act of 2015, information "retained by an event data recorder . . . is property of the [car] owner, or . . . lessee."[53] In addition, the Data Privacy Act of 2015 limits, who besides the owner and lessee, may access EDR data. A few states have enacted their own legislation on EDRs.

To date, only fourteen states have passed laws addressing privacy and EDRs.[54] Of these states, Arkansas, North Dakota, Oregon, and Virginia prohibit insurance companies from requiring drivers to consent to disclosure of EDR data or from requiring drivers to submit EDR data in order to settle an insurance claim.[55] Virginia goes one step further and prohibits insurers from adjusting rates solely because a driver refuses to submit EDR data.[56]

---

51.   49 C.F.R. §§ 563.6–.7.
52.   *Id.*
53.   49 U.S.C. § 30101 (Driver Privacy Act of 2015).
54.   Privacy of Data Event from the Data Recorders: State Statutes, NAT'L CONFERENCES OF STATE LEGISLATURES, www.ncsl.org/research/telecommunications-and-information-technology/privacy-of-data-from-event-data-recorders.aspx (as of Nov. 18, 2019).
55.   ARK. CODE ANN. § 23-112-107(e)(3)–(4) (2014); N.D. CENT. CODE § 51-07-28(6) (2007); OR. REV. STAT. § 105.932 (2013); VA. CODE ANN. § 38.2-2212(C.1)(s) (2007).
56.   VA. CODE ANN. § 38.2-2213.1 (2007).

§ 3:4.2   *Connected Televisions*

Responding to increased concerns about privacy and smart televisions, California, in 2015, passed AB 1116, which became the first-ever law to specifically target an IoT device.[57] AB 1116 mandates that user consent must be obtained prior to the activation of voice recognition features. The law also requires warnings to be given to consumers during initial set-up or installation of their smart-TV that alert the user that the device could be recording their voice. Finally, the law prohibits manufacturers of smart-TV's from recording consumer voices for advertising purposes.

There is no private right of action for violation of this law, but the California Attorney General can impose fines of up to $2,500 for each infraction. The law also limits manufacturer liability to the point of sale. Thus, the manufacturer is not liable if the consumer subsequently installs or downloads an app that records the consumer and then transmits that information to another or uses it for advertising.[58]

§ 3:4.3   *Smart Meters*

A smart meter offers real-time readings of electricity consumption in a home or business. Among other things, electricity usage can indicate the number and identities of people in the home and how often occupants "cook, clean, shower or watch television."[59] According to the National Institute of Standards and Technology (NIST),

> [p]ersonal energy consumption data . . . may reveal lifestyle information that could be of value to many entities including vendors of a wide range of products and services. Vendors may purchase attribute lists for targeted sales and marketing campaigns that may not be welcomed . . . Such profiling could extend to . . . employment selection, rental applications, and other situations that may not be welcomed by those targets.[60]

---

57.   CAL. BUS. & PROF. CODE ch. 35 § 22948.20.

58.   *See* Brandon Johnson, *New California Law Regulates Voice Recognition Technology in Smart TVs*, COVINGTON, INSIDER PRIVACY (Oct. 9, 2015), www.insideprivacy.com/advertising-marketing/new-california-law-restricts-smart-tv-recognition-recording-and-transmission-of-users-speech/.

59.   Scott Peppet, *Regulating the Internet of Things: First Steps Toward Managing Discrimination, Privacy, Security, and Consent*, 93 TEX. L. REV. 85 (2014).

60.   Cyber Security Working Group National Institutes of Standards and Technology NISTIR 7628, *Guidelines for Smart Grid Cyber Security: Vol. 2, Privacy and Smart Grid 28* (Aug. 2010).

To date, the California Public Utilities Commission and NIST have worked together to issue a report detailing privacy concerns with regard to smart meter technology.[61]

Certain states have also taken action to safeguard the privacy of their residents. New Hampshire mandates that utility companies obtain a homeowner's consent prior to installing a smart meter device.[62] New Hampshire, Vermont, Michigan, Rhode Island, and New York allow consumers to opt out of using smart meter technology.[63] Additionally, California, Oklahoma, and Colorado limit the ability of utility companies to sell or share smart meter data to others.[64] As discussed in chapter 9, some residents have brought legal challenges to the required use of smart meters in their homes.

§ 3:4.4 California Consumer Privacy Act (CCPA)

Generally speaking, the California Consumer Privacy Act of 2018 (CCPA) restricts how businesses collect and sell the "personal information" of California consumers.[65] The law, effective July 1, 2020, was passed in a very rushed fashion in order to stave off a statewide proposition that, if enacted, would have had even stronger privacy protections for consumers.[66] Modifications to the act will continue into the foreseeable future.[67]

[A] Personal Information

The CCPA's broad definition of "personal information" covers most data that businesses collect from consumers and "includes any information capable of being associated with or reasonably linked to

---

61. *Id.*
62. N.H. REV. STAT. ANN. § 374:62(II)(a) (Supp. 2013).
63. N.H. REV. STAT. ANN. § 374:62(II)(a) (Supp. 2013); VT. STAT. ANN. tit. 30, § 2811(b)(2)–(3) (Supp. 2013); H.R. 4315, 97th Leg., Reg. Sess. (Mich. 2013); H.R. 5027, 2013 Gen. Assemb., Reg. Sess. (R.I. 2013); S. 7184, 235th Leg., Reg. Sess. (N.Y. 2012).
64. CAL. PUB. UTIL. CODE § 8380(b), (e) (West 2013); OKLA. STAT. ANN. tit. 17, §§ 710.4, 710.7 (West Supp. 2014); and H.R. 11-1191, 68th Gen. Assemb., 1st Reg. Sess. (Colo. 2011).
65. Consumer Privacy Act of 2018 (A.B. 375), CAL. CIV. CODE §§ 1798.100–.199.
66. *Id. See also* Adam Schwartz, Lee Tien & Corynne McSherry, *How to Improve the California Consumer Privacy Act of 2018*, ELEC. FRONTIER FOUND. (Aug. 8, 2018), www.eff.org/deeplinks/2018/08/how-improve-california-consumer-privacy-act-2018.
67. Jeewon Kim Serrato & Susan Ross, *California Governor Signs All 5 CCPA Amendments*, DATA PROT. REPORT (Oct. 14, 2019); Grant Ross, *Potential Impact of Two IoT Security and Privacy Laws on Tech Industry*, HPE. COM (Dec. 19, 2018).

a consumer or household."[68] The CCPA's definition of "personal information," does not require the presence of an individual identifier.[69] Instead, the CCPA takes an expansive view and defines "personal information" as "information that identifies, relates to, describes, or is capable of being associated with, or could reasonably be linked, directly, or indirectly, with a particular consumer or household." However, "personal information" does not include:

• anonymized information;

• aggregate consumer information; and

• publicly available information.

Examples of "personal information" include "electronic network activity [such as] browsing history, search history, and information regarding a consumer's interaction with an Internet Web site, application, or advertisement" and "inferences drawn" from this data.

[B]   Businesses Covered Under the CCPA

The CCPA applies to a for-profit business that:

(1)   has $25 million in annual revenues (not limited to revenue earned in California);

(2)   engages in the buying, selling, or receipt of the personal information of 50,000 or more California residents; or

(3)   derives 50% of annual revenues from the sale of California residents' personal information.

The act also covers entities that control or are controlled by a covered business.[70]

[C]   Exclusions from the CCPA

CCPA does not cover:

(1)   commercial conduct occurring entirely outside of California;

(2)   non–personally identifiable or aggregated information;

---

68.   Consumer Privacy Act of 2018 (A.B. 375), CAL. CIV. CODE §§ (1798.100–.199). *See also Client Alert: The California Consumer Privacy Act of 2018: Don't Wait Until 2020 to Get Started*, Schumaker, Loop & Kendrick (Jan. 23, 2019), www.jdsupra.com/legalnews/client-alert-the-california-consumer-72255/.

69.   Consumer Privacy Act of 2018 (A.B. 375), CAL. CIV. CODE §§ (1798.100–.199).

70.   *Id. See also* Wilson C. Freeman, *California Dreamin' of Privacy Regulation: The California Consumer Privacy Act and Congress*, CRS (Nov. 1, 2018), https://fas.org/sgp/crs/misc/LSB10213.pdf.

(3) compliance with a legal obligation or federal statute like HIPAA, GLBA, FRCA, etc.;

(4) certain health/clinical trial information and healthcare entities; and

(5) rights of other consumers, or the "noncommercial activities" of a person or entity "as described in" the free expression provision of the California Constitution.[71]

[D] Protections for California Residents Under the CCPA

The CCPA provides California residents with four main rights: the right to know, the right to opt out, the right to delete, and the right to equal service.[72] Under the *right to know*, businesses, prior to collecting data, must provide consumers with the following information:

(1) sources from which data is collected;

(2) purposes for collection or sale of data;

(3) types of data collected; and

(4) categories of third parties with whom data is shared.

Under the *right to opt out*, businesses must let consumers know that they can prevent the selling of their information. Businesses must provide an obvious link on their homepage entitled "Do Not Sell My Personal Information." If a consumer opts out, the business is prohibited from selling or sharing the consumer's information without express authorization from the consumer. Businesses need an opt-in or prior consent for those under the age of sixteen.

Under the *right to delete*, consumers may request that a business delete information collected about them. Upon receipt of the request, the business must delete the information and direct its service providers to do the same. There are exceptions to this right, for example, such as when the information is needed to complete a particular transaction, to detect security incidents, or to maintain "the right of another consumer to exercise his or her free speech."

Pursuant to the *right to equal service*, businesses are prohibited from discriminating against consumers who exercise their rights under the CCPA. For example, a business, with certain limitations, cannot:

(1) deny the consumer goods or services;

---

71. Consumer Privacy Act of 2018 (A.B. 375), CAL. CIV. CODE §§ (1798.100–.199).
72. *Id.*

(2) provide a different level or quality of goods or services to the consumer;

(3) charge different prices or rates for goods or services; or

(4) suggest that the consumer will receive a different price or rate for goods or services or a different level or quality of goods or service.[73]

However, businesses may offer consumers "financial incentives" for the collection, sale, or non-deletion of personal information.[74] Furthermore, the CCPA allows businesses to "charge a different price or rate, or to provide a different quality of goods or services" so long as the difference is reasonably related to "the value provided to the consumer" by his or her data. Not surprisingly, many have found the exceptions to the *right to equal service* to be confusing and contradictory.[75]

[E] Obligations for Businesses Under the CCPA

Businesses must inform consumers of their rights under the CCPA to include providing their privacy policy or a description of a consumer's *right to know*.[76] In addition, businesses must inform consumers of the method by which they may submit their requests. The CCPA also imposes recordkeeping requirements on businesses that include mapping data flows of consumer information. Recordkeeping starts twelve months prior to the effective date of the law.

[F] Enforcement of the CCPA

The California Attorney General is the primary enforcer of the CCPA. The law allows the California Attorney General to impose a $2,500 fine for each violation of the law and a $7,500 fine for each intentional violation.

In a private right of action, consumers can bring a claim for a data breach when a company fails to "implement and maintain reasonable

---

73. *Id. See also* Cooley, *CCPA FAQs Part 2b: CCPA Rights and Material Provisions* (Oct. 1, 2018), https://cdp.cooley.com/ccpa-faqs-part-2b-ccpa-rights-and-other-material-provisions/.

74. Consumer Privacy Act of 2018 (A.B. 375), Cal. Civ. Code §§ (1798.100–.199).

75. *Id. See also* Lydia de la Torre, *GDPR Matchup: The California Consumer Privacy Act 2018*, IAPP (July 31, 2018).

76. Consumer Privacy Act of 2018 (A.B. 375), Cal. Civ. Code §§ (1798.100–.199). *See also* Data Guidance and Future of Privacy Forum, *Comparing Privacy Laws: GDPR v. CCPA*, https://fpf.org/wp-content/uploads/2018/11/GDPR_CCPA_Comparison-Guide.pdf.

security procedures and practices." Absent actual pecuniary damages, the consumer must give the business thirty days' written notice and the opportunity to cure. Consumer recovery damages are limited to $750 per incident or actual damages, whichever is greater. The law also allows for injunctions.

[G] Similarities with the GDPR

The EU's General Data Protection Regulation (GDPR), discussed in depth in chapter 10, shares many similarities with the CCPA:

1. Both have extra-territorial reach and use broad definitions of personal info/data.

2. Both incorporate data subjects'/consumers' rights of access, deletion, and portability of their data.

3. Both require consumers to be notified of privacy practices prior to, or at the time of, data collection.

4. Both require that consumers receive notice of changes to privacy practices.

5. Both provide time limits for fulfilling data subjects' requests: thirty days under the GDPR and forty-five days under the CCPA.

6. Both grant specific protections for children.

7. Both impose penalties upon businesses for failing to safeguard privacy.

[H] Differences with the GDPR

While numerous similarities exist, there are also noticeable differences between the CCPA and GDPR:

1. The GDPR focuses on the collection of consumer data and its use, while the CCPA is more concerned with how businesses use consumer data after collection.[77]

2. The GDPR does not include a consumer's right to opt-out.[78]

3. The CCPA establishes specific communication channels for consumers, for example, a toll-free telephone number and a conspicuous website link.[79]

---

77. Grant Ross, *Potential Impact of Two IoT Security and Privacy Laws on Tech Industry*, HPE.COM (Dec. 19, 2018).
78. DATA GUIDANCE AND FUTURE OF PRIVACY FORUM, *supra* note 76.
79. *Id.*

4.   The CCPA extends "personal information" protections to information about devices and households.[80]

5.   The CCPA provides the means to a private right of action for breaches of consumer data.[81]

6.   The CCPA imposes few restrictions on the activities that businesses are allowed to carry out internally with consumer data.[82]

[I]   Criticisms of the CCPA

As the first omnibus data privacy bill passed in decades, the CCPA is not without critics, and many believe that the law will continue to be amended.[83] The major criticisms of the CCPA may be summarized as follows:

1.   The right to equal service contains unclear and contradictory terms.

2.   Consumers have limited ability to bring private causes of action.

3.   CCPA requires users to opt-out rather than opt-in for data collection.

4.   The terms "de-identified" and "aggregate consumer information" lack clarity.[84]

§ 3:5   Litigation

The FTC, state attorneys general, and private individuals have all brought privacy actions against manufacturers of IoT devices. In many instances, those cases raised both privacy and security issues.[85] This chapter focuses on those cases where IoT privacy was the main concern. For cases that centered on IoT security, see chapter 4.

---

80.   *Id.*
81.   *Id.*
82.   Lydia de la Torre, *GDPR Matchup: The California Consumer Privacy Act 2018*, IAPP (July 31, 2018).
83.   Adam Schwartz, Lee Tien & Corynne McSherry, *How to Improve the California Consumer Privacy Act of 2018*, EFF (Aug. 8, 2018).
84.   *Id.* Timothy Tobin, et al., *California Consumer Privacy Act: The Challenge Ahead—The Impact of the CCPA on Data-Driven Marketing and Business Models*, HOGAN LOVELLS (Nov. 30, 2018).
85.   Nikole Davenport, *Smart Washers May Clean Your Clothes, But Hacks Can Clean Out Your Privacy, and Underdeveloped Regulations Could Leave You Hanging on a Line*, 32 J. MARSHALL J. INFO. TECH. & PRIVACY L. 259 (2016).

In *FTC v. Vizio*, the FTC, along with the state of New Jersey, claimed that Vizio smart TVs captured "viewing information and device level information about the television and nearby wireless devices."[86] The complaint further alleged that Vizio sold consumer viewing profiles for audience measurement and to determine advertising effectiveness. According to the complaint, the software was turned on by default on new TVs and remotely installed on TVs already in consumers' possession. The complaint asserted that the actions of Vizio went beyond what a reasonable consumer would expect from a tv manufacturer and the notice and choice provided to consumers was "vague, misleading, and ephemeral."

The final consent order with the FTC required Vizio to pay $2.2 million dollars split between the FTC and the New Jersey Attorney General. Vizio was also required to display and obtain affirmative consent for its data collection and sharing practices, and is prohibited from future misrepresentations about privacy, security, or the collection of confidential consumer information. Finally, Vizio must delete all information collected prior to March 1, 2016, and implement comprehensive data privacy programs and biennial assessments of that program.

Arguably, the most significant aspect of the Vizio decision was the classification of consumer viewing activity as "sensitive data." Historically, the FTC had a narrower definition of "sensitive data," applying it to health and financial information, Social Security numbers, geolocation, and data about children. This new, expansive view of "sensitive data" was not shared by all of the FTC commissioners who voted for the complaint and consent order. Acting FTC Chairwoman Maureen Ohlausen in her concurrence was skeptical of expanding the definition of "sensitive data" beyond the traditional notions because "people have widely varying privacy preferences."[87] Ohlausen went on to note that expanding the definition of "sensitive data" places undue burdens on businesses.[88] She argued that the FTC should perform a balancing test, weighing the harm against business versus that caused to consumers. In this case, it appears that the FTC, which found that "collection and sharing of sensitive data without consumers' consent has caused or is likely to cause substantial injury to consumers," did not go far enough to determine whether consumers were actually injured.[89] It remains to be seen whether future FTC complaints will

---

86. FTC v. Vizio, No. 2:17-cv-00758 (D.N.J.), complaint filed Feb. 6, 2017. *See also* Christin S. McMeley et al., *The Real Takeaway from Vizio's Privacy FTC Settlement*, DAVIS WRIGHT TREMAINE (Feb. 27, 2017).

87. *Id.*

88. *Id.*

89. *Id.*

require such additional information, showing that consumers have suffered an actual privacy injury.

In 2015, the FTC brought an action against Nomi Technologies, Inc. (Nomi) alleging that Nomi's 'Listen Service' "uses mobile device tracking technology to provide analytics services to brick and mortar retailers."[90] The Listen Service relied on a beacon placed inside retail stores to collect information released from individuals' smartphones when they entered or passed by specific stores.[91] The data gathered included:

(1) the percentage of consumers merely passing the store versus entering the store;

(2) the average duration of consumers' visits;

(3) types of mobile devices used by consumers visiting a location;

(4) the percentage of repeat customers within a given time period; and

(5) the number of customers who also visited another location within the client's chain.[92]

Apparently, the FTC was not necessarily concerned with the actual tracking and data collection, but rather Nomi's violation of its privacy policy which claimed that consumers could opt-out of the tracking system either online or in the retail store. However, Nomi did not require retailers to post in-store disclaimers about the Listen Service nor information about how consumers could opt-out of the tracking.

Ultimately, the FTC imposed disclosure and reporting requirements upon Nomi. In addition, the FTC prohibited Nomi from engaging in any future inadequate notices of tracking or misrepresentations about consumers maintaining control over tracking.[93]

Like in *Vizio*, the FTC Acting Chairwoman Maureen Ohlausen wanted to see actual harm to the consumer in order to punish the business.[94] Thus, she dissented in the consent order, writing that the FTC "should have exercised its prosecutorial discretion" because the "partially inaccurate statement [privacy policy] harmed no consumers."[95]

In the case of *N.P. v. Standard Innovation Corp.*, the manufacturer of a smart vibrator (We-Vibe) settled a privacy class action for

---

90. *In re* Nomi Techs. Inc., No. 132 3251 (Fed. Trade Comm'n Aug. 28, 2015).
91. Sarah H. Bruno et al., *Big Brother for Hire: FTC Cracks Down on Consumer Tracking Company*, ARENT FOX (June 12, 2015).
92. *In re* Nomi Techs. Inc., *supra* note 90.
93. *Id.*
94. Dissenting Statement of Commissioner Maureen K. Ohlhausen, *In re* Nomi Techs., Inc. Matter, No 1323251 (Apr. 23, 2015).
95. *Id.*

$3.75 million.[96] Plaintiffs alleged violations of the Federal Wiretap Act, Illinois Eavesdropping Statute, intrusion upon seclusion, unjust enrichment, and consumer fraud. The product in question, We-Vibe, connects to the user's smartphone through Bluetooth and permits users to interact with others via video chat and text messages. The product also allows users to control another user's We-Vibe remotely.

The company was alleged to have collected data about the users of the product to include (1) date and time of each use; (2) the vibration intensity; (3) the vibration mode or pattern selected by the user; and (4) where available, the email addresses of users who registered the app. Plaintiffs claimed that the information collected by Standard Innovation was done without permission. Consumers became aware of the data gathered by Standard Innovation shortly after Def Con 2016, where white-hat hackers discovered a security flaw that allowed the device to be remotely seized and activated at will. The hackers also discovered that the "app itself was phoning home, letting the manufacturer discover some very intimate information about users." Since Def Con, Standard Innovation has patched the vulnerability and updated its terms and conditions to be more explicit about the information it is collecting.[97]

§ 3:6   Conclusion

As illustrated herein, IoT devices have raised a number of privacy issues. In a limited number of instances, the industry has attempted to respond to customers when additional privacy is demanded.[98] For example, Fitbit embedded privacy into their technology because they wanted their standards to meet the specific needs of their customers based on the sensitivity of the data collected.[99] In fact, Fitbit devices are now HIPAA-compliant.[100] The efforts of Fitbit unfortunately are not reflective of the industry as a whole, which is why the CCPA was enacted. Most believe that additional privacy legislation is likely to be passed in the near future. However, uncertainty still exists as to the favored regulatory approach by legislators—either sectoral or omnibus—and whether new laws will be passed at the state or federal level.

---

96.   N.P. v. Standard Innovation Corp., No. 1:16-cv-08655 (N.D. Ill. Mar. 9, 2017).

97.   Molly Redden, *Tech Company Accused of Collecting Details of How Customers Use Sex Toys*, THE GUARDIAN (Sept. 14, 2016).

98.   Christine Bannan, *The IoT Threat to Privacy*, TECHCRUNCH (Aug. 14, 2016), https://techcrunch.com/2016/08/14/the-iot-threat-to-privacy/.

99.   *Id.*

100. Michael McAlpin, *Fitbit Is Now HIPAA Compliant—Is Your Business?*, CIO (Oct. 2, 2015).

Chapter 4

Security

§ 4:1   Overview

Ten years ago, most people only had to worry about protecting one device, their computer, from a cyberattack.[1] Half a decade later, users had to add smartphones to the list.[2] Today, cybersecurity concerns have expanded to cars, home appliances, wearables, and numerous other IoT devices.[3] With so many products now connected to the Internet, security concerns increase exponentially as hackers have a virtual treasure trove of attack points to target.[4] A journalist attending a Black Hat Conference in 2013 even predicted that IoT hacking or "thing hacking" would eventually be the subject of its own conference in upcoming years because of increasing popularity.[5]

In addition to the sheer number of IoT targets now potentially vulnerable to cyber-attacks, the issues of interconnectivity and interdependence also arise.[6] One single attack on an IoT device has the potential to impact other connected or co-dependent systems, creating the dangerous paradigm of "attack once; affect many."[7] This chapter examines the risks raised by unsecured IoT devices, discusses the challenges in securing those devices, and analyzes potential IoT security solutions, including recent legislative efforts.

§ 4:2   Security Breach

Broadly speaking, an IoT device with compromised security may lead to:

1. unauthorized access and misuse of personal information;

2. attacks on other systems; and

3. physical harm.

---

1. Gary Eastwood, *4 Critical Security Challenges Facing IoT*, DIG. DIRECTORSHIP (2017), https://digitaldirectorship.com/4-critical-security-challenges-facing-iot/ (last visited July 6, 2020).
2. *Id.*
3. *Id.*
4. *Id.*
5. E. Lundquist, *Black Hat 2013: Five Security Trends That Will Draw Most Attention*, EWEEK (July 31, 2013), www.eweek.com/security/black-hat-2013-five-security-trends-that-will-draw-most-attention/(language)/eng-US.
6. Robert Metzger, *Security and the Internet of Things: The Role of the Federal Government to Reconcile Opportunity and Risk*, SCITECH LAW. (Mar. 1, 2018).
7. *Id.*

§ 4:2.1   Unauthorized Access and Misuse of Personal Information

As discussed in chapter 2, the FTC is the primary governmental agency responsible for regulating the IoT, especially with respect to security lapses that impact consumers. One of the first cases brought by the FTC against an IoT manufacturer for a security breach involved TRENDnet, which sells video cameras that allow people to remotely monitor their homes.[8] TRENDnet's marketing materials claimed that their cameras were secure, but the FTC found otherwise. According to the FTC's complaint, TRENDnet failed to test certain privacy settings in their cameras. Furthermore, consumer login credentials were stored in clear text on users' mobile devices and subsequently transmitted in clear text over the Internet.

As a result of these lapses, hackers accessed live feeds of TRENDnet security cameras and conducted "unauthorized surveillance of infants sleeping in their cribs, young children playing, and adults engaging in typical daily activities." In one instance, a hacker posted links to the live feeds of nearly 700 cameras, online.[9] Ultimately, TRENDnet settled with the FTC. While the company escaped a monetary fine, it agreed to make a number of security improvements and to obtain a third-party assessment of its security procedures.

§ 4:2.2   Attacks on Other Systems

One of the first large-scale examples of employing IoT devices to attack other systems occurred between December 23, 2013, and January 6, 2014. During this time, approximately 100,000 devices ranging from computers to smart televisions to wireless speaker systems, and at least one refrigerator, sent 750,000 bogus emails.[10] Most of the devices were compromised due to either a misconfiguration of the device or the use of a default password, not because of a sophisticated hacking effort. It appears that the object of the attack was merely to get the compromised devices to send out emails worldwide.[11] While the overall damage was insignificant, it set the stage for future attacks.

Today, attackers no longer limit themselves to sending malicious email, but instead create botnet armies to execute Distributed Denial of Services (DDoS) attacks. The harm caused by a DDoS attack, discussed in greater detail in section 9:2.3, can be quite significant.

---

8.   *In re* TRENDnet, Inc., No. C-4426 (F.T.C. Jan. 16, 2014), www.ftc.gov/system/files/documents/cases/140207trendnetcmpt.pdf.

9.   *Id.*

10.   Press Release, Proofpoint, Proofpoint Uncovers Internet of Things (IoT) Cyberattack (Jan. 16, 2014).

11.   *Id.*

§ 4:2.3   *Physical Harm*

Compromised IoT security can also lead to physical harm. In 2015, Chrysler announced a recall of more than a million vehicles after hackers remotely hijacked the digital systems in their Jeep, enabling the hijackers to disable brakes at low speeds and paralyze the vehicle.[12] A year later, the same hackers returned to demonstrate that they could now tamper with acceleration, brakes, and steering. Hackers were able to bypass safeguards that prevented the vehicle from performing potentially deadly actions. Similar to the first hack, the new attack involved entering the network and taking the main "computer" offline to override safeguards that prevent dangerous maneuvers. Fortunately, the larger, more serious hack required a direct connection to the vehicle and it could not occur wirelessly— yet. While these vehicle hackers did not find a way to hack remotely in their second attempt, others have. Their methods include: connecting via OnStar, using a compromised smartphone to reach the network via Bluetooth, playing a CD with a malicious file inside the CD player, and even accessing insurance dongles plugged into a vehicle dashboard.[13]

The hacking attempts of autonomous cars illustrate the importance of back-up systems and sophisticated security, both of which are essential safeguards to protecting IoT devices and other products with IoT parts. While an autonomous vehicle can be extremely complex and sophisticated, it may be nonetheless defeated through a side-channel attack involving leaked information.[14]

§ 4:3   Challenges of Securing IoT Devices

Despite the universal acceptance of the importance of securing IoT devices, a number of challenges exist to prevent this from routinely occurring. These impediments, found throughout the lifecycle of many IoT devices, start at the initial design stage and carry through to consumer use. These challenges involve:

- inexperience of IoT manufacturers;

- costs and design;

---

12.   Steven Overly, *What We Know About Car Hacking, the CIA and Those WikiLeaks Claims*, WASH. POST (Mar. 8, 2017), www.washingtonpost.com/news/innovations/wp/2017/03/08/what-we-know-about-car-hacking-the-cia-and-those-wikileaks-claims/?utm_term=.9c129d808e9c.

13.   *Id.*

14.   *Understanding the Evolution of Side-Channel Attacks*, RAMBUS PRESS (Apr. 11, 2017), www.rambus.com/blogs/understanding-the-evolution-of-side-channel-attacks/.

- speed of adoption;

- updates of IoT products;

- lack of coordination and interoperability; and

- inadequate data breach notification laws.

§ 4:3.1   *Inexperience of IoT Manufacturers*

At present, IoT devices are often built by traditional consumer hardware and software firms who have limited cybersecurity experience.[15] Thus, unlike smartphone manufacturers who think about security from inception, an IoT-device manufacturer may be unaware of the security risks that come with connecting devices to the Internet. Additionally, these same manufacturers may struggle to identify vulnerabilities or may not fully understand the consequences of a breach.[16] All of these factors collectively make it that much more challenging for many companies to get their corporate leadership on board with implementing security measures.[17]

§ 4:3.2   *Costs and Design*

Consumers obtain IoT devices because they are generally inexpensive, simple to install and use, and can provide a convenient solution to many common problems. The desire for affordable IoT devices causes the market to "prioritize[ ] features and cost over security."[18] Adding security protections, especially to a device that is small in size or limited in functionality, may cause the price of a product to

---

15.   Swaroop Poudel, *Internet of Things: Underlying Technologies, Interoperability, and Threats to Privacy and Security*, 31 BERKELEY TECH. L.J. 996, 1013 (2016).

16.   Bruce Schneier, *Click Here to Kill Everyone*, NYMAG.COM (Jan. 27, 2017). "Our computers and smartphones are as secure as they are because companies like Microsoft, Apple, and Google spend a lot of time testing their code before it's released, and quickly patch vulnerabilities when they're discovered. Those companies can support large, dedicated teams because those companies make a huge amount of money, either directly or indirectly, from their software—and, in part, compete on its security. Unfortunately, this isn't true of embedded systems like digital video recorders or home routers. Those systems are sold at a much lower margin, and are often built by offshore third parties. The companies involved simply don't have the expertise to make them secure."

17.   *Id. See also* Dep't of Homeland Sec., National Protection and Programs Directorate Office of Cyber and Infrastructure Analysis (OCIA), *Why Is the Internet of Things Insecure?* (Aug. 15, 2017) (with author).

18.   Sara Sun Beale & Peter Berris, *Hacking the Internet of Things: Vulnerabilities, Dangers, and Legal Responses*, 16 DUKE L. & TECH. REV. 161 (2018).

increase to such an extent that it is no longer economically feasible to produce.[19]

The prioritization of features and cost over security is also apparent in the designing of IoT devices.[20] By way of example, many IoT devices are designed to have very small batteries with limited life. As a result, the computing systems and power resources of such devices are insufficient to support robust security measures like encryption and authentication.[21]

§ 4:3.3   Speed of Adoption

Another challenge with providing security to IoT devices is the pressure companies feel to get devices to market quickly.[22] Many IoT devices are released as faster and newer models, but do not necessarily receive the same robust security testing and patch management as more mature, established products.[23] With the enhanced speed of adoption, IoT security becomes a secondary concern.[24] Put differently, when companies rush to get devices to market, many take shortcuts, some of which involve security. Examples include sending IoT devices to market with default and identifiable passwords that can be easily exploited, which is precisely what occurred with the Mirai botnet, discussed in depth in chapter 9.[25]

§ 4:3.4   Updates of IoT Products

Some IoT manufacturers believe that they can alleviate any initial security concerns by later pushing updates through once the device is in the hands of the end-user. However, updates raise their own unique issues. First, since IoT manufacturers regularly release new or revised models, some older products are neglected and left unpatched. In fact, a few older devices are so out-of-date they cannot even support an update and are left unprotected.[26] Thus, legacy software that outlives security updates becomes extremely vulnerable to attack.[27]

---

19.   *Id.*
20.   Schneier, *supra* note 16.
21.   *Id.*
22.   *Id.*
23.   *Id.*
24.   *Id.*
25.   Josh Fruhlinger, *The Mirai Botnet Explained: How Teen Scammers and CCTV Cameras Almost Brought Down the Internet* (Mar. 9, 2018), www.csoonline.com/article/3258748/security/the-mirai-botnet-explained-how-teen-scammers-and-cctv-cameras-almost-brought-down-the-internet.html.
26.   *Id.*
27.   Dep't of Homeland Sec., National Protection and Programs Directorate Office of Cyber and Infrastructure Analysis (OCIA), *Why Is the Internet of Things Insecure?* (Aug. 15, 2017) (with author).

For example, the devices targeted by the WannaCry malware were running older versions of Windows, such as Windows XP, that were no longer supported.[28]

Another concern with updates is the frequency of their occurrence; some updates require immediate implementation while others can wait. For example, researchers hacked into the Samsung SmartThings platform by eavesdropping on the PIN code and then using the PIN code during a new install that gave them control of the entire home automation system.[29] A security flaw of this magnitude requires an immediate firmware upgrade, but companies often want to wait to avoid disrupting their user base.[30] In many instances, researchers find device vulnerabilities and report them but end up waiting for the vulnerability to be patched, which, depending on the manufacturer, can take time.[31]

Also, not all devices support "over-the-air" updates or the devices must shut down in order to accept the update; in these instances, the manufacturer might have to access the device physically.[32] Finally, some users decline to participate in updates no matter what the format and instead opt out.[33]

§ 4:3.5   *Lack of Coordination and Interoperability*

As discussed in chapter 1, there is no consensus among industry stakeholders and standards organizations regarding how IoT devices communicate with each other.[34] This lack of interoperability is a double-edged sword. On one side, it makes implementing a universal security plan difficult if not impossible, which in turn makes the entire IoT ecosystem vulnerable to an attack.[35] According to the CEO of one security company, "[w]hen we look at our workspaces today there are already a number of wireless devices, from Bluetooth mice to wireless keyboards, and we have very little knowledge of who develops the firmware that runs on them or where . . . it com[es] from."[36] On the other side, lack of interoperability may make it more difficult

---

28.   *Id.*
29.   John Brandon, *Security Concerns Rising for Internet of Things Devices,* CSO Online (June 1, 2016), www.csoonline.com/article/3077537/internet-of-things/security-concerns-rising-for-internet-of-things-devices.html.
30.   *Id.*
31.   *Id.*
32.   *Id.*
33.   *Id.*
34.   Stephanie Lynn Sharon & Nikita A. Tuckett, *The Internet of Things: Interoperability, Industry Standards & Related IP Licensing Approaches,* Socially Aware Blog (Feb. 2, 2016).
35.   *Id.*
36.   *Id.*

to design one form of malware to take down every device if those devices are unable to communicate with each other.

Another potential problem area related to IoT coordination and interoperability involves the relationship between hardware and software.[37] In some instances, the owner of an IoT device may be completely unaware of the fact that the software within their device has been corrupted. This is because the device itself still functions. This was the case with the Mirai botnet, where many of the IoT devices, despite operating without a problem, had been compromised and used in DDoS attacks to take down an Internet infrastructure company by flooding it with nuisance signals.

§ 4:3.6   *Inadequate Data Breach Notification Laws*

In addition to being unaware that their IoT device has been compromised, consumers may also be in the dark about the loss of personal information from those devices. At present, consumer data security is regulated through either the FTC or state data breach notification statutes. While there has been much discussion about a federal data breach notification law, it has yet to come to fruition.[38]

With the passage of the Alabama Data Breach Notification Act of 2018, every state now has a law requiring companies to alert users when their personal information has been revealed as a result of a data breach.[39] However, the challenge with most state data breach

---

37.   Beale & Berris, *supra* note 18.

38.   Will Oremus, *Beware of Tech Companies Bearing Privacy Laws*, SLATE. COM (Aug. 28, 2018).

39.   ALASKA STAT. § 45.48.010 (2012); ARIZ. REV. STAT. ANN. § 44-7501 (2013); ARK. CODE ANN. § 4-110-105 (2011); CAL. CIV. CODE §§ 1798.29, 1798.82 (West Supp. 2014); COLO. REV. STAT. ANN. § 6-1-716 (West Supp. 2013); CONN. GEN. STAT. ANN. § 36a-701b (West Supp. 2014); DEL. CODE ANN. tit. 6, § 12B-102 (2013); FLA. STAT. ANN. § 817.5681 (West 2006); GA. CODE ANN. § 10-1-912 (2009); HAW. REV. STAT. ANN. §§ 487N-1 to -7 (LexisNexis 2012); IDAHO CODE ANN. § 28-51-105 (2013); 815 ILL. COMP. STAT. ANN. 530/10 to 530/12 (West 2008); IND. CODE ANN. §§ 24-4.9-3-1 to -3-2 (West Supp. 2013); IOWA CODE ANN. § 715C.2 (West Supp. 2014); KAN. STAT. ANN. § 50-7a02 (Supp. 2013); LA. REV. STAT. ANN. § 51.3074 (2012); ME. REV. STAT. ANN. tit. 10, § 1348 (Supp. 2013); MD. CODE ANN., LAB. & EMPL. §§ 14-3501 to -3508 (LexisNexis 2013); MASS. GEN. LAWS ANN. ch. 93H, §§ 1–6 (West Supp. 2014); MICH. COMP. LAWS ANN. § 445.72 (West 2011); MINN. STAT. ANN. § 325E.61 (West 2011); MISS. CODE ANN. § 75-24-29 (Supp. 2013); MO. ANN. STAT. § 407.1500 (West 2011); MONT. CODE ANN. § 30-14-1704 (2013); NEB. REV. STAT. § 87-803 (2008); NEV. REV. STAT. § 603A.220 (2013); N.H. REV. STAT. ANN. § 359-C:20 (2009); N.J. STAT. ANN. § 56:8-163 (West 2012); N.Y. GEN. BUS. LAW § 899-aa (McKinney 2012); N.C. GEN. STAT. § 75-65 (2013);

notification laws is that many were not drafted with the IoT in mind.[40] While every state data breach notification law covers "personal information," generally defined as an individual's first or last name, Social Security number, driver's license number, or bank or credit card information, these laws may not cover the type of "personal information" regularly gathered or recorded by IoT devices, e.g., biometric or sensor data.[41] Thus, the theft or loss of biometric or sensor data without the inclusion of other "personal information" may not trigger state data breach notification laws.[42]

A few jurisdictions have data breach laws, which, if interpreted broadly, might cover sensor data. These jurisdictions can be placed into two groups. In the first group, Arkansas, California, Missouri, and Puerto Rico include medical information in their definition of personal information.[43] Missouri defines "medical information" as "any information regarding an individual's medical history, mental or physical condition or medical treatment or diagnosis by a healthcare professional." Missouri's broad definition appears to cover Fitbit-type of information under their data breach notification laws.[44] In contrast, Arkansas and California define "medical information" more narrowly to include only information "regarding the individual's medical history or medical treatment or diagnosis by a health care professional."[45] This definition, which follows the one found in HIPAA, would probably not include Fitbit-related information.[46]

N.D. CENT. CODE §§ 51-30-02 to -30-03 (Supp. 2013); OHIO REV. CODE ANN. §§ 1347.12, 1349.19 (West Supp. 2014); OKLA. STAT. tit. 74, § 3113.1 (2011); OR. REV. STAT. § 646A.604 (2013); 73 PA. CONS. STAT. ANN. §§ 2301–08, 2329 (West Supp. 2014); R.I. GEN. LAWS § 11-49.2-3 (Supp. 2013); S.C. CODE ANN. § 39-1-90 (Supp. 2013); TENN. CODE ANN. § 47-18-2107 (2013); TEX. BUS. & COM. CODE ANN. § 521.053 (West Supp. 2014); UTAH CODE ANN. § 13-44-202 (LexisNexis 2013); VT. STAT. ANN. tit. 9, § 2435 (Supp. 2013); VA. CODE ANN. § 18.2-186.6 (2014), § 32.1-127.1:05 (2011); WASH. REV. CODE ANN. § 19.255.010 (West 2013), § 42.56.590 (West Supp. 2014); W. VA. CODE ANN. §§ 46-2A-101 to -2A-05 (LexisNexis Supp. 2014); WIS. STAT. ANN. § 134.98 (West 2009); WYO. STAT. ANN. § 40-12-502 (2013).

40. Scott R. Peppet, *Regulating the Internet of Things: First Steps Toward Managing Discrimination, Privacy, Security, and Consent*, 93 TEX. L. REV. 85 (2014).

41. *Id.*

42. *Id.*

43. ARK. CODE ANN. § 4-110-103(7)(D) (2011); CAL. CIV. CODE §§ 1798.29(e)(4), .82(e)(4) (West Supp. 2014); MO. ANN. STAT. § 407.1500 (9)(e) (West 2011); P.R. LAWS ANN. tit. 10, § 4051(a)(5) (2012).

44. MO. ANN. STAT. § 407.1500(9)(e) (West 2011).

45. ARK. CODE ANN. § 4-110-103(7)(D) (2011); CAL. CIV. CODE §§ 1798.29(e)(4), .82(e)(4) (West Supp. 2014).

46. Peppet, *supra* note 40.

In the second group, Nebraska, Texas, and Wisconsin include unique biometric data in their definition of "personal information."[47] The "unique biometric data" definitions used by Nebraska and Wisconsin include fingerprint, voice print, retina or iris image, and "other unique biometric data."[48] Broadly speaking, this definition would encompass Fitbit-related data.[49] The far more expansive Texas statute requires disclosure if the data breach involves "sensitive personal information" to include "information that identifies an individual and relates to: (i) the physical or mental health or condition of the individual."[50] This definition would most certainly apply to Fitbit-related data.[51]

While a few states have data breach notification laws covering Fitbit-related information, most do not. In addition, other types of data created by IoT devices would most likely not be covered by state data breach notification laws. Consider the following IoT devices and all the various types of information created by them:

- accelerometers

- smart meters

- thermostats

- home appliances

- automobiles.[52]

§ 4:4   Potential Solutions

Currently, there are a variety of solutions for improving the security of IoT devices under consideration. These solutions range from security by design to government intervention. The biggest challenge with most solutions is the impact they will have on IoT adoption and innovation. This in turn raises the recurring question of whether any proposed solution should be voluntary or mandatory. Some also believe that no market solution exists, because insecurity is an "externality" and considered to be "an effect of the purchasing decision that

---

47. IOWA CODE ANN. § 715C.1(11)(e) (West Supp. 2014); NEB. REV. STAT. § 87-802(5)(e) (2008); TEX. BUS. & COM. CODE ANN. § 521.002(a)(b)(5) (West Supp. 2014); WIS. STAT. ANN. § 134.98 (1)(b)(5) (West 2009).

48. NEB. REV. STAT. § 87-802(5)(e) (2008); WIS. STAT. ANN. § 134.98 (1)(b)(5) (West 2009).

49. Peppet, *supra* note 40.

50. TEX. BUS. & COM. CODE ANN. § 521.002(a)(2)(B)(i) (West Supp. 2014).

51. Peppet, *supra* note 40.

52. *Id.*

affects other people."[53] Similar comparisons can be drawn to historical and contemporary attempts to solve the problem of pollution.

§ 4:4.1   *Security by Design*

One solution, security by design, requires manufacturers to think
about security at the front end rather than the back end.[54] According
to one security expert, "IoT security must be baked in, not bolted
on."[55] With security by design, manufacturers do not add measures or
modify the product right before it is ready to go to market, but instead
think about security at the initial stages of development.

Security by design, should at a minimum, include:

(1) *Testing:* Prior to entering the market, testing the security features of each IoT device.[56]

(2) *Information for consumers:* Packaging should: provide clear
warnings about the dangers associated with inappropriate
use of the device's technologies; give consumers sufficient
information about the device to make an informed decision;
and alert consumers that they will be required at the point
of set-up to change passwords, e.g., the device will not work
unless default credentials are modified.[57]

(3) *Safeguarding data:* Measures should include collecting only
necessary data, thus reducing the loss of information if
security is compromised; and encrypting, anonymizing, and
de-identifying (i.e., "storing and sharing the data without
revealing the identity of the individuals involved").[58]

---

53. Bruce Schneier, *Click Here to Kill Everyone*, NYMAG.COM (Jan. 27,
2017), https://nymag.com/intelligencer/2017/01/the-internet-of-things-
dangerous-future-bruce-schneier.html. "The market can't fix this because
neither the buyer nor the seller cares. The owners of the webcams and
DVRs used in the denial-of-service attacks don't care. Their devices were
cheap to buy, they still work, and they don't know any of the victims of
the attacks. The sellers of those devices don't care: They're now selling
newer and better models, and the original buyers only cared about price
and features."

54. Ashley Brooks, *'Internet of Things' Security Concerns: How IT Pros Can
Save the Day* (July 26, 2016), www.rasmussen.edu/degrees/technology/
blog/internet-of-things-security-concerns/.

55. Rich Nass, *IoT Security Must Be Baked In, Not Bolted On*, INSIGHT.TECH
(Oct. 17, 2017).

56. Internet of Things: Privacy & Security in a Connected World, FTC Staff
Report (Jan. 2015).

57. *Id. See also* Wendy Zamora, *Internet of Things (IoT) Security: What Is
and What Should Never Be*, MALWAREBYTES.COM (Dec. 22, 2017).

58. FTC Staff Report, *supra* note 56.

§ 4:4.2   *Dedicated Network*

Another potential solution is to place IoT devices on their own network with a firewall separating them from other networks or equipment.[59] Thus, if an IoT device is compromised, attackers are still unable to reach other equipment or networks.

§ 4:4.3   *Manage Updates*

As previously discussed, manufacturers rely on online updates to justify sending IoT devices to market with inadequate security protections. If manufacturers continue to follow this practice, they need to ensure that consumers routinely receive security patches along with firmware, software, and other updates in order to keep devices secure.[60] This includes setting up automatic updates.

In addition, manufacturers need to come up with a plan to address so-called legacy systems that have been around for decades but have been only recently connected to the Internet.[61] Legacy systems are difficult to update because doing so can lead to unintended consequences.[62] For example, an engineer at a nuclear plant in Georgia updated the plant's business network with new software.[63] This in turn forced a data reset on the control systems, which was misinterpreted by the safety system as a lack of cooling water that then led to an automatic shutdown of the reactor.[64] At the time, the engineer did not know that the "software was designed to synchronize data between machines on both networks, or that a reboot in the business system computer would force a similar reset in the control system machine."[65] Clearly, legacy systems have to be accounted for in future updates.

§ 4:4.4   *Government Intervention*

The most often discussed solution to improving IoT security is governmental intervention. The challenge, of course, is maintaining the balance between security and innovation. When intervening in

---

59.   Anna M. Gerber, *Top 10 IoT Security Challenges*, THE DEVELOPER-WORKS BLOG (Mar. 26, 2020), https://developer.ibm.com/dwblog/2017/iot-security-challenges/?lnk=hm.
60.   *Id.*
61.   Dep't of Homeland Sec., National Protection and Programs Directorate Office of Cyber and Infrastructure Analysis (OCIA), *Why Is the Internet of Things Insecure?* (Aug. 15, 2017) (with author).
62.   *Id.*
63.   Brian Krebs, *Cyber Incident Blamed for Nuclear Power Plant Shutdown*, WASH. POST (June 5, 2008).
64.   *Id.*
65.   *Id.*

any particular industry, the government generally does so as a purchaser, regulator, or legislator.

[A] Government As Purchaser

In 2015, the government, primarily the Department of Defense (DoD), spent nearly $9 billion on sensor-enabled IoT technologies.[66] As one of the largest purchasers of IoT equipment, the government can play an outsized role in imposing requirements on the IoT industry. For example, the government can refuse to buy from certain manufacturers and/or create specific requirements for IoT products. Recently, the DoD created a "'do not buy' list to block vendors using software code originating from Russia or China."[67] The list was primarily created to prevent the DoD and industry partners from purchasing "problematic code."[68] The Internet of Things Cybersecurity Act of 2017, discussed later in this chapter, illustrates the government's ability to legislatively impose security requirements on the IoT equipment it purchases.

[B] Government As Regulator

As discussed in chapter 2, the government primarily regulates the IoT industry through the FTC. One of the first litigated cases involving security and the IoT was *FTC v. D-Link*.[69] Here, D-Link, a global manufacturer of computer networking equipment to include routers and Internet protocol cameras, claimed that their routers were "easy to secure" and equipped with "advanced network security." The government, however, found these statements to be deceptive to consumers. In addition, the government claimed that D-Link engaged in unfair practices that put consumers' privacy at risk.

The FTC's complaint against D-Link alleged that the company failed to correct preventable security flaws to include:

(1)   "hard-coded" login credentials integrated into D-Link camera software—such as the username "guest" and the password "guest"—that could allow unauthorized access to the cameras' live feeds;

---

66.   Robert Metzger, *Security and the Internet of Things: The Role of the Federal Government to Reconcile Opportunity and Risk*, ABA THE SCITECH LAW. (Spring 2018).

67.   Mike Stone, *Pentagon Creating Software 'Do Not Buy' List to Keep Out Russia, China*, REUTERS (July 27, 2018).

68.   *Id.*

69.   Fed. Trade Comm'n v. D-Link Sys. Inc., 2017 WL 4150873 (N.D. Cal. Sept. 19, 2017). *See also* Press Release, Fed. Trade Comm'n, D-Link Case Alleges Inadequate Internet of Things Security Practices (Jan. 5, 2017).

(2)   a software flaw known as "command injection" that could enable remote attackers to take control of consumers' routers by sending them unauthorized commands over the Internet;

(3)   private key code used to sign into D-Link software was openly available on a public website for six months; and

(4)   leaving users' login credentials for D-Link's mobile app unsecured in clear, readable text on their mobile devices, even though there is free software available to secure the information.

The FTC asserted that a bad actor could exploit these vulnerabilities; for example, a hacker could use a compromised router to obtain information stored on the router's attached storage device. The complaint also claimed that a hacker could use the router in a DDoS attack or redirect it to a bogus website.

D-Link filed a motion to dismiss and three of the six claims brought by the FTC were struck. According to the court,

> [t]he FTC does not identify a single incident where a consumer's financial, medical or other sensitive personal information has been accessed, exposed or misused in any way, or whose IP camera has been compromised by unauthorized parties, or who has suffered any harm or even simple annoyance and inconvenience from the alleged security flaws in the DLS [Direct Link] devices. The absence of any concrete facts makes it just as possible that DLS's devices are not likely to substantially harm consumers, and the FTC cannot rely on wholly conclusory allegations about potential injury to tilt the balance in its favor.[70]

The FTC faced standing issues because no consumer information was in fact lost; there was just the potential for loss. Nonetheless, the court allowed three counts related to deceptive claims about the security of D-Link's products to continue. Additionally, the judge allowed the FTC to amend its complaint. Specifically, the court stated:

> [i]f the FTC had tied the unfairness claim to the representations underlying the deception claims, it might have had a more colorable injury element. A consumer's purchase of a device that fails to be reasonably secure—let alone as secure as advertised—would likely be in the ballpark of a "substantial injury," particularly when aggregated across a large group of consumers.[71]

---

70.   *D-Link Sys. Inc.*, 2017 WL 4150873 at *5.
71.   *Id.* at *6.

While *FTC v. D-Link* was the first litigated case involving an IoT device, the FTC had previously gone after companies for unsecured routers, which, according to the FTC's Bureau of Consumer Protection Director, "play a key role" in "connecting smart devices to their home networks."[72] One of the first cases involving unsecured routers was brought against computer maker, Asus.[73] The case stemmed from security flaws in Asus's routers that put the home networks of hundreds of thousands of consumers at risk. According to the FTC, Asus failed to deliver patches promptly to devices or notify consumers of security risks. The FTC also claimed that Asus allowed users to retain default login credentials of "admin" for both username and password. In 2014, hackers identified thousands of vulnerable Asus routers and subsequently published 12,937 IP addresses of those Asus routers. Also, the Asus software update tool informed consumers that their routers used the latest software—which was untrue—as the software had actually been replaced by newer versions.[74]

Asus ultimately settled with the FTC in 2016. The FTC consent order requires Asus to establish and maintain a comprehensive security program subject to independent audits for twenty years.[75]

[C] Government As Legislator

At present, there does not appear to be a strong desire by Congress to regulate in the IoT arena.[76] While Congress has introduced a number of bills concerning IoT security, few have passed.[77] Of those that have been enacted into law, most are advisory in nature.[78] One bill that has gained some attention is the bipartisan Internet of Things Cybersecurity Act of 2017. At the state level, California, in 2018, passed the first ever law related to IoT security, SB 327. Both of these bills are discussed below.

---

72.   Liam Tung, *ASUS Hit by FTC with 20-year Audit Bungled Router Security*, ZDNET (Feb. 24, 2016).

73.   *Id.*

74.   *Id.*

75.   Press Release, Fed. Trade Comm'n, Asus Settles FTC Charges That Insecure Home Routers and "Cloud" Services Put Consumers' Privacy at Risk (Feb. 23, 2016), www.ftc.gov/news-events/press-releases/2016/02/asus-settles-ftc-charges-insecure-home-routers-cloud-services-put.

76.   Derek Johnson, *Why Is No One Raising a Hand to Regulate the Internet of Things*, FCW.COM (Mar. 16, 2018).

77.   Katharine Goodloe, *U.S. Legislative Roundup of IoT*, INSIDE PRIVACY (May 9, 2018).

78.   IoT Consumer TIPS Act of 2017 (S. 2234), SMART IoT Act (H.R. 6032), Security IoT Act of 2017 (H.R. 1324), Cyber Shield Act of 2017, House (H.R. 4163) and Senate (S. 2020), DIGIT Act, Senate (S. 88) and House (H.R. 686), and Internet of Things Cybersecurity Improvement Act of 2017 (S. 1691).

[C][1]   *Internet of Things Cybersecurity Act of 2017*

The proponents of the Internet of Things Cybersecurity Act of 2017, which was introduced in the U.S. Senate, had several objectives with this legislation.[79] First and foremost, the sponsors wanted greater security for IoT devices used by the federal government, and to that end, the bill imposes "minimum security requirements for federal procurements of connected devices."[80]

Sponsors of the bill also wanted to encourage research into IoT device vulnerabilities. To accomplish this goal, the bill amends the Computer Fraud and Abuse Act (CFAA) and the Digital Millennium Copyright Act (DMCA) to create so-called Safe Harbor provisions for vulnerability researchers, also known as white-hat hackers.[81] When conducting research or security testing, these researchers must "act[ ] in good faith" and in compliance with National Protection and Programs Directorate (NPPD) guidelines.[82] Furthermore, the research must be on the "same class, model, or type of the device" the government purchases and "not on the actual device provided to the United States Government."[83]

In addition, the sponsors wanted to know the total number of IoT devices used by the federal government; therefore, the bill requires the director of each executive federal agency to establish and maintain an IoT device inventory.[84] The bill also directs the head of the National Institute for Standards and Technology (NIST) to establish and maintain a National Vulnerability Database.[85]

This bill hopes to achieve its primary goal by imposing five new contractual obligations on vendors of "Internet-connected devices" who contract with the federal government "for the acquisition of

---

79.   S. 1691, Internet of Things (IoT) Cybersecurity Improvement Act of 2017, 115th Congress (2017–2018). *See also* Jennifer Huddleston Skees, *Liberty and Security in the Proposed Internet of Things Cybersecurity Improvement Act of 2017*, TECHLIBERATION.COM (Aug. 23, 2017).

80.   *See* Skees, *supra* note 79.

81.   *Id. See also* Schneier, *supra* note 53. Pursuant to the DMCA "it is a crime to bypass security mechanisms that protect copyrighted work, even if that bypassing would otherwise be legal. Since all software can be copyrighted, it is arguably illegal to do security research on these devices and to publish the result."

82.   S. 1691, Internet of Things (IoT) Cybersecurity Improvement Act of 2017, 115th Congress (2017–2018).

83.   *Id. See also* Randy Milch, *A First Legislative Step in the IoT Security Battle*, LAWFARE (Aug. 4, 2017).

84.   S. 1691, Internet of Things (IoT) Cybersecurity Improvement Act of 2017, 115th Congress (2017–2018).

85.   *Id.*

Internet-connected devices."[86] Specifically, the bill requires vendors to certify in writing that IoT devices purchased by the government:

(a)   do not have any known security vulnerabilities or defects listed in the NIST database of vulnerabilities or other such national database;

(b)   have no fixed or hardcoded credentials used for remote administration, delivery of updates, or communication;

(c)   rely only on standard protocols and technologies; and

(d)   have components capable of being updated securely from the vendor.[87]

Vendors are also required to

(a)   notify the purchasing agent of any known security vulnerabilities or defects that are later discovered;

(b)   provide software and firmware updates "to fix or remove any future security vulnerability or defect in any part of the software or firmware";

(c)   repair or replace any device in a timely manner when a new security vulnerability cannot be remedied through an update; and

(d)   provide the purchasing agent with

   (i)   the manner in which the device receives security updates,

   (ii)   the anticipated timeline for ending security support,

   (iii) the formal notification when security support has ceased, and

   (iv)   any additional information recommended by National Telecommunications and Information Administration (NTIA).[88]

Exceptions to the aforementioned rules may be granted by the relevant executive agency head.[89] For example, the director of a federal

---

86.   Randy Milch, *A First Legislative Step in the IoT Security Battle*, Lawfare (Aug. 4, 2017).

87.   S. 1691, Internet of Things (IoT) Cybersecurity Improvement Act of 2017, 115th Congress (2017–2018).

88.   *Id.*

89.   *Id.*

agency can waive the "no known vulnerabilities" clause if the vendor discloses a known vulnerability and provides mitigation actions limiting "the ability for an adversary to exploit the vulnerability."[90] If the waiver is granted, the agency head must state in writing that the "executive agency accepts such risks resulting from use of the device with the known vulnerability as represented by the contractor."[91] These types of waivers may be common, at least early on, because software and firmware builders often use libraries with known vulnerabilities.[92]

Other exceptions to the requirements imposed by the bill may be granted if the IoT device in question has "severely limited functionality" as defined by the NIST.[93] Exceptions also arise if the third-party standards provide equivalent or greater security than what is recommended in the legislation.[94] These same third-party exceptions are available if agency security evaluations exist.[95]

The bill is not without detractors; first and foremost are concerns that the legislation only applies to the those who do business with the government.[96] Thus, many consumer IoT devices will be left unaffected by the bill.[97] Another critique is that this bill is primarily directed at vendors and contractors and not necessarily the manufacturers who build the IoT products.[98] Other criticisms target the NIST vulnerability database and whether it will be available to the public.[99] Also, some are bothered by the legislation's lack of criminal penalties; however, violators face the potential loss of government contracts.[100] Yet, despite these criticisms, many feel that this initial

---

90.   *Id.*
91.   *Id.*
92.   Randy Milch, *A First Legislative Step in the IoT Security Battle*, LAWFARE (Aug. 4, 2017).
93.   S. 1691, Internet of Things (IoT) Cybersecurity Improvement Act of 2017, 115th Congress (2017–2018).
94.   *Id.*
95.   *See* Milch, *supra* note 92.
96.   Ersin Domangue, *Explaining the Internet of Things Cybersecurity Improvement Act of 2017*, SEC. EVALUATORS (Sept. 25, 2017); Jennifer Huddleston Skees, *Liberty and Security in the Proposed Internet of Things Cybersecurity Improvement Act of 2017*, TECHLIBERATION.COM (Aug. 23, 2017).
97.   *See* Domangue, *supra* note 96.
98.   *Id.*
99.   *Id.*
100.   *Id. See also* Skees, *supra* note 96.

attempt to regulate IoT security on the federal level is a step in the right direction.[101]

[C][2] *California SB 327*

California Senate Bill (SB) 327 was the first IoT security bill enacted into law at any level of government.[102] SB 327, which took effect on January 1, 2020, does not create any private right of action for individuals and instead leaves enforcement solely with state or local officials.[103]

SB 327 mandates that IoT-device "manufacturers," defined as "the person who manufacturers, or contacts with another person to manufacture on the person's behalf, connected devices that are sold or offered for sale in California" have "reasonable security features to proactively implement 'security by design' (that is, at an early stage, and built into the product development process, rather than added reactively later as a 'patch' or as an optional or voluntary industry best practice)." A "connected device" is broadly defined as "any device, or other physical object that is capable of connecting to the Internet, directly or indirectly, and that is assigned an Internet Protocol address or Bluetooth address." For the most part, all devices connected to the Internet receive either an IP or Bluetooth address upon connection.

The law does not delve into what are "reasonable security features." Instead, the law takes a risk-based approach requiring the security features to be:

1. appropriate to the nature and function of the device;

2. appropriate to the information the device may collect, contain, or transmit; and

3. designed to protect the device and any information contained in it from unauthorized access, destruction, use, modification, or disclosure.

SB 327 also states that if an IoT device uses authentication, defined as "a method of verifying the authority of a user, process, or device

---

101.   *See* Domangue, *supra* note 96.

102.   SB-327 Information Privacy: Connected Devices, an Act to Add Title 1.81.26 (commencing with Section 1798.91.04) to Part 4 of Division 3 of the Civil Code, relating to information privacy (2017–2018). *See also* David M. Stauss, *California Poised to Enact Internet of Things Information Security Law*, NAT'L L. REV. (Sept. 6, 2018).

103.   It should be noted that other California laws do provide a private right of action for data breaches, e.g., the California Consumer Privacy Act of 2018.

to access resources in an information system," beyond a local area network, a "reasonable security feature" is one that either: (1) allows a pre-programmed password unique to each device (no default login credentials); or (2) generates a new method of authentication before providing access to the device for the first time.

Finally, the law provides for a number of exemptions, including:

1. a "manufacturer of a connected device related to unaffiliated third-party software or applications that a user chooses to add to a connected device";

2. "any connected device the functionality of which is subject to security requirements under federal law, regulations, or guidance promulgated by a federal agency pursuant to its regulatory enforcement authority"; and

3. HIPAA-covered entities and business associates for activity related to this law.

Like with other technology-related legislation passed in California, SB 327 could significantly impact the entire IoT industry.[104] First, a number of the major IoT companies like Amazon, Google, Tesla, and Fitbit are located in California. Second, California is arguably the largest commercial market for emerging technology.[105] Third, this legislation requires manufacturers to rewrite their software.[106] Once manufacturers make this initial security update with their software, they are unlikely to make two different versions, one for California and one for the rest of the United States.[107] Rather, they will likely pick one, the California standard, and that will be used as the default for everyone.[108]

While some have praised this new law as a good first step, others have found it to be flawed.[109] For example, some critics state that although well-intended, the law is misguided and focuses on the wrong area of security.[110] They argue that rather than add "security features" which increases the "attack surface," manufacturers should

---

104. Douglas G. Bonner & Richard J. Caira, *California Bill Mandates Privacy by Design for IoT Devices*, NAT'L L. REV. (Apr. 27, 2017).

105. *Id.*

106. Bruce Schneier, *We Need Stronger Cybersecurity Laws for the Internet of Things*, CNN.COM (Nov. 10, 2018).

107. *Id.*

108. *Id.*

109. Catalin Cimpanu, *First IoT Security Bill Reaches Governor's Desk in California*, ZDNET (Sept. 11, 2018).

110. Robert Graham & David Maynor, *California's Bad IoT Law*, ERRATA SEC. (Sept. 10, 2018).

focus on removing "insecure features" like listening ports and cross-site/injection issues."[111] Others wanted the law to require encryption or "clear standards per the device's components that a manufacturer will be able to follow."[112] Finally, SB 327 will have a significant R&D and budgetary impact on IoT device development, transforming what was once a manufacturer's afterthought into a key component at the design and production stages of any IoT device produced for sale to consumers in California.

§ 4:4.5   Private Litigation

In addition to the actions brought by the FTC and state attorneys general, individuals have brought civil lawsuits against manufacturers of insecure IoT devices. At present, there are numerous grounds for a consumer to assert damages caused by a security breach. The most common theories of recovery are breach of contract, breach of fiduciary duty, public disclosure of private facts, negligence, and strict liability. Federal and state statutes also provide a basis for civil actions, e.g., Gramm-Leach-Bliley, HIPAA, SCA, and the FCRA. In addition, public companies that experience data breaches may also be subject to shareholder derivative lawsuits asserting that company officials did not take sufficient steps to prevent the cybersecurity breaches that harmed the company.[113]

[A]   In the Home

To date, IoT devices sold to consumers for use in and around the home have been the subject of numerous civil actions alleging inadequate security. These civil suits, brought by consumers, the FTC, and state attorneys general, have involved IoT devices ranging from children's toys to home security monitoring systems.

In the case of *In re VTech Data Breach Litigation*, consumers brought a class action against the maker of children's learning toys when a hacker illegally bypassed VTech's security measures and obtained customer data including profile pictures, emails, passwords, and nicknames.[114] The hacker, who was arrested, provided the data to

---

111.   *Id.*
112.   Jennifer Kang, *A New California Bill Would Require Better Passwords for Internet of Things Devices*, SLATE.COM (Sept. 21, 2018); Jerry Bowles, *SB-327 Passes As California Steps Up with Nation's First IoT Security Bill—Is It Useful?*, DIGINOMICA.COM (Sept. 24, 2018).
113.   Torres v. Wendy's Int'l, LLC, 2016 WL 7104870 (M.D. Fla. Nov. 29, 2016); Complaint, Havron v. Yahoo, No. 16-cv-01075 (S.D. Ill. Sept. 22, 2016), assigned, Case No. 16-cv-07031-LHK.
114.   *In re* VTech Data Breach Litig., No. 1:15-CV-10889 (N.D. Ill. Dec. 3, 2015).

a technology journalist.[115] Plaintiffs alleged breach of contract, breach of the implied covenant of good faith and fair dealing in contract, and breach of implied warranty of merchantability The plaintiffs also claimed violation of the Illinois Consumer Fraud and Deceptive Business Practices Act and sought declaratory judgment on VTech's obligations.

In their motion to dismiss, the defendants claimed that the plaintiffs lacked standing because they suffered no harm.[116] According to the defendants, there was no evidence that the hacker did anything more than point out the vulnerability.[117] While the court ultimately dismissed the suit, the defendants could not escape the reach of the FTC, which brought its own complaint against VTech under COPPA.[118] VTech ultimately settled with the FTC for $650,000, and agreed to create an extensive data security program to ensure future compliance with COPPA and to protect the personal information of consumers.[119] This was the FTC's first-ever children's security/privacy case involving IoT toy products.[120]

Similarly, in *Archer-Hayes v. ToyTalk, Inc.*, consumers brought a class action against Mattel, the makers of Hello Barbie, a doll that recorded conversations when children played with it, and collected and stored the recordings in the cloud.[121] Plaintiffs claimed, among other things, that the doll could not distinguish between children whose parents consented to recordings and those who did not. Thus, the doll violated the COPPA because it made, stored, and used information from children whose parents did not grant Mattel prior permission. The complaint, which was ultimately dismissed, was based on negligence, unfair competition, and privacy violations.

Furthermore, *In re Sony Gaming Networks & Customer Data Security Breach Litigation* involved a class action lawsuit brought by PlayStation users concerning a data breach.[122] Shortly after the attack, sixty-five class action lawsuits were filed against Sony which were

---

115.   John Clabby & Joseph Swanson, *A Look at Manufacturer Liability for the Internet of Things*, Carlton Fields (Oct. 4, 2016).

116.   *Id.*

117.   *Id.*

118.   Erin Bosman, Julie Park & Benjamin Kagel, *Digital Toy Product Company Ducks Data Breach Class Action*, Class Dismissed (May 8, 2018), https://classdismissed.mofo.com/consumer-products/digital-toy-product-company-ducks-data-breach-class-action/.

119.   *Id.*

120.   *Id.*

121.   Archer-Hayes v. ToyTalk, Inc., 2015 WL 8304161 (Cal. Super. Ct. Dec. 7, 2015), *notice of removal*, No. 2:16-cv-02111 (C.D. Cal. Mar. 29, 2016).

122.   *In re* Sony Gaming Networks & Customer Data Sec. Breach Litig., 903 F. Supp. 2d 942 (S.D. Cal. 2012) (Settlement Agreement).

ultimately consolidated. The compromised information included confidential personal and financial account information. Plaintiffs claimed that Sony not only failed to protect consumer information, but did not tell consumers that their data has been compromised. Plaintiffs also claimed that Sony should have been aware of their inadequate security measures which were below the industry standard.

Sony's initial motion to dismiss was granted; however, plaintiffs were allowed to file an amended complaint. In the amended complaint, most of the plaintiffs' claims were again dismissed, but the court did allow some consumer protection claims brought under state law to remain. The court determined at the motion to dismiss stage that Sony misrepresented its network security. Sony ultimately settled the lawsuit, agreeing to provide users with $15 million in games, online currency, and identity theft reimbursement.

In *Baker v. ADT Corp.*, the plaintiff brought a class action against ADT's wireless security and monitoring system.[123] The plaintiff claimed that ADT's equipment could be remotely turned on or off by basic technology available to the general public, that he was hacked at least twice, and his alarm was falsely triggered which led to the police coming to his house. The plaintiff also alleged that hackers could "hack into ADT's wireless system and use customers' own security cameras to unknowingly spy on them." Rather than focus on a particular harm that arose from the so-called "false alarms," the plaintiff's claims focused on ADT's marketing which advertised its systems as secure and reliable. The plaintiff, who brought claims under strict product liability and unjust enrichment, further argued that ADT violated both Florida and Illinois consumer fraud statutes.

In a motion to dismiss, ADT challenged the legal sufficiency of the plaintiff's claims, asserting that his statements were mere "puffery." The trial court granted the motion to dismiss for the strict liability count but denied it for the unjust enrichment claim. Also, the court allowed the portions of the consumer fraud counts that were based on ADT's "secure communications links" advertisement to continue.

[B] Medical

In *Ross v. St. Jude Medical Inc.*, the plaintiff brought a putative class action suit claiming that the defendant's products to include implants, pacemakers, defibrillators and heart re-synchronizers, were vulnerable to potential hackers who could cause a "crash attack" or "battery drain attack."[124] The devices in question used radio frequency wireless technology to allow remote collection of medical information

---

123. Baker v. ADT Corp., No. 2:15-cv-02038 (C.D. Ill. Nov. 9, 2014).
124. Ross v. St. Jude Med. Inc., No. 2:16-cv-06465 (C.D. Cal. Aug. 26, 2016).

via the Internet.[125] While remote collection cuts down on trips to the doctor's offices, it also opens up another potential attack vector.

According to the plaintiff, who had a St. Jude defibrillator, the defendant owed patients a "duty of care to ensure that the devices safeguarded against potential hacking."[126] The plaintiff further argued that "[i]t is foreseeable that if defendants did not take reasonable security measure[s], the devices could be accessed and viewed or controlled by unauthorized persons." The plaintiff's class action lawsuit stemmed in large part from a report by MedSec Holdings, which found security vulnerabilities in St. Jude devices. St. Jude defended these claims aggressively, even bringing a defamation claim against MedSec Holdings. Ultimately, the plaintiff voluntarily dismissed his case without prejudice.

[C] Smart Vehicles

Several civil actions have been brought against manufacturers of so-called "smart" cars. In *Cahen v. Toyota*, one of the first putative class action lawsuits against Toyota, Ford, and General Motors, the plaintiffs brought claims of fraud, breach of contract, common law warranty, and implied warranty of merchantability.[127] According to the plaintiffs, the defendants' vehicles were vulnerable to hacking due to design flaws. The complaint alleged that someone could interact remotely through Bluetooth or a smartphone with the network of devices that operated the vehicle, resulting in complete loss of driver control over steering, accelerating, and braking. The plaintiffs claimed that the manufacturers were aware of these security vulnerabilities but nonetheless claimed their products were safe.

The defendants argued that the plaintiffs failed to "allege any hacking incidents that have taken place outside of the controlled settings, and that the entire threat rests on the speculative premise that a sophisticated third-party cybercriminal may one day successfully hack one of the plaintiffs' vehicles. Following traditional automobile and products liability precedent, the court dismissed the case, stating that the alleged risk was too speculative to constitute actual injury, and thus consumers lacked Article III standing to assert claims against the defendant vehicle manufacturers. The plaintiffs' privacy claims were also dismissed, with the court finding that, under California law, vehicle manufacturers' alleged tracking of vehicles' driving history, performance, or location, if proven, did not violate the consumers' privacy interests.

---

125.   Julie Steinberg, *St. Jude Sued Over Security of Connected Devices*, BLOOMBERG LAW (Sept. 7, 2016).
126.   *Ross, supra* note 124.
127.   Cahen v. Toyota, 147 F. Supp. 3d 955, 966 (N.D. Cal. 2015).

A similar case was brought by owners of Chrysler automobiles in *Flynn v. FCA US LLC*.[128] Here, the plaintiffs alleged that Chrysler and Harmon Industries (a software manufacturer) improperly sold the defectively designed uConnect system, which allowed for control over the phone, navigation, and entertainment functions throughout the affected Chrysler vehicles. According to the plaintiffs, the uConnect system had a number of design vulnerabilities that could allow hackers to take remote control of the vehicles while they were in operation. The complaint raised claims for breach of warranty, violation of the Magnuson-Moss Act, common law fraud, negligence, unjust enrichment, and violation of state consumer protection statutes, each separately predicated on Michigan, Illinois, and Missouri law. The defendants maintained that there was no defect in the vehicles and they were safe.

The court dismissed certain claims and ruled that the plaintiffs lacked standing to seek damages for the risk of future hacking. But, unlike in *Cahen*, the court found the plaintiffs had standing to sue for damages for the diminished value of the car. Some of the warranty claims were compelled to arbitration while others were permitted to proceed.

[D]   Non-IoT Security Breaches

On November 12, 2013, Target was the victim of a cyber data breach that impacted forty million credit and debit card accounts.[129] The attack forced top Target officials to resign, including the CEO, as Target's profits fell 46% during the holiday season of that year. Target's data breach illustrates how a security lapse, albeit done by a third party, can result in unauthorized access and misuse of personal information.

There are several theories surrounding the specifics of how exactly Target was attacked, but none have been confirmed.[130] Most believe that the initial breach arose outside of Target and through a third-party vendor, Fazio Mechanical Services, a heating, ventilation, and

---

128.   Flynn v. FCA US LLC, 2016 WL 5341199, at *1 (S.D. Ill. Sept. 23, 2016) and 2016 WL 5341749 (S.D. Ill. Sept. 23, 2016).

129.   *See* G. Markowsky & L. Markowsky, *From Air Conditioner to Data Breach*, Kevin Daimi & Hamid R. Arabnia (eds.), Proceedings of the 2014 International Conference on Security and Management, SAM 2014, http://docplayer.net/7778877-George-markowsky-ashu-m-g-solo-kevin-daimi-samiha-ayed-michael-r-grimaila-hanen-idoudi-editors-hamid-r-arabnia.html.

130.   *See* Xiaokui Shu, Ke Tian, Andrew Ciambrone & Danfeng Yao, *Breaking the Target: An Analysis of Target Data Breach and Lessons Learned* (Jan. 17, 2017), http://arxiv.org/abs/1701.04940.

air-conditioning firm.[131] The attackers gained access to Fazio through a Citadel Trojan which was installed through phishing. Once inside Fazio, the attackers had access to Target's external billing system, Ariba, which included the business section of the Target network. Upon accessing the business section, the attackers could enter other parts of the Target network.

Ultimately, Target faced a number of class action lawsuits brought by different groups of plaintiffs, ranging from consumers to financial institutions to shareholders.[132] In total, approximately seventy lawsuits were filed between December 2013 and January 2014.[133]

The class of financial institutions claimed out-of-pocket expenses related to the actual fraud caused by the data theft.[134] The court found that the financial institutions had to reissue nearly every Target credit card. Thus, the risk of harm to them went beyond the "risk of future harm," as argued by Target, and was actual harm. Target settled the class action with the financial institutions for $39.4 million.

The class action brought by forty-seven state attorneys general was settled in 2017 for $18.5 million.[135] As part of the settlement, Target was required to appoint an executive to manage a "comprehensive security program." In addition, Target had to hire an outside third party to conduct a comprehensive security assessment. Target also had to implement additional cybersecurity measures to include: (1) encrypting payment information; (2) separating cardholder data from the rest of the computer network; and (3) requiring two-factor authentication and password rotation within its business network system.

§ 4:4.6   Insurance

As demonstrated by the foregoing, IoT devices are vulnerable to security breaches which in turn expose manufacturers, sellers, installers, and others to civil liability. Valuable data may be lost, stolen, or compromised by poorly designed, improperly installed, incorrectly

---

131.   *Id.*
132.   *See* Joel Schectman, *Target Faces Nearly 70 Lawsuits Over Breach*, WSJ. COM (Jan. 15, 2014).
133.   *Id.*
134.   Jonathan Stempel & Nandita Bose, *Target in $39.4 Million Settlement with Banks over Data Breach*, REUTERS (Dec. 2, 2015); *In re* Target Corp. Customer Data Sec. Breach Litig., Settlement Agreement and Release, 66 F. Supp. 3d 1154 (Mar. 18, 2015).
135.   *In re* Target Corp. Customer Data Sec. Breach Litig. (Financial Institutions Case), 309 F.R.D. 482 (Sept. 15, 2015). *See also* Sruthi Ramakrishnan & Nandita Bose, *Target Pays Millions to Settle State Data Breach Lawsuits*, FORTUNE (May 23, 2017).

monitored, or outdated IoT devices. In addition to theft or loss of data, security breaches have the potential to disable or disrupt IoT-connected devices that can completely incapacitate a whole firm or enterprise.[136] Online businesses have repeatedly been affected by malicious denial of service attacks that use IoT devices to overload the servers of a target. One survey showed peak-time distributed denial-of-service attacks cost organizations more than $100,000 per hour.[137] Documented security breaches have impacted automobiles, thermostats that control heating and cooling, and a steel mill's blast furnaces.[138] The potential liability for such security breaches has led to increased reliance on insurance policies in an effort to protect enterprises from the financial risks of security breaches.[139]

The availability of cybersecurity coverage varies by policy. Certain policies do not cover so-called "breachless" claims where security issues are identified prior to any actual exploitation.[140] This is due to the fact that the insured cannot demonstrate that "an actual or reasonably suspected breach—is present." However, as previously discussed, breachless claims may be brought by private litigants[141] and regulatory authorities.[142]

In contrast, if the insured can show actual harm to persons or organizations whose data was compromised, then those claims will most likely be covered.[143] Most insurance policies require the policyholder to prove that the policy has been triggered by some conduct discovered during the policy period.[144] The triggering conditions of

---

136. Steve Reilly, *Records: Energy Department Struck by Cyber Attacks*, USA TODAY (Sept. 11, 2015). Cyber attackers successfully compromised the security of U.S. Department of Energy computer systems more than 150 times between 2010 and 2014.

137. Joe Loveless, *DDOS Attacks Are Costing Business Victims Cash*, NEUSTAR (June 28, 2017), www.home.neustar/blog/ddos-attacks-are-costing-business-victims-hard-cash.

138. Kim Zetter, *A Cyberattack Has Caused Confirmed Physical Damage for the Second Time Ever*, WIRED (Jan. 8, 2015). Mill personnel were unable to shut down a blast furnace when required, resulting in "massive damage to the system."

139. Mary Borja & Edward Brown, *The Problem with Breachless Cyberinsurance Claims*, LAW360 (Oct. 24, 2016).

140. *Id.*

141. *See* Cahen v. Toyota Motor Corp., 147 F. Supp. 3d 955 (2015), and Ross v. St. Jude Med. Inc., 2016 WL 4527336 (C.D. Cal. 2016).

142. *In re* Dwolla, Inc., No. 2016-CFPB-0007, 2016 WL 4523122 (Administrative Proceeding filed Mar. 2, 2016).

143. P.F. Chang's China Bistro, Inc. v. Fed. Ins. Co., 2016 WL 3055111 (D. Ariz. May 31, 2016).

144. Wiley Rein, *The Problem with Breachless Cyberinsurance Claims*, LAW360 (Oct. 24, 2016).

many policies replicate the reporting and notice obligations under state breach notification laws, which may not capture all IoT-related breaches.

Courts have recently examined the issue of whether a general liability insurance policy covers acts by third parties. As previously discussed in this chapter, tens of millions of Sony PlayStation users were the victims of a data breach in which hackers obtained their confidential information.[145] Upon discovering the hack, Sony turned to their insurance providers to cover the costs associated with the breach. The insurance companies balked at paying and took the matter to court. The issue before the court was essentially how the phrase "in any manner" was defined. The insurance companies argued that the phrase "refers to the medium used for publication, not to what party is doing the dissemination." Thus, for the insurance policy to be applicable, Sony would have had to publicize the confidential information of its users. In contrast, Sony argued that its general liability policy "provided coverage for publication of the information 'in any manner,' regardless of whether the publication was carried out by the policyholder or by a third party."

The judge in this case determined that the insurers did not have to defend Sony against the scores of suits stemming from the data breach. While the judge held that theft of sensitive data by hackers constituted a "publication" of private information, he found that, as required by the general liability insurance policy, that coverage could not be triggered through the actions of third parties, i.e., the hackers. Sony appealed, but the parties settled before the appellate court rendered a decision.[146] Nonetheless, this case puts those seeking cyber breach policies on notice that they should not rely on or expect general liability policies to cover cyber risks.

The best cyber breach policies cover costs associated with:

1. alerting customers;

2. forensics;

3. call center set-up;

4. consumer identity monitoring;

5. legal fees; and

---

145.   Zurich Am. Ins. Co. v. Sony Corp. of Am., 2014 WL 3253541 (N.Y. Sup. Ct. Feb. 21, 2014). *See also* Robert Siciliano, *Cyber Attackers & Data Leaks: Do You Need Data Breach Insurance*, BUSINESS.COM (Feb. 22, 2017).

146.   *See* Jeff Sistrunk, *Sony, Zurich Settle Data Breach Coverage Battle*, LAW360 (Apr. 30, 2015).

6. using a crisis management firm.[147]

At present, there are numerous challenges facing both those seeking cybersecurity insurance and those offering it. First, there is currently insufficient information in this area to adequately predict the likelihood of when someone will be hacked.[148] Due to the growing number of security breaches, this problem will likely be resolved in the near future. Second, it is challenging to economically quantify "reputational damage" and "loss of customer loyalty."[149] However, as with predicting the likelihood of being hacked, this problem may soon be resolved because of the increasing number of companies who are forced to deal with the aftermath of a security breach. For those who can obtain adequate coverage, many insurance companies cap policies at $300 million, but claims can actually reach into the billion-dollar territory.[150]

Finally, those seeking cyber insurance must ensure that they closely adhere to their specific policy. In 2013, Cottage Health, which operates a network of hospitals in Southern California, suffered a data breach involving 32,500 confidential medical records.[151] Their insurance provider, Columbia Casualty, went to court seeking a declaratory judgment against Cottage Health for losses associated with the policy. Columbia Casualty claimed that they did not have to defend or indemnify Cottage Health because Cottage Health failed to follow the insurance policy. The pertinent portions of the policy read as follows:

> exclusion entitled Failure to Follow Minimum Required Practices that precluded coverage for any loss based upon, directly or indirectly arising out of, or in any way involving [a]ny failure of an Insured to continuously implement the procedures and risk controls identified in the Insured's application for this Insurance and all related information submitted to the Insurer in conjunction with such application whether orally or in writing.

In essence, Columbia Casualty argued that the data breach was caused "by Cottage's failure to continuously implement the procedures and risk controls identified in its application."[152] While the plaintiff here

---

147. Robert Siciliano, *Cyber Attackers & Data Leaks: Do You Need Data Breach Insurance*, BUSINESS.COM (Feb. 22, 2017).

148. *Id.*

149. *Id.*

150. *Id.*

151. Columbia Cas. Co. v. Cottage Health Sys., 2015 WL 4497730 (C.D. Cal. July 17, 2015).

152. *See also* Francesca Giannoni-Crystal, Columbia Casualty v. Cottage Health System, *When Your Cyber Insurance Is Not What It Seems*, TECHNOETHICS (July 7, 2015).

was ultimately unsuccessful, this case nonetheless illustrates some of the challenges that arise with obtaining and maintaining cyber-security insurance.

§ 4:5   Conclusion

As this chapter demonstrates, today's ever connected world raises numerous IoT risks. While complete security is unrealistic, steps are currently being taken to safeguard IoT devices. The challenge is to strike the proper balance between security and innovation. At present, most appear to favor allowing the IoT industry to determine, create, and maintain their own security standards. However, a water-shed security incident in the future may cause some to rethink this position, and thus trigger a push for more government regulation.

Chapter 5

Contracts

---

§ 5:1   Overview

This chapter examines the various issues that arise in litigation over contracts involving the IoT. The issues discussed herein include: complexities in defining the applicable law in the context of IoT; the different legal approaches toward blended IoT contracts that cover both goods and services; problems that arise when determining whether Article 2 of the Uniform Commercial Code (UCC) applies to service and software components of IoT contracts; and how the

IoT impacts contract formation through mutual assent, unconscionability, fraud, material misrepresentation, and mistake, depending on
which law applies. This chapter also analyzes the debate surrounding
how traditional contract law deals with hybrid IoT technologies and
examines the complexities of emerging smart technologies and automated contracting.

§ 5:2   Contract Law Applicable to the IoT

As in all contract claims, the first issue the court must consider is
determining which law should apply to IoT transactions.

§ 5:2.1   *IoT As Product or Service*

As discussed throughout this book, IoT relates to the technology
concept of connecting electronic devices, products, or other everyday
objects to the Internet and to other IoT enabled devices. In the process of connecting IoT devices in this manner, IoT devices relate not
just to their users, but to other objects and data collected by those
objects. IoT devices can range from ordinary items such as electrical
plugs, lightbulbs, electricity meters, household appliances, and wearables (such as Fitbits), to complex items such as automated cars, medical devices, or home security systems. As the number of connected
objects increases, more information is gathered and stored about
those who use them. By 2021, estimates place the number of IoT
devices connected online to soar past 35 billion.[1] These estimates go
on to suggest "that, by that point, machine-generated data will exceed
Internet traffic generated by humans, as growing numbers of sensors,
servers, and computers are collecting and sharing information back
and forth."[2]

These IoT devices are intended to connect or link to other smart
objects; for example, smart thermostats, light bulbs, smoke detectors,
washing machines, and door locks are capable of connecting or linking together to create a "smart device 'ecosystem'" in which billions of
sensors record, process, store, and exchange data with other devices.[3]
In this interconnected IoT economy, consumers are often unaware of

---

1.   *See* www.statista.com/statistics/471264/iot-number-of-connected-devices-
      worldwide/.
2.   Senator Mark Warner, *Reflections on the Internet of Things*, THE
      INTERNET OF THINGS: LEGAL ISSUES, POLICY, AND PRACTICE STRATEGIES,
      at xxv (ABA 2019).
3.   Jenna Lindqvist, *New Challenges to Personal Data Processing
      Agreements: Is the GDPR Fit to Deal with Contract, Accountability and
      Liability in a World of the Internet of Things?*, 26 INT'L J. L. INFO. TECH.
      1, 3 (Mar. 1, 2018).

both the volume of data gathered by these devices and the full scope of the content of the data that has been stored online or in databases about the consumer and their personal behavior.[4] Furthermore, consumers are often woefully unaware of their rights or responsibilities under the terms of contract for these IoT products and devices.

Additional contracting concerns arise with the growing popularity of digital or voice controlled assistants or mobile devices.[5] Users of home devices such as Google Home and Amazon Echo command their IoT-enabled devices to "adjust the thermostat, lock the doors, print an e-mail, order more dish soap, play music, or converse with someone at the door."[6] While these types of digital assistants have the potential to provide many benefits to their users, they also introduce risks in security, privacy, and contracting.[7] In regard to contracting, the interconnectedness of these IoT objects can be maintained with little to no human interaction with either the device itself or with a computer, such as with Amazon's Dash Replenishment Services (DRS).[8] This passive engagement with IoT-connected objects could be problematic for courts when determining whether or not users are bound by the contracts formed by these devices.

In the United States, contract law for the sale of goods is regulated by Uniform Commercial Code (UCC) Article 2. However, service and intangible contracts are governed by common law. Before applying the law in an action for breach of contract to these IoT devices, it is necessary to engage in a threshold discussion regarding which law applies in the particular circumstance. In the IoT context, smart objects are embedded with both hardware and software components which are inextricably tied to the functioning of the product: the hardware, including the device itself; the sensors collecting the data; the servers and routers used to transmit and store information; and the software, including the data collection, real-time analytics, and device integration features, are all connected.[9] Having both hardware and

---

4. Michael Chertoff, *Foreword, in* THE INTERNET OF THINGS: LEGAL ISSUES, POLICY, AND PRACTICE STRATEGIES (Cynthia Cwik et al., eds. 2019).

5. Mark E. Budnitz, *Article and Survey: Touching, Tapping, and Talking: The Formation of Contracts in Cyberspace*, 43 NOVA L. REV. 235, 236 (Spring 2019).

6. Christopher Bradley, *Disrupting Secured Transactions*, 56 HOUS. L. REV. 965, 987–88 (Spring 2019).

7. *See* Budnitz, *supra* note 5, at 239.

8. *The Internet of Things, An Overview: Understanding the Issues and Challenges of a More Connected World*, THE INTERNET SOCIETY, at 17 (Oct. 2015), www.internetsociety.org/wp-content/uploads/2017/08/ISOC-IoT-Overview-20151221-en.pdf.

9. *See* https://mindmajix.com/hardware-software-of-iot (last visited May 28, 2020).

software features makes it difficult to classify IoT objects and devices as either a product or service and leaves several threshold questions unanswered: Are IoT products goods or non-goods? Should Article 2 of the UCC apply to transactions involving IoT devices or should the transactions be governed by common law contract principles? Or, due to the nature of these complex questions, is it recommendable to develop a totally new IoT-specific law to address the complexities of the IoT industry?

[A] Contracts for Goods Under the UCC

The idea to develop a uniform code of law that governs commercial transactions came about due to inadequate sales law for the industrial economy.[10] The drafting of the UCC then arose in an effort to create a set of basic rules of commercial law that would allow for better accuracy and flexibility in transactions.[11] The UCC was meant to be business-friendly and easy to understand so that transactions could be more readily formed in the growing industrial economy.[12] Yet, commercial law and the courts' applications of this law have failed to keep up with the radical ways that constantly evolving technology has transformed the consumer marketplace.[13] Traditionally defined, Article 2 of the UCC generally only applies to transactions for the sale of real, tangible goods—otherwise defined as movable goods.[14] Whether or not goods are movable is determined by their "mobility" at the time of identification to the contract, subject to a limited number of exceptions. Yet, Article 2 may also be applicable to "blended" transactions that involve both the sale of goods *and* services in certain situations. Courts determine applicability of UCC Article 2 through various tests such as the "predominant purpose" or the "gravamen of the claim" test.

Whether a contract is governed by the UCC or the common law can affect a court's determination regarding the formation of the contract, a breach of the contract, and the defenses that may be available to the buyer or seller under the contract. For example, an important aspect in all goods contracts governed by UCC Article 2 is that of the implied warranties. Under Article 2, the implied warranties include

---

10.   Stacy-Ann Elvy, *Hybrid Transactions and the Internet of Things: Goods, Services, or Software?*, 74 WASH. & LEE L. REV. 77, 104 (2017).

11.   *See* Bradley, *supra* note 6, at 967 (quoting Grant Gilmore, *The Uniform Commercial Code: A Reply to Professor Beutel*, 61 YALE L.J. 364, 378 (1952)).

12.   *Id.* (citing Karl Llewellyn, *Why a Commercial Code?*, 22 TENN. L. REV. 779, 783 (1953)).

13.   *See* Budnitz, *supra* note 5, at 235–36.

14.   *See* U.C.C. § 2-105.

the warranty of merchantability and usage of trade.[15] To fall under the implied warranty of merchantability/usage of trade, the seller must be a merchant with regards to the goods at issue. Further, the goods must conform to the contract and be fit for the ordinary purposes for which the goods are generally used. The implied warranty of merchantability is a warranty that could easily change the outcome of a legal dispute. However, the IoT object must fall explicitly under Article 2 or an approved exception in order to apply. Thus, the question remains, do IoT products properly fit into an Article 2 exception, or is it improper to apply Article 2?

[B] Service Contracts and Intangible Goods Under Common Law

Common law, unlike the UCC, generally applies to service contracts, employment contracts, and intangible goods such as real estate, patents, or trademarks.[16] The common law elements of contract formation, include offer, acceptance, and consideration, all of which are necessary to make a contract legally binding.[17] Acceptance under common law includes the "mirror image rule," meaning that the acceptance must exactly match the offer in order to form a legally enforceable contract. If the acceptance contains new or modified terms and is not a mirror image of the original offer, then it is considered a counter-offer, and must be accepted under those new or modified terms by the original offeror. This is not true of transactions between merchants under the UCC. As mentioned previously, courts determine the applicability of either the common law or the UCC through various tests including the predominant purpose test, the gravamen of the claim test, or the component test. To add to the confusion, some courts break contracts down into component parts—depending on the tangible and intangible components in the transaction—and then apply both the common law and the UCC to resolve a party's dispute.[18]

When courts determine that the common law principles of contract formation apply to an issue, the outcome of the case can be greatly affected. As in the example given above, generally, common law

---

15. *See* U.C.C. § 2-314.

16. UPCOUNSEL, *Common Law Contracts vs. UCC: Everything You Need to Know*, www.upcounsel.com/common-law-contracts-vs-ucc (last visited May 29, 2020).

17. LUMEN, *Common Law and Uniform Commercial Code Contracts*, https://courses.lumenlearning.com/workwithinthelaw/chapter/formation-and-types-of-contracts/ (last visited May 29, 2020).

18. *See* Elvy, *supra* note 10, at 114 (citing Foster v. Colo. Radio Corp., 381 F.2d 222, 226 (10th Cir. 1967)).

contracts do not include the same implied warranties of merchantability and fitness for a particular purpose, as those implied in contracts governed by the UCC.[19] Although some courts have extended these implied warranties to contracts involving professional services, other courts have held that implied warranties are not applicable to service contracts.[20] Instead, under the common law, contracts are subject to express warranties.[21] Yet, in the context of IoT transactions, devices not only contain hardware that may be subject to the warranty, but many retailers provide ongoing embedded services, such as DRS replacement services. Complications arise with express warranties if, for example, a manufacturer of a device provides an express warranty for the device's hardware and accessories, but that warranty does not extend to the replacement services (such as DRS services) or firmware that the device uses.[22] Therefore, because of reluctance of the courts to extend implied warranties to service contracts, scholars have questioned the applicability of common law warranties to these hybrid IoT transactions.

[C] Mixed Contracts—The Reality of Hybrid IoT Transactions

If UCC Article 2 generally only applies to real, tangible goods, and the common law generally applies to intangible goods and service contracts, which law should apply when a product contains aspects of both? In IoT products, the hard and software components maybe inextricably combined. In the IoT context, courts have struggled with whether to apply UCC Article 2 or the common law to these hybrid IoT products because they combine both goods and services in one transaction.

Part of the problem relates to the fact that the contract rules of the UCC were largely drafted in the 1940s and the last major amendments to Article 2 took place in 1958.[23] Hence, the UCC's main principles were drafted and amended long before the development of stand-alone software applications that are sold separately from computer hardware systems. Although there were attempts in the 1990s to further amend Article 2 to include provisions covering the transfer

---

19.   *Id.* at 115.

20.   *Id.* at 115–16 (citing Albion Coll. v. Stockade Buildings, Inc., No. 322917, 2016 Mich. App. LEXIS 998, at *6 (Mich. Ct. App. May 17, 2016); *but see* Cargill, Inc. v. Ron Burge Trucking, Inc., No. 11-2394, 2013 U.S. Dist. LEXIS 22139 (D. Minn. Feb. 19, 2013).

21.   Elvy, *supra* note 10, at 115.

22.   *Id.* at 115.

23.   Michael L. Rustad & Elif Kavusturan, *A Commercial Law for Software Contracting*, 76 WASH. & LEE L. REV. 775, 777–78 (2019).

of data, text, and other such information, those amendments failed, leaving the courts to fill in the gaps about how and when to apply the UCC in hybrid transactions for themselves.[24] For example, in *SAS Institute, Inc. v. World Programming Ltd.*, involving Article 2's role in a software transaction, the court mused:

> The applicability of the Uniform Commercial Code to software is a question that has confounded courts in the digital age. For every court that finds that the weight of authority favors application of common law and not the UCC with regard to software licenses, another finds that courts nationally have consistently classified the sale of a software package as the sale of a good for UCC purposes.[25]

Therefore, it is obvious that the problems related to applicability of the UCC to technological advances did not start with IoT devices, but with the advent of computer and software technologies as early as the 1970s and into the current technological boom of the IoT economy.[26] In the current state, critics point to the myriad laws that failed to keep up with the technological transformation which, in turn, has left consumers vulnerable when contracting with IoT tech companies.[27]

Today, with the advent of the IoT, companies are offering services, goods, and software to consumers all in a single transaction.[28] "Almost any product, including cars, everyday household items, office goods, and manufacturing equipment, can be accompanied by cloud or fog computing services, firmware, software updates, and ongoing online services that facilitate interconnectivity between individuals, companies, and systems."[29] For example, the Ring video doorbell connects to a consumer's home Wi-Fi network and allows a user to: stream a video of the person at their door; carry on a conversation with the visitor; and receive real-time notifications to the consumer's phone when someone presses the button on the doorbell or when motion is detected.[30] Ring provides this service through a free app, but also provides: email reminders when the Ring battery runs low; software updates; and an optional subscription service, Ring Video Recording Plan, that allows owners to record video when motion is detected but

---

24.   *Id.* at 779–80.
25.   SAS Inst., Inc. v. World Programming Ltd., 2016 WL 3435196, at *10 (E.D.N.C. June 17, 2016).
26.   *See* Rustad & Kavusturan, *supra* note 23, at 779.
27.   *See generally* Budnitz, *supra* note 5.
28.   *See* Elvy, *supra* note 10, at 83.
29.   *Id.*
30.   RING, *Frequently Asked Questions*, https://shop.ring.com/pages/faq (last visited May 29, 2020).

they cannot view the motion in real time. The Ring doorbell is also compatible with smart lock systems.

However, which law should apply when problems arise with IoT devices like the Ring video doorbell? Which body of law governs the issue if a service offered for an IoT product was acquired by another company and subsequently discontinued? For example, the manufacturer of a smart home hub called Revolv announced in 2016 that it would no longer provide support to the device.[31] Revolv was an innovative home hub that enabled a smartphone to control multiple devices in the home under one app, encompassing several big device brands into a small package for a relatively low cost.[32] The Revolv hub simplified the complexity of uniting smart home objects under a single system, no matter the brand. In 2014, only one year after its release on the market, Nest acquired the Revolv company and product and subsequently stopped selling the smart home hub while still maintaining the app that allowed purchasers to control their multiple, interfaced devices. When Revolv announced in 2016 that all support and service for Revolv would cease, Nest also shut down the Revolv app service, rendering the expensive product moot and effectively useless to consumers.[33] In this case, would the owners of Revolv devices have a legal action under UCC Article 2 because the manufacturer elected to terminate the service and software updates integral to the operations of the Revolv devices? Because, if Article 2 does not apply, then the common law would dictate how to handle the transaction.

§ 5:2.2   Legal Tests to Determine the Applicable Law for Hybrid IoT Transactions

Hybrid IoT transactions involving hardware, services, and software create even more challenges in determining which body of law should apply.[34] A leading scholar in contract issues involving IoT transactions, Professor Stacy-Ann Elvy, states:

> A buyer of an IOT device may be subject to three separate contracts and potentially multiple sources of law: (1) an end user licensing agreement (EULA) subject to intellectual property law, the common-law or potentially the Uniform Computer Information

---

31.   *See* Elvy, *supra* note 10, at 83.

32.   Matt Paulson, *Revolv Offers Promising Home Automation Solutions IoT Evolution World* (Dec. 18, 2013), www.iotevolutionworld.com/m2m/articles/364119-revlov-offers-promising-home-automation-solutions.htm.

33.   *See* Nick Statt, *Nest Is Permanently Disabling the Revolv Smart Home Hub*, THE VERGE (Apr. 4, 2016), www.theverge.com/2016/4/4/11362928/google-nest-revolv-shutdown-smart-home-products.

34.   *See* Elvy, *supra* note 10, at 94.

Transactions Act (UCITA) for the software that allows the IOT device to function; (2) a contract subject to Article 2 or the common-law, which is provided by the manufacturer or retailer for the sale and purchase of the IOT device—this contract may include a limited warranty that covers the device but excludes software and services—and (3) a licensing agreement for the use of the company's product ordering, monitoring, or other application services.[35]

Thus, a hybrid software transaction may arise when software is bundled with hardware or another product, or if software is provided with services such as installation, debugging, or support.[36] Hybrid software transactions are complex and courts to date continue to struggle with determining which laws apply to them.[37]

Despite the fact that the software field has skyrocketed into a multi-billion-dollar industry in the last half century, the laws governing the two types of software contracting methods today—software licensing and software-as-a-service (SaaS)—have not kept pace with this technological revolution. Drafted in the 1940s, UCC Article 2 does not even directly mention software, leaving Article 2 woefully outdated in regards to software contracts since it has not been significantly updated in nearly seventy years.[38] Although most courts have held that computer software sales, such as transactions in which software is purchased on a CD, fall within the definition of goods under UCC Article 2, they have been inconsistent in evaluating hybrid software transactions under the UCC.[39] Some courts consider the totality of the circumstances surrounding the purchase to decide whether a software transaction qualifies as either a good or service.[40] Other courts have stated that Article 2 only applies to the sale of software but not to the licensing of software.[41] In these jurisdictions,

---

35. *Id.* at 95.
36. *Id.* at 125.
37. *See* Richard Raysman & Peter Brown, *Applicability of the UCC to Software Transactions*, N.Y.L.J. ONLINE (Mar. 8, 2011); *see also* Elvy, *supra* note 10, at 79.
38. *See* Rustad & Kavusturan, *supra* note 23, at 789. SaaS services, also referred to as cloud computing, is based on the model that software applications are delivered to the user over the Internet or on networks on an on-demand basis. *Id.* at 778–79.
39. *See* Richard Raysman & Peter Brown, *Applicability of the UCC to Software Transactions*, N.Y.L.J. ONLINE (Mar. 8, 2011); *see also* Elvy, *supra* note 10, at 135.
40. *See* Elvy, *supra* note 10, at 133 (citing Rottner v. AVG Techs. USA, Inc., 943 F. Supp. 2d 222, 230 (D. Mass. 2013)).
41. *Id.* at 126–27 (citing Digital Ally, Inc. v. Z3 Tech., LLC, Case No. 09-2292-KGS, 2010 U.S. Dist. LEXIS 103715, at *32 (D. Kan. Sept. 30, 2010); Adobe Sys. Inc. v. One Stop Micro, 84 F. Supp. 2d 1086

if the court finds that the transaction is for the licensing of software, the terms of the licensing agreement control as to which rules are applicable for contract formation and which defenses are available.[42] However, if the court holds that the software transaction is considered a sale of a good, it would be subject to Article 2, and thus the parties may be able to negotiate to exclude certain contract provisions.

Inconsistent application by the courts may stem from an attempt to overextend Article 2, which was created to deal with transactions involving the one-time purchase of tangible goods.[43] In trying to apply UCC Article 2 principles to software transactions, complications arise as both software licensing agreements and SaaS are relational contracts paired with support services that only transfer software usage rights to the consumer, but do not transfer the title of a tangible good.[44] When a user obtains a license, title does not truly pass to the user, but instead only transfers a contractual permission or right to use that license without triggering infringement concerns under intellectual property law.[45] Yet under UCC Article 2, the very definition of a sale is a transaction in which the buyer transfers title to the buyer for a price.[46] The fact that the title does not transfer to the buyer in software transactions has left many legal scholars critical of the applicability of Article 2 to software licensing claims.[47] Furthermore, in the IoT context, services provided in connection with the sale of the device muddles the Article 2 analysis.[48] IoT devices are built to interact with other devices, owners, and the environment, while performing specific functions and adapting to accommodate the needs of the owner.[49] This is further complicated by the fact that software technologies have expanded to cloud computing or SaaS.[50] Whereas with traditional software licensing, the licensee purchases the right

---

	(N.D. Cal. 2000); Kane v. Fed. Express Corp., No. CV990078971S, 2001 Conn. Super. LEXIS 2536 (Conn. Super. Aug. 28,2001)).
42.	*See* Nancy S. Kim, *The Software Licensing Dilemma*, 2008 BYU L. REV. 1103, 1135–36 (2008).
43.	*See* Rustad & Kavusturan, *supra* note 23, at 790, 792.
44.	*Id.* at 790.
45.	Holly K. Towle, *Enough Already: It Is Time to Acknowledge That UCC Article 2 Does Not Apply to Software and Other Information*, 52 S. TEX. L. REV. 531, 542 (2011).
46.	*See* Elvy, *supra* note 10, at 128 (citing U.C.C. § 2-106 (Am. Law Inst. & Unif. Law Comm'n 2002)).
47.	*Id.*; *see generally* Towle, *supra* note 45.
48.	Elvy, *supra* note 10, at 134.
49.	*Id.* (citing Jacob Morgan, *A Simple Explanation of The Internet of Things Jacob Morgan* (Apr. 5, 2018), https://thefutureorganization.com/simple-explanation-internet-things/).
50.	*See* Towle, *supra* note 45, at 557.

to use the software on their own equipment, with SaaS, the licensee only purchases the right to access a centralized software application stored in a proprietary service or cloud, not on their individual device.[51] Therefore, as the developers of IoT devices provide software solely through cloud computing and service contracts, SaaS licenses are further distanced from the application of UCC Article 2. Courts will now be hard-pressed to use the software-CD-sale analogy to apply UCC principles to these hybrid transactions.[52]

Despite scholars' recommendations to move toward a new legal framework to better deal with hybrid IoT transactions, neither changes that would include new, specialized UCC Articles, nor a commitment to developing specific legislation to address these hybrid transactions, has been agreed upon.[53] Therefore, courts have used the following tests to determine whether the hybrid transaction is covered by the common law or by UCC Article 2: the predominant purpose test, the gravamen of the claims test, and the component parts test.[54]

[A]   The Predominant Purpose Test

The predominant purpose test is the majority approach test in the United States and applies only in situations where the transaction is hybrid in nature.[55] Under the predominant purpose test, the purpose of the contract must be predominantly regarding goods in order for UCC Article 2 to apply. Therefore, the courts will evaluate the essential purpose of the contract—whether it is for goods or services. In *Neibarger v. Universal Cooperatives, Inc.*, the court stated, "[i]f the purchaser's ultimate goal is to acquire a product, the contract should be considered a transaction in goods . . . . Conversely, if the purchaser's ultimate goal is to procure a service, the contract is not governed by the UCC, even though goods are incidentally required in the

---

51.   *See* Rustad & Kavusturan, *supra* note 23, at 790.

52.   *See* Elvy, *supra* note 10, at 135.

53.   *See* Rustad & Kavusturan, *supra* note 23, at 791; *see generally* Budnitz, *supra* note 5.

54.   *See, e.g.*, Raymond T. Nimmer, *Symposium on Approaching E-Commerce Through Uniform Legislation: Understanding the Uniform Computer Information Transactions Act and the Uniform Electronic Transactions Act: Through the Looking Glass: What Courts and UCITA Say About the Scope of Contract Law in the Information Age*, 38 DUQ. L. REV. 255, 279 (2000); Ellen Taylor, *Applicability of Strict Liability Warranty Theories to Service Transactions*, 47 S.C. L. REV. 231, 253 (1996). *See also* Elvy, *supra* note 10, at 105–14.

55.   Abby J. Hardwick, Note: *Amending the Uniform Commercial Code: How Will a Change in Scope Alter the Concept of Goods?*, 82 WASH. U. L.Q. 275, 280 (2004).

provision of this service."[56] Courts evaluate the transaction using different factors including: the express language of the contract, the comparison of the costs of goods to the total price of the contract, the value of the goods without the service component, the nature of the supplier's business, whether the contract billed separately for the prices of goods and labor or contained an overall price, and whether the consumer had a reasonable expectation in acquiring a property interest.[57]

Despite the common use of the predominant purpose test, it can be applied quite differently depending upon the court's interpretation of "predominant purpose," and therefore does not guide parties in advance of litigation as to which law will apply. The test creates the framework for the courts to follow, but only after the court decides the purpose of the contract.[58] Because the outcome of the test cannot be predicted in advance by the parties, it forces the parties to assume risks in transacting without providing prior guidance about which body of law will apply in advance of the transaction.[59] "[T]he test also ensures that in all cases when it is used, the wrong law will be applied to some aspects of a transaction (e.g., goods law applied to services aspect of a mixed transaction)."[60] Furthermore, Professor Elvy points out that not all courts addressing these issues provide clear explanation of their rationale and instead "often simply 'state the facts and then declare an answer'" as to which law applies, making it difficult to analogize in future cases.[61]

The uncertainty that has resulted under the predominant purpose test is further demonstrated by the fact that courts in different jurisdictions have issued opposing rulings using the same purported test. Because courts have inconsistently applied the predominant purpose test even before the introduction of hybrid IoT devices, this complication is exacerbated by cases involving hybrid IoT products, where courts have come to different conclusions regarding whether the transaction constitutes a transaction in goods or not.[62] For example, in *TK Power v. Textron*, the court held that the contract for the provision of mechanical items and prototypes was primarily for the developer's "knowledge, skill, and ability" to develop software code

---

56.   Neibarger v. Universal Coops., Inc., 486 N.W.2d 612, 622 (Mich. 1992).
57.   *See* Elvy, *supra* note 10, at 106; *see also* Hardwick, *supra* note 55, at 280.
58.   *See* Nimmer, *supra* note 54, at 278.
59.   *Id.*
60.   *Id.*
61.   *See* Elvy, *supra* note 10, at 107 (quoting LINDA J. RUSCH & STEPHEN L. SEPINUCK, COMMERCIAL LAW: PROBLEMS AND MATERIALS ON SALES AND PAYMENTS 24 (2012)).
62.   *Id.* at 130.

and test prototypes and the price paid on the contract was that for services rather than for the goods, thus making Article 2 inapplicable for the situation.[63] In contrast, the court found in *Audio Visual Industry v. Tanzer* that Article 2 applied to the sale and installation of a customized smart home system because it was primarily a goods sale based on the comparison of cost of services versus the cost of the equipment, the nature of the seller's business, and the intent of the parties.[64] This inconsistent application by courts has led scholars to conclude that "[t]he predominant purpose test along with the various factors used by courts applying this test has created a lack of uniformity and clarity in decisions addressing the applicability of Article 2 to hybrid transactions, which contradicts the stated goals of the UCC."[65]

[B] The Component Test

Another approach used by the courts in hybrid IoT transactions is the component test, which applies regardless of whether the primary purpose of the transaction is for the sale of goods.[66] The component test protects consumers through implied warranties for goods bought even when the service component was the predominant portion of the transaction.[67] For example, in *Newmark v. Gimbel's Inc.*, the court applied the UCC to the goods portion of the service allowing the consumer to sue a beauty parlor operator for violating implied warranties regarding a defective solution that had been used as part of the beauty treatment.[68]

The component test creates additional work for the courts because it requires splitting the contract into two parts; this may be one reason why the test is used only in a minority of jurisdictions.[69] This approach can require a court to decide on issues such as the statute of frauds, parol evidence, the statute of limitations, and other legal questions beyond the traditionally implied warranties.[70] How would a court resolve a dispute if a seller offered installation services of a smart home hub system and damaged it while in the process of

---

63.   TK Power v. Textron, 433 F. Supp. 2d 1058, 1062 (N.D. Cal. 2006).

64.   Audio Visual Indus. v. Tanzer, 403 S.W.3d 789, 799–805 (Tenn. Ct. App. 2012).

65.   Elvy, *supra* note 10, at 108.

66.   Jesse M. Brush, *Mixed Contracts and the U.C.C.: A Proposal for a Uniform Penalty Default to Protect Consumers*, YALE STUDENT SCHOLARSHIP PAPERS, Paper 47, at 14 (2007), http://digitalcommons.law.yale.edu/student_papers/47.

67.   *Id.*

68.   Newmark v. Gimbel's Inc., 54 N.J. 585 (1969).

69.   *See* Taylor, *supra* note 54, at 253.

70.   *See* Brush, *supra* note 66, at 15.

installing it? Under the component test, the court would be required to segregate the claim into component parts to determine whether the warranty of merchantability applies under UCC Article 2 because the object (the smart home hub) was damaged or if the warranty does not apply because the damage occurred during the installation (service).[71] Like the predominant purpose test, the component test does not guide parties in advance of litigation as to which law will apply. Parties may even need to seek court resolution of issues arising out of whether specific elements of the transaction are a service or a good, tying up court resources and increasing costs to the taxpayers.[72] If the parties cannot determine which law applies, they may waste needless resources and time just to determine, for example, which relevant statute of limitations applies in their case.[73]

[C] The Gravamen of the Claims Test

Finally, the gravamen of the claims test is also used by a minority of jurisdictions in determining which body of law to apply in hybrid IoT transactions.[74] *Merriam-Webster Dictionary* defines a gravamen as "the material or significant part of a grievance or complaint." Under the gravamen test, the court examines the party's grounds for complaint and determines if the party's discontent lies with the portion of the contract relating to the goods, thereby allowing the courts to apply UCC Article 2, or the portion relating to the service components, allowing the courts to apply common law contract principles.[75]

This test was created to avoid conflicts arising from the predominant approach or the component approach.[76] If strictly applied, the gravamen test would allow for both sellers and buyers to know which law governs in advance of litigation depending upon how the plaintiff drafts the complaint.[77] However, there are still difficulties that arise when IoT transactions are at issue. For instance, if a consumer-plaintiff is unsatisfied with the services provided by an IoT device but drafts the complaint in a way that implies that the goods are defective, the gravamen test might determine that the gravamen relates to the goods and thus apply Article 2.[78] However, if a consumer is dissatisfied with the automatic subscription service for their smart printer, but inadvertently drafts the complaint in a manner expressing

---

71.   *Id.*
72.   *Id.*
73.   *Id.*
74.   *See* Hardwick, *supra* note 55, at 281.
75.   *Id.*
76.   *See* Brush, *supra* note 66, at 16.
77.   *See* Elvy, *supra* note 10, at 112.
78.   *Id.*

dissatisfaction with the goods by predominantly referring to dissatisfaction with the printer itself, the gravamen test could lead to an improper application of UCC Article 2; really the true gravamen should have applied common law as a result of the defective refill subscription service. Therefore, it is possible that the gravamen test would yield inconsistent determinations when applied in the IoT context.[79]

§ 5:3   Determining Contract Formation

The basic principles of contract law have been developed over time and intentionally designed to allow for freely negotiated agreements between rational and informed parties with equal bargaining power.[80] The following requisite elements must be established in order to demonstrate proper formation of a legally binding contract: offer, acceptance, consideration, mutuality of obligation, competency and capacity, and on occasion a written instrument. The following is a discussion of topics related to the IoT and mutual assent to a contract. Although consideration is an important element within common law contracts, this topic will not be addressed in the IoT context.

§ 5:3.1   *Mutual Assent—Offer and Acceptance in IoT Transactions*

The laws governing the formation of a contract will differ significantly depending upon whether the contract is a goods contract governed by UCC Article 2 or a services contract governed by the common law. The common law elements of contract formation—offer, acceptance, and consideration—are much more stringent than the requirements for contract formation under the UCC.[81] If all three elements are not fulfilled, then the contract may either be void or voidable under the common law. To establish mutual assent, first an offer is proffered by the offeror through a manifestation of willingness to enter into a bargain which justifies the offeree in understanding that his assent to that bargain is invited and will conclude in a contract.[82] In response to this offer, the offeree must proffer an acceptance through the manifestation of assent to the terms of the offeror.[83] Under common law, acceptance of a contract must be a mirror image

---

79.   *Id.* at 114.

80.   Stacy-Ann Elvy, *Contracting in the Age of the Internet of Things: Article 2 of the UCC and Beyond*, 44 HOFSTRA L. REV. 839, 870 (2016).

81.   *Common Law and Uniform Commercial Code Contracts*, LUMEN, https://courses.lumenlearning.com/workwithinthelaw/chapter/formation-and-types-of-contracts/ (last visited May 29, 2020).

82.   *See* RESTATEMENT (SECOND) OF CONTRACTS § 24.

83.   *See id.* § 50.

of the offer in order to form a legally enforceable contract.[84] If the acceptance contains new or modified terms and is not a mirror image of the original offer, then it is considered a counter-offer, and must be accepted under those new or modified terms by the original offeror. Furthermore, contracts under the common law must be made by parties who have the legal capacity to enter into a contract.

On the other hand, the UCC, including Article 2, was specifically developed to facilitate freedom of contract while assuring that parties act in good faith, diligence, or reasonableness in their obligations to the other party.[85] Hence, the common law mirror image rule does not apply to transactions between merchants under the UCC.[86] Therefore, parties may fulfill their obligations of offer and acceptance in any reasonable manner under the UCC.[87] The UCITA, like the UCC, allows for acceptance to be made in any manner and by any reasonable medium under the circumstances, but also allows acceptance to be made by electronic means.[88] "The UCC and the [Uniform Computer Information Transactions Act (UCITA)] define an agreement as a bargain of the parties, in fact, as found in their language or by implication from other circumstances, including course of dealing, usage of trade, and course of performance."[89] Generally, in order for UCC Article 2 to apply, the parties must qualify as either a buyer, seller, merchant, or third party with rights to the goods.[90]

Additionally, further considerations govern the formation of IoT contracts in the virtual world because of the very different relationship between the buyer and the seller of IoT products than the conditions traditionally present in more typical, face-to-face transactions of goods or services.[91] Whereas the terms of a contract in prior consumer transactions were often laid out in a written agreement that could be referenced later, in the IoT context, the terms of the agreement are often found on websites, and might have been replaced by subsequent,

---

84.   *See Common Law and Uniform Commercial Code Contracts, supra* note 81.

85.   *See* Elvy, *supra* note 80, at 869 (citing U.C.C. § 1-302 cmt. 1, 1-302(b) (Am. Law Inst. & Unif. Law Comm'n 2013)).

86.   *See Common Law and Uniform Commercial Code Contracts, supra* note 81.

87.   *Id.*

88.   *See* Elvy, *supra* note 80, at 872 (citing U.C.C. § 2-206(1)(a) & Unif. Comput. Info. Transactions Act §§ 203(4), 206).

89.   *Id.* (citing U.C.C. § 1-201(b)(3) & Unif. Comput. Info. Transactions Act § 12(a)(4) (amended 2002), 7 pt. 2 U.L.A. 212 (2009)).

90.   *Id.* at 871 (citing U.C.C. § 2-102 (Am. Law Inst. & Unif. Law Comm'n 2013)).

91.   *See* Budnitz, *supra* note 5, at 265.

modified versions, or may not have been readily accessible to the consumer at the time of formation.[92]

Furthermore, issues arise regarding whether the elements of contract formation are satisfied by adhesion or form contracts which are frequently used in e-commerce. Contracts of adhesion typically offer consumers little bargaining power and are presented on a "take-it-or-leave-it" basis.[93] For years, a debate has raged over whether contracts of adhesion have impacted the traditional concept of mutual assent by displacing the notion of rational and informed parties.[94] On one side, scholars who oppose form contracts argue that these contracts increase risk for consumers. On the other side, scholars who support the use of form contracts believe that businesses will treat consumers more fairly, based upon the theory that pro-seller contract terms would hurt the seller's reputation.[95] These concerns have only been exacerbated by the rise of internet retailers who can use their websites to draft one-sided contract terms and then make it difficult for consumers to discover those terms on the site.[96] The concerns about adhesion contracts will presumably only increase as more IoT devices connect over the Internet and end-user contracts proliferate.

Lastly, courts also wrestle with issues regarding whether clickwrap, shrinkwrap, or browsewrap agreements can fulfill the elements of assent to contract terms. For example, if the seller uses a shrinkwrap agreement, the buyer accepts the terms of the license agreement by unwrapping the packaging or by using the software; the terms are generally included alongside a CD containing the software. If the seller uses a clickwrap agreement, the buyer is required to click a button stating that they accept the terms of use; these types of agreements are generally used when downloading software and transacting for goods. Finally, should the seller use a browsewrap agreement, the terms of the contract are only available if the buyer clicks on the provided links, and the buyer is assumed to have consented to the terms by continuing to use the website.[97] Here, a consumer is never affirmatively given the opportunity to indicate their consent, through an "I agree" button or the like.[98]

---

92.   *Id.* at 266.
93.   Lucian A. Bebchuk & Richard A. Posner, *Boilerplate in Consumer Contract: One-Sided Contracts in Competitive Consumer Markets*, 104 MICH. L. REV. 827, 828 (2006).
94.   Ronald J. Mann & Travis Siebeneicher, *Just One Click: The Reality of Internet Retail Contracting*, 108 COLUM. L. REV. 984, 984–85 (May 2008). *See also* Elvy, *supra* note 80, at 870.
95.   *See* Mann & Siebeneicher, *supra* note 94, at 984–85.
96.   *Id.* at 985–86.
97.   *See* Elvy, *supra* note 80, at 872.
98.   *See* Budnitz, *supra* note 5, at 265.

Cases involving clickwrap and browsewrap agreements must be considered on a case-by-case basis as they are extremely fact-specific.[99] These types of contracts can pose significant issues with contract formation under general contract law and Article 2.[100] Courts have typically addressed transactions involving consumer assent to online contract terms by focusing on constructive notice and the opportunity to read, but this does not necessarily always equate to mutual assent.[101] For example, this approach does not work well for clickwrap agreements where the terms are displayed and the consumer must click an "I agree" button.[102] Further, consumers regularly fail to actually read the terms of a contract.[103] In 2007, a study found that less than a single percentage of users access a company's terms of use, less than half of those who did access the terms of use spent less than thirty seconds on the terms page, and 90% of those who spent longer than thirty seconds on the page did not remain for longer than two minutes while reviewing the terms and conditions.[104] The court in *Ting v. AT&T* noted that when sent a separate mailing on updated terms of a contract, only 30% of AT&T customers read the entire updated agreement, while 10% did not read the terms at all.[105] Despite these figures, most courts have held that consumers are generally bound by the terms of clickwrap agreements.[106]

Courts have been even more restrictive in affirming browsewrap agreements than clickwrap agreements.[107] In these cases, courts will also evaluate the website's content, placement of the notice of link in relationship to the terms of the agreement, and the accessibility of the agreement (i.e., if it requires several steps to arrive at the page).[108] The effectiveness of these types of agreements is dependent on the location of the hyperlink and whether it would place a reasonably prudent person on notice of the terms of the contract.[109] Browsewrap agreements also create new issues concerning lack of notice and assent due to the use of obscure terms and hyperlinks that may prevent consumers from clicking on the terms. The simple fact that the buyer might

---

99.   *Id.*
100.   *See* Elvy, *supra* note 80, at 872.
101.   *Id.*
102.   *Id.*
103.   *Id.*
104.   *Id.* (citing Yannis Bakos et al., *Does Anyone Read the Fine Print? Consumer Attention to Standard-Form Contracts*, 43 J. Legal Stud. 1, 10, 19–24 (2014)).
105.   Ting v. AT&T, 182 F. Supp. 2d 902, 930 (N.D. Cal. 2002).
106.   *See* Budnitz, *supra* note 5, at 266.
107.   *Id.* at 268.
108.   *Id.*
109.   *See* Elvy, *supra* note 80, at 875.

not take the extra steps necessary to find the link, click on it, and then read and understand the terms makes the issues of notice and assent unclear.[110] Thus, courts must review the design and content of the website in order to effectively assess whether a reasonable person would have notice of the terms of use. However, this test requires judges to assume the perspective of the consumer when assessing the clarity of the website design, and further assumes that those judges are indeed the best-suited to so judge these conditions.[111]

§ 5:3.2   Mutual Assent—"Contract Distancing" in IoT Transactions

Problems can occur when the constructive notice standard is applied to IoT contracts. The mutual assent issue created by the use of IoT devices is referred to by Professor Stacy-Ann Elvy as "contract distancing," which is defined as the "lack of proximity between consumers, contract terms, and the contract formation process." This distancing can complicate the analysis of consumer assent to contract terms because of the nature of IoT devices.[112] This distance is created because the device places the order for the consumer, either through its programming or at the direction of the consumer, creating a rift between consumer, contract terms, and contract formation. Professor Elvy offers the example of an IoT product placed by order through the use of Amazon's DRS (Dash Replenishment Service). In order to activate the DRS on the device, the consumer must activate the device, select the item that the device is allowed to order, and enable the one-click payment option. From that point on, the customer may re-order a product with a click of the button. Therefore, the consumers no longer need to go to a store, website, or application to place an order, nor does the consumer need to review terms of use or click an "I agree" button prior to a purchase.

Traditional tests in the courts fail to adequately take contract distancing into consideration.[113] Under the traditional "notice and opportunity to review" test, the consumer would be held to have consented to the conditions when placing consecutive orders through the IoT devices, even if the consumer may not have been given another opportunity to review and agree to new or altered contract terms and conditions. Furthermore, the "constructive notice and opportunity to review" test is still applied by courts despite evidence that consumers fail to read terms at the bottom of a website or may click a button

---

110.   *Id.*
111.   *Id.* at 844.
112.   *Id.* at 876–77.
113.   *Id.* at 878.

but nevertheless fail to review or understand any of the terms.[114] The steadily rising use of IoT devices is predicted to increase the levels of contract distancing. Because IoT technology was developed to make devices and people more interconnected and in turn to facilitate more speedy transactions, it stands to reason that a growing number of consumers will not review contract terms before placing future orders.[115]

Professor Elvy also suggests that the contract distancing created by IoT devices may also create more "battle of the forms" problems under UCC Article 2.[116] For example, an IoT device could purchase a consumable good from an online seller while the seller's website fails to include all the terms and conditions; however, the full set of terms and conditions might then be sent to the consumer's email along with the order of confirmation. Under Article 2, if one individual in the contract is a non-merchant, any additional terms proposed in an acceptance are viewed only as a proposal to add terms.[117] Thus, if a merchant were to add additional contract terms to a proposed acceptance via a confirmation email, the consumer should have the ability to accept or reject those terms under Article 2, and the failure of the consumer to expressly accept would cause the additional terms to be dropped out of the contract.[118] However, courts have increasingly been accepting a "terms-later" contracting style despite Article 2's battle of the forms rules.[119] Thus, a court is more likely to view the ordinary confirmation email as reasonable notice of additional contract terms to the average consumer, and failure to expressly reject those additional terms constitutes an acceptance of the additional terms.[120] Also, courts have refused to apply the battle of the forms rules to consumer contracts based solely on the fact that only one form is involved in the transaction and not multiple forms.[121]

§ 5:4   Available Defenses

To determine whether a party may avail themselves of an affirmative defense to the enforcement of a contract, it is necessary to analyze whether the contract was entered into in good faith through the defenses of unconscionability, mistake, and misrepresentation.[122]

---

114.   *Id.*
115.   *Id.*
116.   *Id.* at 883–84.
117.   *Id.* (citing SAMUEL WILLISTON & RICHARD A. LORD, A TREATISE ON THE LAW OF CONTRACTS § 4:16 (4th ed. 2007).
118.   *Id.*
119.   *Id.*
120.   *Id.*
121.   *Id.*
122.   *Id.*

Due to the issues discussed below, IoT transactions will likely only exacerbate the preexisting information asymmetry that currently plagues contract enforceability.[123]

§ 5:4.1 *Unconscionability in IoT Contracts*

As an exception to the duty to read and understand the contract terms, unconscionability can be asserted as an affirmative defense to contract enforcement.[124] Under common law, UCC Article 2, and the UCITA, a court is permitted to refuse to enforce a contract, in whole or in part, if it is found to be unconscionable.[125] Unconscionable contracts "[are ones] which no man in his senses, not under delusion, would make, on the one hand, and which no fair and honest man would accept, on the other."[126] Therefore, in order for a court to find a contract or clause unconscionable, the term must be extremely oppressive or shocking to the conscience.[127]

Because of this high standard to prove unconscionability, scholars and courts are at odds as to whether this doctrine adequately protects consumer rights in adhesion contracts. Most scholars believe that unconscionability is sufficient, but as empirical studies have shown, courts routinely fail to find contract terms unconscionable in order to protect the freedom to contract.[128] In some scholars' views, the courts' reticence to find contracts unconscionable is alarming, as businesses frequently use adhesion contracts that define "class action waivers, arbitration clauses, liability limitations, and forum-selection clauses to insulate themselves from liability, thereby restricting the ability of consumers to obtain legal redress."[129] These adhesion contracts routinely allow sellers to unilaterally amend contracts and place the risk of loss upon consumers.[130]

123.　*Id.*
124.　Steven W. Feldman, *Mutual Assent, Normative Degradation, and Mass Market Standard Form Contracts—A Two-Part Critique of Boilerplate: The Fine Print, Vanishing Rights and the Rule of Law (Part I)*, 62 CLEV. ST. L. REV. 373, 425 (2014).
125.　Larry A. DiMatteo & Bruce Louis Rich, *A Consent Theory of Unconscionability: An Empirical Study of Law in Action*, 33 FLA. ST. U. L. REV. 1067, 1071–72 (2006).
126.　*See* Feldman, *supra* note 124, at 425 (quoting Smith v. Mitsubishi Motors Credit of Am., Inc., 721 A.2d 1187, 1190 (Conn. 1998)).
127.　*See* Elvy, *supra* note 80, at 889.
128.　*Id.*
129.　*Id.* (citing MARGARET JANE RADIN, BOILERPLATE: THE FINE PRINT, VANISHING RIGHTS AND THE RULE OF LAW 33–34, 41–42 (Princeton University Press 2013)).
130.　*Id.*

Courts analyze unconscionability under a two-prong review: substantive unconscionability and procedural unconscionability.[131] Substantive unconscionability relates to contract terms themselves and whether they are unreasonably favorable to the party with superior knowledge or bargaining ability or whether the terms go against public policy.[132] Procedural unconscionability relates to the circumstances surrounding the procedural formation of the contract, including the bargaining power of the parties, deceptive practices, unfair surprises, and contracts of adhesion.[133] But it is not necessary that the evidence of substantive and procedural unconscionability be present in the same degree, because after evaluating both prongs, courts use a "sliding scale" analysis to weigh the evidence.[134] Therefore, if there is ample evidence of procedural unconscionability, then courts will require less evidence of substantive unconscionability, and vice versa.[135]

[A] Substantive Unconscionability

Generally, evidence of a substantively unconscionable contract term points to one party having unreasonable bargaining power over another party.[136] The court in *Williams v. Walker-Thomas Furniture Co.* held "[b]ut when a party of little bargaining power, and hence little real choice, signs a commercially unreasonable contract with little or no knowledge of its terms, it is hardly likely that his consent, or even an objective manifestation of his consent, was ever given to all the terms."[137] When a court is deciding a substantive unconscionability question, the case may involve terms defining unfair prices or warranties.[138] Additionally, these cases can involve contracts with clauses for penalties or limitations on remedies in the form of liquidated damages, exculpatory damages, and non-compete clauses.[139]

Contracts pertaining to IoT devices are subject to the same substantive unconscionability problems as more traditional contracts for other products. Many IoT manufacturers also use limitation of remedy clauses, such as requirements that consumers submit claims to arbitration. Scholars have hypothesized that, given the courts' reticence

---

131.   *Id.* at 890.
132.   *See* Feldman, *supra* note 124, at 427.
133.   *Id.* at 426.
134.   *Id.* at 427.
135.   *Id.*
136.   *See* Elvy, *supra* note 80, at 890 (citing RESTATEMENT (SECOND) OF CONTRACTS § 208, cmt. d (Am. Law Inst. 1981)).
137.   Williams v. Walker-Thomas Furniture Co., 350 F.2d 445, 449–50 (D.C. Cir. 1965).
138.   *See* Elvy, *supra* note 80, at 890 (citations omitted).
139.   *See* DiMatteo & Rich, *supra* note 125, at 1079.

to rule against one-sided contract amendments, sellers of IoT devices may be able to hold consumers to unfair contract terms by unilaterally amending their terms and conditions.[140] Also, due to the nature of bundled services for smart products, such as hardware components bundled with a DRS-enabled reorder feature, a consumer may be subject to multiple agreements to terms which are all crafted in favor of the seller, severely limiting consumer bargaining power.[141] Further, since DRS-enabled IoT devices have the capability of automatically reordering products upon depletion, it is unlikely that a consumer will review amendments to the terms of use before the goods are purchased by the IoT device.[142] Even if consumers receive advanced notice of changes to the terms, it is likely that consumers would not understand the impact of such amendments.[143] Further, the constant influx of advanced notices from different online retailers, service providers, banks, and credit card companies would be overwhelming, rendering advanced notice essentially useless and ineffective in providing sufficient notice to consumers.[144]

[B] Procedural Unconscionability

Courts generally are more likely to find unconscionability on procedural grounds than on substantive ones.[145] In *Wille v. Southwestern Bell Telephone Co.*, the court defined a ten-factor test which included both procedural and substantive factors regarding the enforceability of a clause. In *Wille*, the particular clause limited the telephone company's liability for either printing or content errors in a business's advertisement in their yellow-pages directory.[146] The procedural factors mentioned in the case were: (1) whether standardized form or boilerplate contracts were employed; (2) whether the placement of the clause was inconspicuous, either hidden in the fine print or hidden within the contract; (3) whether the language of the clause was easy for a layperson to understand; (4) whether one party had superior bargaining power over another; and (5) whether one party exploited an unsophisticated, uneducated, or illiterate party.[147]

In the past, courts would generally focus their procedural unconscionability evaluation on whether the parties had a meaningful choice in signing the contract: in other words, if the purchaser had

---

140. *See* Elvy, *supra* note 80, at 893.
141. *Id.*
142. *Id.*
143. *Id.*
144. *Id.*
145. *See* DiMatteo & Rich, *supra* note 125, at 1076.
146. Wille v. Sw. Bell Tel. Co., 549 P.2d 903 (Kan. 1976).
147. *Id.* at 906–07.

both the ability to understand the contract terms or to find a suitable alternative product.[148] Yet, in today's society, many form contracts have the same terms, whether offered by different sellers/providers, leaving consumers with little option to walk away from a contract in order to find a suitable replacement.[149] Therefore, today's courts focus more intently on unfair surprise due to hidden provisions or confusing language.[150]

Information asymmetry that gives way to a party's superior bargaining power is exacerbated in IoT contracts because IoT companies are able to track an incredible amount of data regarding consumer practices and personal information.[151] The data garnered from the IoT allows companies to track consumer visits to their websites, generate databases from interconnected goods, monitor the rate of product consumption, and much more.[152] It is speculated that the data provided by IoT devices can contain an "overall assessment of observations of daily living" for individual users, as well as provide information pertaining to the unique biometrics and health conditions of the user.[153] Using the wealth of information gathered from interconnected devices, companies that manufacture and sell IoT devices will be able to better market their products and make product recommendations to consumers.[154]

§ 5:4.2   Misrepresentation, Mistake, and Fraud

Generally, in common law, parties are bound by the terms of their contract unless the contract is found to be illegal, unconscionable, or based on misrepresentation, fraud, or mistake.[155] Consumers can use the avoidance defenses of mistake, misrepresentation, and fraud in order to allow courts to monitor bad-faith conduct in e-commerce under the UCC, the UETA, and UCITA as well.[156]

In applying the defense of misrepresentation, a contract may be void if the party was induced to enter into the contract by fraud or

---

148.   *See* Elvy, *supra* note 80, at 893.
149.   *Id.*
150.   *Id.*
151.   Scott R. Peppet, *Regulating the Internet of Things: First Steps Toward Managing Discrimination, Privacy, Security, and Consent*, 93 TEX. L. REV. 85, 120–22 (2014).
152.   *Id.* at 98–104, 114–17.
153.   *See* Elvy, *supra* note 80, at 895.
154.   *Id.*
155.   Mellon Bank, N.A. v. Aetna Bus. Credit, Inc., 619 F.2d 1001, 1009 (3d Cir. 1980).
156.   *See* Elvy, *supra* note 80, at 901 (citing U.C.C. § 1-103; Elec. Transactions Act § 3 legis. note 4 & § 9 cmt. 2, 7A pt. 1 U.L.A. 239 (2002); Unif. Comput. Info. Transactions Act § 206(a)).

material misrepresentation caused by the other party, coupled with justifiable reliance on the misrepresentation.[157] In a case for fraudulent misrepresentation, the seller must have the intent to deceive the consumer, making it a fairly onerous defense to prove.[158] But, fraudulent misrepresentation by a third party involves a party's manifestation of assent to be bound by a contract which was induced by either a fraudulent or a material misrepresentation by a third party to the transaction, upon which the seller is justified in relying.[159] These contracts are voidable by the purchaser, unless the seller in the transaction in good faith and without reason to know of the misrepresentation, either provides value or materially relies on the transaction.[160]

In the IoT context, fraudulent misrepresentation might become an issue arising from the security breach of a device.[161] As a result of such a breach, a third party could order products through another's IoT device, directing delivery to the consumer, the hacker, or to other third parties.[162] In such a case, neither the consumer nor the electronic agent has the necessary intent or knowledge to defraud the seller; rather it is the third party, the hacker, who uses the electronic agent to facilitate the fraud to the detriment of both the consumer and seller.[163] Manufacturers of IoT devices are more prepared to bear the risks and costs associated with this type of fraud.[164] However, with the increasing frequency of security breaches, consumers who use IoT devices should also be aware of the potential security risks. On the other hand, it might be argued that the seller's reliance on orders placed by the IoT device may not be reasonable; in light of past security breaches of IoT devices, perhaps the occurrence of a security breach should be reasonably foreseeable to the seller.

Material misrepresentation is demonstrated when a reasonable recipient would have been induced to make the contract, or when the maker of the contract had special knowledge that the misrepresentation would be likely to induce that specific party to assent.[165] With the vast amount of consumer information made available to companies through interconnected IoT devices, it is likely that that consumers could make a successful case for material misrepresentation against companies that have the requisite knowledge about individual consumers

---

157.　*See* RESTATEMENT (SECOND) OF CONTRACTS § 164(1).
158.　*Id.* § 162(1).
159.　*Id.* § 164(2).
160.　*Id.*
161.　*See* Elvy, *supra* note 80, at 906.
162.　*Id.*
163.　*Id.*
164.　*Id.*
165.　*Id.* § 162(2).

and their purchasing profiles.[166] However, consumers would need to prove the company's knowledge of the consumer's special circumstances and that the manufacturer's knowledge about the consumer was shared with the retailer.[167] Furthermore, the party would need to prove justifiable reliance on the misrepresentation.[168]

Lastly, in using the defense of mistake, though one party to the contract is unilaterally mistaken, that party cannot escape its obligation under the contract unless the contract is unconscionable or the non-mistaken party had reason to know of the mistake or caused the mistake.[169] When both parties are mistaken, the *Restatement of Contracts* authorizes avoidance of the contract by the adversely affected party. Otherwise, reformation of the contract is also authorized as long as the mistake: is made by both parties at the time of the contract; relates to the basis on which the contract was formed; and has a material effect on the contract.[170] However, both the *Restatement* and the UCITA allow for the parties to freely allocate the risk of mistake or fraud between themselves.[171]

If an electronic agent malfunctions and subsequently orders the wrong product erroneously, the consumer is not likely to escape performance of the contract.[172] A mistaken order by an IoT device acting as the electronic agent will most likely be classified as a unilateral mistake. While some may claim that a seller should be charged with knowledge of the product descriptions that they provide to consumers, the court is more likely to find that a consumer assumes the risk that a web-enabled IoT device could commit an error. However, it is still a question whether consumers truly assume the risk of mistake if an IoT device malfunctions due to no fault of the consumer.

§ 5:5   Conclusion

As seen throughout this chapter, IoT innovations have created an intense need to update contract law to reflect the complexities inherent in these emerging technologies and their hybrid natures. Current contract law is difficult to apply to IoT transactions, as it was not written with such complex technologies in mind and has not been updated to take these new factors into consideration. Lawmakers must begin to

---

166.   *See* Elvy, *supra* note 80, at 905.
167.   *Id.*
168.   *Id.* (citing RESTATEMENT (SECOND) OF CONTRACTS § 164).
169.   RESTATEMENT (SECOND) OF CONTRACTS § 153.
170.   *Id.* § 152(1).
171.   *Id.* § 154; *see also* Unif. Comput. Info. Transactions Act § 206 cmt. 3 (amended 2002), 7A pt. 2 U.L.A. 306 (2009).
172.   *See* Elvy, *supra* note 80, at 904.

search for resolutions to the current lack of clarity surrounding which body of law should apply to IoT contract claims and the approach the law should take to hybrid IoT transactions. Furthermore, lawmakers should take a proactive and reformative approach to contract law by looking to the future when considering the best methods to address complexities of emerging smart technologies and automated contracting as the field of interconnected IoT devices continues to proliferate.

Chapter 6

Ownership and Intellectual Property

§ 6:1   Overview

This chapter examines ownership of data collected by IoT devices and the types of data that may be protected as intellectual property under copyright, trade secret, and patent law.

§ 6:2   Ownership

For many businesses, the real value of the IoT lies in data monetization; that is, retrieving, analyzing, and exploiting the data collected by the IoT.[1] But, who owns the data collected by the IoT? Legal ownership of IoT data is generally predetermined through the agreements between individual persons and the entities involved in the creation and manufacturing of the IoT device, and/or in the creation

---

1.   Mauricio Paez & Mike La Marca, *The Internet of Things: Emerging Legal Issues for Businesses*, 43 N. KY. L. REV. 29, 65 (2016).

and processing of IoT data.[2] However, in situations where such agreements are non-existent or fail to anticipate the allocation of rights, legal ownership of IoT data becomes complicated. This is especially true when numerous proprietary devices or objects interact with each other and create new and unique data sets.[3] For example, when an IoT-enabled milk carton transmits to the IoT-enabled refrigerator in which it sits that its contents are running low, the IoT-enabled refrigerator responds by adding milk to the grocery list or by ordering milk for delivery from the local grocer. Such a transaction collects data as to the type of milk, the producer of the milk, the name and address of the recipient, and other personal information including financial accounts.[4] This data may then be combined with other datasets to reveal further information or to gain power through accretion.[5] Thus, questions arise as to whether this data belongs to the consumer, the carton creator, the milk producer, the refrigerator manufacturer, the Internet service provider, the local grocer, or the bank.[6] Currently, there is no simple or uniform answer.

Each unanswered question ultimately leads to the overarching issue of IoT data ownership—is the data owned by the person who created or provided it, the manufacturer whose sensors collected it, or the company whose platforms aggregate and analyze it?[7] It is instinctive to assume that data generated by and about the consumer should belong to the consumer. However, at present, there is no legal concept that conveys sole ownership of personal data to the individual, nor that considers the mere collection of personal information (that which is unprotected by statute) to be a violation of that individual's

---

2. Thomas A. Walsh, *What Can I Do with All This Data? How to Monetize 'Internet of Things' Data*, INSIDE IND. BUS. (Jan. 27, 2017), www.insideindianabusiness.com/story/34366554/what-can-i-do-with-all-this-data-how-to-monetize-internet-of-things-data.

3. Charles E. Root & Nancy E. Cronin, *The Internet of Things and Intellectual Property: Who Owns the Data?*, IP CAPITAL GRP. (2016), www.ipcg.com/?file=The_Internet_of_Things_and_Intellectual_Property:_Who_Owns_the_Data (last visited May 29, 2020).

4. *Id.*

5. Paul Ohm, *Broken Promises of Privacy: Responding to Surprising Failure of Anonymization*, 57 UCLA L. REV. 1701, 1705 (2010). This process is referred to as re-identification—a process in which two datasets, meant to be kept apart, are combined, and in doing so, gain power through accretion. This process breaks any anonymization as a person is able to reidentify anonymized data by linking anonymized records to outside information, revealing the true identity of the data subjects.

6. Root & Cronin, *supra* note 3.

7. *The Great IoT Data Ownership Debate*, IOT AGENDA (Apr. 23, 2018), https://internetofthingsagenda.techtarget.com/feature/The-great-IoT-data-ownership-debate.

rights.[8] To put this another way, if Google hired an employee for the sole task of observing and recording facts and habits of all bystanders in a park, Google is permitted to do so.[9] In fact, certain types of psychological research and private investigations are conducted in this very manner.[10] Importantly, data collected by IoT devices differs in that it is not generic, as in the Google example, but rather it may be specifically identifiable. Even with promises of data anonymization, re-identification is plausible.[11] End-users, unlike in the Google example, must consent to data collection prior to using an IoT device.

Within the technology industry, there are various views about ownership of data collected by IoT devices. Some companies operate from the view that the generator of the data—the consumer—owns the data. For example, Dennis Groseclose, President and CEO of TransBoyant, takes this view and, in fact, TransBoyant pays for the consumer data integrated into its platform.[12] Similarly, John Licciardello, Managing Director of the Ecosystem Development Fund at the IOTA Foundation, believes that the individuals who produce the data, own the data, and are thereby free to sell that data if they so choose to.[13] However, this is not the trend for a majority of companies. Among those who follow the majority view, Melanie Nuce, Senior Vice President of Corporate Development at GS1 US, stated that it is critical for all manufacturers to clearly indicate to consumers just how data is collected, used, and shared.[14] Additionally, users need to have the option of a clear "opt-out" strategy. Nuce further noted that companies also need to consider uncollected data. She explained that in the supply chain, certain entities may believe they own all the data therein; however, once data is decentralized and democratized, the data at issue may be coming from sources that were never anticipated. Additionally, Peter Mehring, CEO of Zest Labs Inc., has also commented on alternative data creation. He stated that even though many people think the company owns the data, generally, it is merely tracking a product and the owner of the product actually owns the data at that time.[15]

---

8. Eric Ravenscraft, *You Don't Own Your Data*, LIFEHACKER (Apr. 1, 2014), https://lifehacker.com/you-dont-own-your-data-1556088120.
9. *Id.*
10. *Id.*
11. *See generally* Ohm, *supra* note 5 (discussing that data is re-identified by linking anonymized records to outside information, revealing the true identity of the data subjects).
12. *See The Great IoT Data Ownership Debate*, *supra* note 7.
13. *Id.*
14. *Id.*
15. *Id.*

In another context—lease holdings—data is considered to be owned by the titleholder.[16] Possession is equated with control, and title is similar to ownership.[17] Every time data sets are copied, re-copied, and transmitted, the individual who has control of the data follows the transmission of data.[18] Despite the ease of transferring control of data, transferring ownership of the data would require a legal mechanism that conveys title.[19] It is similar in nature to car ownership. Whoever is driving the car is exercising control over the car but does not necessarily own it. To have ownership over the car, a legal transfer of title/ownership must take place.

As the previous examples illustrate, currently, no universally accepted means of addressing IoT data ownership exists; each company has its own approach to how ownership should be determined.

§ 6:2.1 Shared Ownership

The concept of sharing encompasses the notion that the split is of equal value.[20] Finding equal value within data is difficult because it can be challenging to determine a fair and accurate way of measuring.[21] Data can range in value from simple details like a user's smart lighting preferences, all the way to complex algorithms to identify a potential failure before a 747 jet takes off the runway.[22] The vast difference in data type and quality leads to difficulties in determining shared ownership because data valuable to one individual or owner may not be valuable to another.

Other challenges surrounding data measurement include the loose approach taken by some entities toward valuing information.[23] A few organizations view data simply as an object to be traded or analyzed. Those critical of this viewpoint believe that traders and users of data need to adopt a disciplined approach towards the valuation and accounting of data in a manner similar to the way money is treated.[24] One result of treating data like money would be the emergence of

---

16. *See* David Knight & IDG Contributor Network, *Who Owns the Data from the IoT?*, NETWORK WORLD (Jan. 30, 2017), www.networkworld. com/article/3152837/internet-of-things/who-owns-the-data-from-the-iot. html.
17. *Id.*
18. *Id.*
19. *Id.*
20. *The Great IoT Data Ownership Debate*, *supra* note 7.
21. *Id.*
22. *Id.*
23. Paul Gillin, *Who Owns Data from the 'Internet of Things'? That's About to Become a Very Big Deal*, SILICON ANGLE (Oct. 15, 2017), https:// siliconangle.com/2017/10/15/owns-iot-data-thats-become-big-deal/.
24. *Id.*

greater guidance for the courts which, to date, have been inconsistent in their treatment of data.[25]

Valuing and measuring online data is also made more complicated by courts who struggle to determine access and control. In *United States v. Microsoft*, Microsoft argued that the U.S. Government had to go through Irish authorities in order to access emails from its servers located in Dublin. In contrast, the United States claimed that a warrant issued in the United States to Microsoft was sufficient because the digital content, although physically located in Ireland, was under Microsoft's control. The government was successful at the District Court level, but Microsoft prevailed at the U.S. Court of Appeals.[26] Ultimately, Congress took the decision out of the hands of the courts and passed the CLOUD Act, which allows warrants for online data located overseas, but also permits companies like Microsoft to challenge the warrant if it violates the laws of the host country.

While measuring, valuing, accessing, and controlling data can be challenging, so too can sharing ownership. In order to find a way to allocate equitably, the industry must first identify the quality and applicability of the data, and those in the industry must be open to the idea of sharing.[27] For example, many supply chain practitioners believe that the data they obtain should remain within their four walls; these companies are not very trusting of others or the crowdsourcing of data.[28]

In order for sharing to flourish, the data must be shared responsibly.[29] For instance, users are not likely to allow free sharing of their information beyond the manufacturer of the device unless they have a reasonable belief that the data will be protected. Providing users with assurances that data will be kept private and that personally identifiable information will be scrubbed creates trust that data is protected and being shared responsibly. This trust is not something to be immediately presumed; a trust relationship between entities evolves over time. Specifically, trust between a user and a business entity grows from consistent internal policies and a company's approach to business operations.[30]

A third concept concerning IoT data ownership involves the extent of the owner's right to use its data. It is important to note that the legal concept of ownership does not convey absolute ownership, as most forms of ownership are encumbered by restrictions and limitations.

---

25.   *Id.*
26.   United States v. Microsoft Corp., 584 U.S. (2018).
27.   *The Great IoT Data Ownership Debate, supra* note 7.
28.   *Id.*
29.   *Id.*
30.   *Id.*

For example, ownership in a home is contingent upon easements and caveats regarding those who may access the home and in what manner the property may be used. Ownership, in most cases, does not convey an absolute right to do with the property whatever the owner may like. For instance, a homeowner may be held liable for creating an attractive nuisance at her house. As such, applying this legal concept of ownership in the digital age means that consumer ownership of the IoT is similarly restricted and limited. These restrictions and limitations are conveyed to consumers in the form of license agreements rather than ownership.[31] The end-user, however, may restrict specific types of datasets, particularly those involving personal health information protected by HIPAA or HITECH.[32] End-users may also restrict or opt-out of specific data collection through their responses to a privacy policy provided by the IoT manufacturer.[33] Moreover, end-users may bring a valid legal claim if their privacy is invaded or intellectual property infringed upon. But end-users presently do not have a claim of ownership to their personal data within the IoT device.

Data ownership by end-users may be possible in the United States in the future. The EU's General Data Protection Regulation (GDPR) aims to protect personal data of EU residents within the EU, and addresses the export of personal data of EU residents outside the EU.[34] Germany has a similar and long-established concept known as "Informationelle Selbstbestimmung" or "informational self-determination," and reflects the right of the individual to decide on their own what personal information should be communicated to others and under what circumstances.[35] Other individual nations have similar concepts, but whether the United States will follow remains to be seen. At present, IoT data ownership ultimately depends upon the specific IoT device involved, the respective contractual provisions, and any intellectual property overlays.

---

31. Bill Rosenblatt, *What Does Ownership Mean in the Digital Age?*, COPYRIGHT & TECH. (Dec. 21, 2016), https://copyrightandtechnology.com/2016/12/21/what-does-ownership-mean-in-the-digital-age/.

32. Christina D. Frangiosa, *Copyright Ownership and IoT Devices*, ABA SCITECH LAW., at 21 (Spring 2016).

33. *Id.*

34. Michael Nadeau, *General Data Protection Regulation [GDPR] Requirements, Deadlines and Facts*, CSO IDGCOMMC'NS, INC. (Jan. 3, 2018), www.csoonline.com/article/3202771/data-protection/general-data-protection-regulation-gdpr-requirements-deadlines-and-facts.html. Similar arguments can be made with the California Consumer Privacy Act of 2018.

35. Ravenscraft, *supra* note 8. *See also* Samuel D. Warren & Louis D. Brandeis, *The Right to Privacy*, HARV. L. REV. vol. IV, no. 5 (Dec. 15, 1890), http://faculty.uml.edu/sgallagher/Brandeisprivacy.htm.

§ 6:3   Intellectual Property

Intellectual property (IP) law aims to strike a proper balance between the unique interests of innovators and the wider public interest.[36] The ideal end result of IP law application is to foster an environment in which creativity and innovation can safely flourish.[37] In a typical IP claim, the party asserting a legal interest in the property is responsible for the property's creation.[38] In contrast, in an IP claim involving IoT data, the party asserting a legal interest may or may not be responsible for the data's creation. Here, the end-user, oftentimes the consumer, is the party responsible for creating and generating the IoT data.[39] The end-user, however, rarely has any ownership interest in the IoT data.[40]

Similarly, intellectual property rights are inherent in data management, as in when a user populates a database with data provided by others, or when an IoT device collects and analyzes data from others. Data management typically has two components: 1) the collection, assembly, and generation of data, and 2) the storage and management of data within a system component.[41] The first component embraces raw data collection, such as hourly temperature readings, survey takers' ages, photographs, recordings, etc., and the second component pertains to the database that holds the raw data. These two components are treated differently under the various branches of intellectual property law—copyright, trade secrets, and patents—discussed below.

§ 6:3.1   *Copyright Law*

The U.S. Constitution authorizes Congress to grant copyrights and patents.[42] Pursuant to this power, Congress enacted the Copyright Act, which protects original works of authorship, fixed in a tangible medium of expression.[43] Ideas, procedures, process systems, methods of operation, concepts, principles, and discoveries, are not copyrightable.[44] Moreover, since copyright requires originality, and since facts are unoriginal, copyright in compilation cannot extend to the facts it contains.[45] A compilation, however, is copyrightable so long

---

36.   *What is Intellectual Property?*, WORLD INTELLECTUAL PROP. ORG, www.wipo.int/about-ip/en/ (last visited May 29, 2020).
37.   *Id.*
38.   Paez & La Marca, *supra* note 1.
39.   *Id.*
40.   Frangiosa, *supra* note 32.
41.   *Id.*
42.   U.S. CONST. art. I, § 8.
43.   17 U.S.C. § 102(a).
44.   17 U.S.C. § 102(b).
45.   Feist Publ'ns, Inc. v. Rural Tel. Serv. Co., 499 U.S. 340, 360 (1991) ("The revisions explain with painstaking clarity that copyright requires originality,

as it features an "original selection, coordination, or arrangement" of those facts.[46] Thus, various authors may create or reproduce different compilations containing the same facts so long as each compilation expresses a different "selection, coordination, or arrangement" of those facts.[47] Further, since the source of the underlying facts—the individual about whom the facts relate—is simply a discoverer of the facts, they are not considered an author under copyright law.[48] By implication, therefore, end-users generating IoT data are not authors for purposes of copyright law. They have not created a protectable compilation of facts, and thus are unable to claim copyright ownership in the IoT data.[49]

The Copyright Office has acknowledged that, generally, data output generated by IoT devices are not copyrightable.[50] However, the device manufacturer who collected, analyzed, and compiled the data into a unique work may claim copyright in compilation.[51] Thus, a business attempting to protect data would have to show that it tracked, selected, and arranged the data in a unique and original fashion in order to show copyright in compilation.[52] Nevertheless, establishing copyright in IoT-related data compilations will prove to be challenging since data is automatically compiled by IoT devices without human involvement, and even in the case of a copyright in compilation, a single data point within the compilation would not be protected by copyright.[53] The end-user may prevent the publication or further dissemination of the data under a right of publicity claim, a right of privacy claim, or under a prohibition of disclosure

---

§ 102(a); that facts are never original, § 102(b); that the copyright in a compilation does not extend to the facts it contains, § 103(b); and that a compilation is copyrightable only to the extent that it features an original selection, coordination, or arrangement, § 101.").

46.   *Id.*
47.   *Id. See also* Frangiosa, *supra* note 32, at 22.
48.   Frangiosa, *supra* note 32, at 22.
49.   *Id.*
50.   Exemption to Prohibition on Circumvention of Copyright Protection Systems for Access Control Technologies, 80 FR 65944-01 (Oct. 28, 2015) ("The Register observed that in many cases, data outputs generated by devices would likely be uncopyrightable, and that in such cases, section 1201(a)(1)—which is limited to works protected under title 17—would not apply. The Register noted, however, that some data outputs could qualify for protection as literary works if they reflect a sufficiently original selection and presentation of data, and that opponents themselves agreed that such outputs could be subject to copyright.").
51.   Frangiosa, *supra* note 32, at 22–23.
52.   Paez & La Marca, *supra* note 1, at 65.
53.   *Id.*

under HIPAA or HITECH—but may not bring a claim under copyright law.[54]

Copyright protection may apply to software code that was written to allow an IoT device to exchange data with other devices, as well as to understand the data.[55] Copyright law can also be used to impede the ability of devices to interact with one another.[56] It can impede this interoperability through the actual software code transmitted by the devices. Thus, there are two questions that emerge about the code that allows the devices to transmit and read the data: will the owner of the code allow it to interact with other devices, and if the data in the device is already in readable format, can other devices access it or will they be prevented by anti-copying mechanisms?[57]

Oracle America, Inc. v. Google, Inc. illustrates the challenges of determining whether software code has been infringed upon.[58] In 2010, Oracle sued Google over its use of Java Application Programming Interface (API) in the Android mobile operating system claiming copyright infringement. An API allows a programmer to use prewritten code to build certain functions into other programs rather than writing their own code to perform the same action. Google claimed that it was only following a "long accepted practice of re-using software interfaces." The federal district court found that the APIs were not subject to copyright protection.

The trial judge based his decision on section 102 of the Copyright Act, which provides that in order to receive copyright protection, a work must be original and it must not be an "idea, procedure, process, system, method of operation, concept, principle, or discovery, regardless of the form in which it is described, explained, illustrated, or embodied in such work." Although the district court found Oracle's API packages both creative and original, it employed an interpretation of the statute as argued by Google—that even if a work is original under section 102(a), section 102(b) removes the protection if the work has a function component.

On appeal, the Federal Circuit Court of Appeals ruled that the creation of APIs requires some level of creativity; therefore, they are copyrightable.[59] In reversing the district court's copyrightable determination, the Federal Circuit Court concluded that the district court's

---

54. Frangiosa, *supra* note 32, at 23.
55. Brian Wassom, *Top 5 Legal Issues in the Internet of Things, Part 4: Copyright*, WASSOM.COM (Feb. 19, 2015), www.wassom.com/top-5-legal-issues-internet-things-part-4-copyright.html.
56. *Id.*
57. *Id.*
58. Oracle Am., Inc. v. Google, 872 F. Supp. 2d 974 (N.D. Cal. 2012).
59. Oracle Am., Inc. v. Google Inc., 750 F.3d 1339 (Fed. Cir. 2014).

analysis was contrary to Congress's intentions for 102(b), which was to not enlarge or contract the scope of copyright protection but to restate that a "basic dichotomy between expression and idea remains unchanged."[60] Thus, section 102(b) does not extinguish the protection on an expression of an idea simply because the expression is part of a method of operation.[61] Section 102(a) and (b) are considered at the same time such that certain expressions are subject to a heightened scrutiny.[62]

Google appealed to the U.S. Supreme Court, and the case will be argued in the Court's October 2020 term. Some commentators believe that, if the Supreme Court agrees with the Federal Circuit Court of Appeals, future innovation may be stifled.[63] They argue that the ruling by the Court of Appeals gives copyright holders a "patent-like veto power" and creates artificial barriers for new players in the market. Further, some claim that prohibiting the reuse of APIs greatly restricts reverse engineering, creation of competing platforms, and interoperability.[64] It is this last category that will have the most lasting impact on IoT.

In order for IoT devices to be effective, they must interact and connect with the world around them. Oftentimes, this interaction requires the sharing and copying of software code, especially with respect to software interfaces.[65] Amazon's Echo serves as an illustrative example; the Echo device uses online sites to respond to requests made by its users. To obtain data from online sources seamlessly, the Echo needs to access, copy, and use certain software interfaces from those third parties. The Echo also internally incorporates software from those third parties in order to better interact with third-party services.

Future litigation and the passage of time will determine whether the IoT will be treated similar to the World Wide Web, which allows users to choose from many different browsers to find the same information, or if, instead, there will be thousands of separate entities that operate in parallel sectors but cannot otherwise communicate.[66]

---

60.   *Id.* (quoting Feist Publ'ns, Inc. v. Rural Tel. Serv. Co., 499 U.S. 340 (1991)).

61.   *Id.* at 1356–57 (quoting Mitel, Inc. v. Iqtel, Inc., 124 F.3d 1366, 1372 (10th Cir. 1997)).

62.   *Id.* at 1357. *See also* Mitel, Inc. v. Iqtel, Inc., 124 F.3d 1366, 1372 (10th Cir. 1997).

63.   *See* Rebecca Hill, *U.S. Supremes Urged by Pretty Much Everyone in Software Dev. to Probe Oracle's 'Disastrous' Java API Copyright Win*, THE REGISTER (Feb. 26, 2019).

64.   *Id.*

65.   *See* Clark D. Asay, *Software's Copyright Anticommons*, 66 EMORY L.J. 265, 288, 289 (2017).

66.   *Id.*

One example of a copyright infringement case in which the court did not enforce a copyright claim is *Balik v. Toy Talk, Inc.* Balik sought to enforce his copyright protection against Toy Talk, Inc. and Mattel, Inc. for his invention of a plush, action-figure doll embedded with mini Bluetooth speakers.[67] The court ruled against Balik on two counts: the first, that he had not properly registered his copyright with the Copyright Office; and the second, that Balik was attempting to copyright an *idea* for a toy design.[68] Balik failed to allege a property right in which Toy Talk, Inc. could and did interfere with or convert, because Balik's complaint only alleged that Toy Talk, Inc. stole or copied his idea. The court, in prior orders, had explained that a claim for conversion cannot be based on an "idea" for a toy design. While Balik asserted that his idea was original and that he had expressed it via PowerPoint, these arguments are irrelevant to the contention of copyright protection. Furthermore, Balik was not asserting any infringement of the text or images used in his PowerPoint documents, only his idea.[69] Because Balik did not present evidence of copyright infringement or even a copyrightable issue, the court granted the defendant's motion to dismiss with prejudice for all claims.[70]

[A]   Digital Millennium Copyright Act (DMCA)

In 1998, the DMCA was passed into law.[71] Initially, the intent behind the DMCA was to update copyright laws in order to effectively regulate digital material and provide protection for both consumers and the copyright holders. It was drafted by a team of publishers, scientists, civil rights groups, and others, in order to form a compromise among these groups whose interests were frequently in conflict. The primary application of the DMCA is to prevent individuals from pirating music and movies.

Many believe that the DMCA inhibits security and compatibility research.[72] Prior to its passage, some of the most prominent computer scientists and technology experts wrote a letter to the U.S. Congress warning that the DMCA, as originally envisioned, would ultimately imperil computer systems and networks, criminalize many current university courses, and severely disrupt the information security

---

67.   Balik v. Toy Talk, Inc., N.D. Cal. No. 15-cv-04556-JST, 2016 U.S. Dist. LEXIS 75969, at *1–2 (N.D. Cal. June 6, 2016).
68.   *Id.* at *6.
69.   *Id.* at *7.
70.   *Id.* at *7–8.
71.   17 U.S.C. § 512.
72.   Bruce Schneier, *DMCA and the Internet of Things*, SCHNEIER ON SEC. (Dec. 29, 2015), www.schneier.com/blog/archives/2015/12/dmca_and_the_in.html.

technology industry.[73] Revisions to the DMCA allowed for specific exceptions, including encryption and security research. In 2003, the Broadband and Internet Security Task Force created a model law, often referred to as the Super DMCA, for states to enact.[74]

Specifically, the DMCA includes an anti-circumvention provision, which prohibits companies from circumventing "technological protection measures" that "effectively control access" to copyrighted works.[75] That means it is illegal for someone to create a Hue-compatible light bulb without Philips' permission, a K-cup-compatible coffee pod without Keurig's, or an HP-printer compatible cartridge without HP's. In the 1990s, Microsoft used a strategy it called "embrace, extend, extinguish," in which it gradually added proprietary capabilities to products that already adhered to widely used standards.[76] More recent examples include: Amazon's e-book format which does not work on other companies' readers; music purchased from Apple's iTunes store that is incompatible with other music players, and every electronic game console with its own proprietary game cartridge format. Because companies can enforce anti-competitive behavior this way, there is a growing litany of things that simply do not exist.

This act of preventing a competitor from designing a similar device is referred to as a DRM (Digital Rights Management) lock.[77] Under section 1201 of the DMCA, any act that weakens or bypasses a lock that controls access to a copyrighted work is banned.[78] The initial use of these locks were to "lock down" the design of DVD players and game consoles in order to prevent activities that would be considered legal activities, such as watching out-of-region discs or playing an independently produced game. The DRM lock was able to "control access" to any copyrighted work thus ensuring that a specific branded device was only compatible with that specific brand's systems. This level of control goes beyond the obvious physical differences in devices, which prevent those designed by different companies from interacting with the system.

---

73.   Edward Felton, *The Chilling Effect of the DMCA*, SLATE (Mar. 29, 2013).

74.   Super DMCA "criminalize[s] the possession, use, development, and distribution of 'unlawful communication and access devices.'" *See, e.g.,* Ark. HB 2361 (2003); 11 DEL. C. sec. 850 (2003); 720 ILCS 5/16-10 through 720 ILCS 5/16-13 (2003); 18 PA. CONS. STAT. § 910 (2003); VA. CODE §§ 18.2-187.1 and 18.2-190.1 *et seq.;* and MD. CRIM. L. CODE ANN. § 7-313 *et seq.*

75.   Bruce Schneier, *DMCA and the Internet of Things*, SCHNEIER ON SEC. (Dec. 29, 2015), www.schneier.com/blog/archives/2015/12/dmca_and_the_in.html.

76.   *Id.*

77.   Cory Doctorow, *EFF vs IoT DRM, OMG!*, ELEC. FRONTIER FOUND. (Feb. 7, 2018), www.eff.org/deeplinks/2018/02/eff-vs-iot-drm-omg.

78.   *See* 17 U.S.C. § 1201.

Another example of DRM in effect is in the video game industry. The different gaming consoles are only able to read the game discs associated with that specific console. Thus, even though the games may all be contained on the same medium, a disc, they cannot be read by differing consoles simply because various companies do not want the consumer to play the game on a console not owned by them.

Despite the use of DRM to prevent security researchers and individual consumers from tinkering with the software and hardware of devices, a victory was achieved in favor of consumers in 2015 when the Electronic Frontier Foundation (EFF) won the right for consumers to "jailbreak" phones and tablets.[79] Thus, consumers are able to change device configuration in order to unlock features that the individual consumer wants, despite the manufacturer's intent, and allows for the removal of other features. Additionally, the EFF won the right for security researchers' to bypass the DRM in order to investigate and test the security of different devices.[80] One linchpin of the EFF's argument for this exemption from the DRM lock and the DMCA was that previously, consumers had always had a right to bypass device bootloaders or activate/disable hardware features. This was the status quo until manufacturers discovered how to use DRM to control their product once it left their possession.[81]

The DMCA has affected, and will continue to affect, IoT devices with its anti-circumvention provision. Relying on this provision, IoT developers can prevent competitors from copying their designs and prevent users from employing third-party items with the IoT device. In addition, the circumvention provision has been cited as grounds to prevent IoT users from even modifying or repairing their own IoT devices.[82] Barring a change to the DMCA text, companies will have the ability to stop outside parties from integrating or communicating with the original IoT device.

§ 6:3.2 *Trade Secret Law*

Trade secret law may also impact the regulation of IoT devices. The Uniform Trade Secrets Act (UTSA) defines a trade secret as information that has economic value and is not generally known to or readily ascertainable by those who could gain value from its use or disclosure, and is subject to reasonable security measures.[83] Trade secrets can

---

79.   Doctorow, *supra* note 77.
80.   *Id.*
81.   *Id.*
82.   Andrew Rens, *Who Is in Charge Here? The Internet of Things, Governance and the Global Intellectual Property Regime*, 23 UCLA J.L. & TECH. 2 (2019).
83.   Unif. Trade Secrets Act § 1(4).

consist solely of information; additionally, they can include a formula, pattern, compilation, program, device, method, technique, or process.[84] However, the common definition of a trade secret dictates that it must be used in business and provide an economic advantage over competitors.[85] Traditionally, trade secret law was generally state law, and every state, except New York, has adopted the UTSA.[86] In 2016, however, the Defend Trade Secrets Act (DTSA) was signed into law creating a federal cause of action for trade secret misappropriation.[87] To claim a trade secret in IoT data under both the UTSA and DTSA, a business or database owner must establish that:

1. the data is secret;

2. value is derived from its secrecy; and

3. the owner used reasonable efforts to safeguard its secrecy or limit access to the data.[88]

Establishing a trade secret claim requires a business or database owner to, first and foremost, compile the data to be protected. Unlike a typical trade secret action in which information is stored on business property, in the context of the IoT, the end-user is both the creator of the information and the owner of the IoT device upon which the data is stored.[89] Therefore, a business or database owner must extract and compile the data, separating it from the IoT device, to preserve trade secret protection.[90] The business or database owner must also maintain secrecy over the compilation by limiting access to only those bound by confidentiality agreements, nondisclosure agreements, and/ or license agreements.[91] Many IoT devices have default credentials hard-coded within, which are widely available on the Internet and

---

84. Office of Policy and International Affairs, *Trade Secret Policy*, United States Patent and Trademark Office—An Agency of the Department of Commerce, www.uspto.gov/patents-getting-started/international-protection/trade-secrets-policy (last visited May 29, 2020).

85. *Id.*

86. Gregory S. Bombard, *Three Key Distinctions Between the Uniform Trade Secrets Act and the Common Law*, 17 COMMERCIAL & BUS. LITIG. 23 (Jan. 26, 2016), www.duanemorris.com/articles/static/bombard_abacommbuslit_winter2016.pdf.

87. Sebastian Kaplan & Patrick Premo, *The Defend Trade Secrets Act of 2016 Creates Federal Jurisdiction for Trade Secret Litigation*, IP WATCHDOG (May 23, 2016), www.ipwatchdog.com/2016/05/23/defend-trade-secrets-act-2016-creates-federal-jurisdiction-trade-secret-litigation/id=69245/. *See also* Defend Trade Secrets Act of 2016, S. 1890, Pub. L. No. 114-153.

88. *Id.*

89. Paez & La Marca, *supra* note 1, at 65.

90. *See generally* Walsh, *supra* note 2.

91. *Id.*

accessible by hackers who may use these credentials to coordinate denial-of-service attacks.[92] To combat such attacks, businesses should continuously change the default credentials or set up an automated system to change passwords periodically throughout the life of the IoT device.[93]

§ 6:3.3 *Patent Law*

"A patent for an invention is the grant of a property right to the inventor by the United States Patent and Trademark Office (USPTO)."[94] A patent is good for twenty years starting on the date that the application for the patent was filed. Further, a patent cannot be obtained on an idea or suggestion; a patent is granted for a concrete object.[95] When obtaining a patent, a full description of the subject matter of the patent is required.[96] By obtaining a patent, the inventor has the right to exclude others from making, using, offering for sale, or selling that invention within the United States or importing the invention into the United States. The USPTO grants the right to exclude others not necessarily the right to make, use, offer for sale, sell, or import that same invention. Additionally, after the patent has been issued, it is up to the patentee to enforce that patent without the use of the USPTO.

When a patent is granted, it must fall into one of three types of patents:

1. utility patent, which is granted to any new and useful process, machine, article of manufacture, or composition of matter, or any new and useful improvement;

2. design patent, which is granted to a new, original, and ornamental design for an article of manufacture; or

3. plant patent, which is granted to the invention or discovery and asexual reproduction of any distinct and new variety of plant.[97]

---

92. Brian Krebs, *Who Makes the IoT Things Under Attack?*, KREBS ON SEC. (Oct. 3, 2016), https://krebsonsecurity.com/2016/10/who-makes-the-iot-things-under-attack/.
93. *Id.*
94. *General Information Concerning Patents*, United States Patent and Trademark Office—An Agency of the Department of Commerce, www.uspto.gov/patents-getting-started/general-information-concerning-patents (last visited May 29, 2020).
95. *Id.*
96. *Id.*
97. *Id.*

There are four subsequent requirements to obtaining a patent: the invention must be statutory, useful, new, and non-obvious.[98] In order for an invention or subject matter to be considered statutory, it must fit into one of the above patent types—of which, the utility patents are most relevant for the IoT context. Delving into the requirements of a utility patent, the term "process" requires further definition. Under patent law, a process is defined as an act or method, which primarily includes industrial or technical processes.[99] The subject matter is considered useful if it has a useful purpose, including its usefulness in operation.[100] Should the subject matter not operate within the intended realm of purpose, it would not be considered useful.[101] In order for an invention to be determined patentable it must not:

1. already be patented, described in a printed publication, or in public use, on sale or otherwise available to the public prior to the filing date of the invention; or

2. already be described in a patent or in the application stage of a patent.[102]

There is a one-year exception for patents that have been disclosed or offered for sale.[103] As long as the sale or disclosure occurred less than one year prior to the patent application, the patent is not barred and the disclosure/sale is "forgiven."[104] The goal of these restrictions is to make sure that the subject matter to be patented is truly something different and not something already available to the public.

If an invention is not "exactly" the same as prior products or processes (prior art), then it can be considered novel.[105] However, for the novel invention to be patentable, the invention must be a non-obvious improvement over the prior art.[106] In other words, the invention must alter the "formula" of the pre-existing patented invention in a way that was not obvious. In determining if the improvement was non-obvious, the previous invention and the new invention are examined side-by-side to determine if the differences would be obvious to a person having ordinary skill with the invention.[107]

---

98.   *See Patent Law in the United States*, BITLAW, www.bitlaw.com/patent/requirements.html (last visited May 29, 2020).
99.   *Id.*
100.   *General Information Concerning Patents, supra* note 94.
101.   *Id.*
102.   *Id.*
103.   *Patent Law in the United States, supra* note 98.
104.   *Id.*
105.   *Id.*
106.   *Id.*
107.   *Id.*

Of all the legal areas impacted by advancements in the IoT, patent law is likely to present some of the greatest challenges. As different industries begin to utilize the IoT, some have started offering IoT communication infrastructures, which in turn creates overlapping utility patents causing an increase in patent infringement suits.[108] Moreover, the interoperability of IoT devices creates uncertainty as to data ownership. Fortunately, this may be overcome by strategic IP policies. Businesses are able to protect their IoT devices and data flow by patenting:

- the data structures and how they are uniquely accessed and used;

- the protocol over which the data is transmitted;

- the topology management schema of the connected devices creating the data;

- the physical connections and the facilitation of data flow through devices/connections;

- the security methods that protect the IoT device and prevent unauthorized access to data; and

- the improved intelligence or results that can be obtained via the IoT data.[109]

Patenting IoT devices and data flow through them has been gaining market popularity with companies applying for patents with the IoT specifically in mind.[110] A recent patent search revealed approximately 62,000 patents that specifically mention the "Internet of Things."[111]

Alice Corp. v. CLS Bank provides an example of an IoT-related patent litigation. The central issue of the case was whether the "invention," a computerized scheme for mitigating "settlement risk," could be patented.[112] The program provided a way for each party to a transaction to know that the other party was able to fulfill its obligation.

---

108. Rob Bloom, *Protecting Your Intellectual Property in the Internet of Things*, IPWATCHDOG (Oct. 5, 2017), www.ipwatchdog.com/2017/10/05/protecting-intellectual-property-internet-of-things/id=88653/ (detailing that various industries are providing services of other industries, such as car companies installing home networks to allow for wireless overnight updates, and power companies connecting homes to smart grids whilst also providing surveillance networks as enticement).

109. Root & Cronin, *supra* note 3.

110. *Id.*

111. *See* https://patents.google.com/?q=%22Internet+of+things%22 (as of Jan. 1, 2018).

112. Alice Corp. Pty. Ltd. v. CLS Bank Int'l, 573 U.S. 208 (2014).

The patent at issue had three parts: 1) the method of exchanging obligations; 2) the computer system to carry out the exchange; and 3) the program code.

The U.S. Supreme Court applied the *Mayo* standard[113] to assess the patent. Under the two-part *Mayo* test, a court must determine 1) if the claim at issue is directed to a patent-ineligible concept, and 2) whether the elements, both in part and combined, transform the nature of the claim into a patentable invention.[114] The Court found that the claims at issue were patent-ineligible concepts because they were an abstract idea of intermediated settlement. The Court in *Alice* ruled that intermediated settlement is an abstract idea beyond the scope of the statute.

The Court further found that the claim failed the second part of the *Mayo* test because the use of the computer is simply a generic implementation and does not contain a transformative property of the abstract idea. The Court relied on *Gottschalk v. Benson*, in which the patent at issue was an algorithm for "a general-purpose digital computer."[115] The Court had found that an algorithm itself was an abstract idea and that in order for the patent to be eligible, it needed to have an inventive concept which it did not have, because this algorithm could be carried out in existing computers that had long been in use. The Court stated that just because something can be used on a computer it is not necessarily an inventive or new procedure.

Applying *Benson*, the Court in *Alice* stated that if the invention is merely applying something onto a computer in order to "implement" it, then it is not transforming an abstract idea; something more is needed to transform an existing technology or process. Therefore, the Court held that the patent at issue was ineligible because it was an abstract idea without any type of transformative aspect to it.

Similarly, *Fitbit Inc. v. Aliphcom* provides another example of a case examining patent eligibility of IoT devices.[116] Aliphcom, doing business as "Jawbone," sued Fitbit for multiple patent infringements in an attempt to block Fitbit from importing Jawbone's products into the United States. The Administrative Law Judge (ALJ) from the International Trade Commission concluded that the patents sought

---

113.   Mayo Collaborative Servs. v. Prometheus Labs., Inc., 132 S. Ct. 1289 (2012).

114.   *Alice Corp.*, *supra* note 112, at 217–18.

115.   *Id.* (citing Gottschalk v. Benson, 93 S. Ct. 253 (1972)).

116.   *In re Certain Activity Tracking Devices, Systems, and Components Thereof*, Inv. No. 337-TA-963, Order No. 54 (Apr. 27, 2016). *See also* Kevin P. Moran, *International Trade Commission Invalidates Patents to Fitness Monitoring Systems as Ineligible Under Section 101*, NAT'L L.J. (May 6, 2016).

to create "a monopoly on the abstract ideas of collecting and monitoring sleep and other health-related data" and that the patents had no innovative concept within them. The ALJ found that Jawbone was attempting to patent systems for organizing human activity, which is already performed by humans, through the use of computer technology. As discussed in *Alice*, simply using a technological device to do the same thing that others can do without any improvement or change is not considered an eligible patent.[117] This first case was decided against Jawbone.

The following year, Fitbit sued Jawbone, claiming that Jawbone infringed on three of Fitbit's patents for technology that collects heart rate information from users of Fitbit products.[118] The court, however, determined that two of the three claims involved ineligible patents. The court deemed the patents ineligible because they did not represent an inventive concept but rather just represented an abstract idea applied to the technology.[119] As for the third patent—which covered specific technology that improved the collection and reporting of heart rate data—the court found that it did represent an inventive concept and was thus eligible for patent protection. Ultimately, all other litigation between the two companies was resolved through a confidential settlement and no official judgment was made as to any other patent or trade secret issues.[120]

As demonstrated in *Alice* and *Fitbit*, using IoT technology as part of the patent process alone does not guarantee a valid patent; transformative uses are required in order for a court to find patent validity. Thus, patents for IoT, and technology in general, require more innovation.

In another case, *DDR Holdings, LLC v. Hotels.com*, the court again cautioned that not every claim that addresses Internet-centric challenges are eligible for patent protection, although it found that the claims at issue in this case did.[121] The claims were "directed to a specific method of advertising and content distribution that was

---

117.   *Id.*; *Alice Corp.*, *supra* note 112, at 223.
118.   Fitbit Inc. v. Aliphcom, 16-cv-00118-BLF (2017), 2017 WL 3129989. *See also* Matthew Renda, *Judge Pares Down Fitbit's Patent War with Jawbone*, COURTHOUSE NEWS SERV. (Mar. 7, 2017), www.courthousenews. com/judge-pares-fitbits-patent-war-jawbone/.
119.   *Id.*
120.   Anthony Dominic, *Fitbit and Jawbone Reach Settlement, End Litigation*, CLUB INDUS. (Dec. 12, 2017), www.clubindustry.com/news/ fitbit-and-jawbone-reach-settlement-end-litigation.
121.   DDR Holdings, LLC v. Hotels.com, L.P., 773 F.3d 1245, 1258 (Fed. Cir. 2014) (in an infringement suit involving patents created to generate a composite web page, the court affirmed that the patents were eligible and reversed the wrongly invalidated patent).

previously unknown and never employed on the Internet before." Distinguishing *Ultramercial, Inc. v. Hulu, LLC*,[122] the court found that the claims in *DDR Holdings, LLC* were specific in their interactions with the Internet. Furthermore, the claims were manipulated to yield a desired result in that the solution offered by the patent amounted to an inventive concept for the resolution for a particular Internet-centric problem.[123]

Advancements in data collection through the use of IoT devices and aggregation of datasets derived therefrom provide value to patent holders of the so-called "data-generating patents"—"patents on inventions involving technologies that by design generate valuable data through their operation."[124] Data-generating inventions are inventions that create mass amounts of data beyond the invention itself, such as IoT devices, or even social media platforms, as the data generated does not relate to the functioning of the IoT itself but instead relates to the end-user.[125] The concept of data-generating patents requires collaboration between patent law and trade secret law, a relatively new phenomenon.[126] Under traditional notions, a patent destroys a trade secret, but here, a patent that covers the IoT and the data flow through it, creates a situation in which, for twenty years, the patentee has complete market power over the invention and the data generated thereby.[127] However, once the patent expires, trade secret law kicks in to protect the data held by the patentee and continues the market power held by the patentee over the data.[128] This intersection of patent law and trade secret law is unique to data-generating inventions.

§ 6:4　　Conclusion

The nature of the IoT is such that there are multiple entities operating as stakeholders in data. These stakeholders include device manufacturers, applications developers, cloud service providers, and third-party data purchasers.[129] Thus, multiple entities may claim exclusive

---

122.　　Ultramercial, Inc. v. Hulu, LLC, 772 F.3d 709 (Fed. Cir. 2014).

123.　　*Id.*

124.　　Brenda M. Simon & Ted Sichelman, *Data Generating Patents*, 111 Nw. U. L. Rev. 377, 378 (2017).

125.　　*Id.* ("In contrast, data-generating inventions by their operation and use may generate large amounts of data beyond the invention itself—for instance, data about users, other persons, or even the world in general—that can then be used to improve the operation of the invention or employed in a field entirely distinct from the invention.").

126.　　*Id.*

127.　　*Id.*

128.　　*Id.*

129.　　Paez & La Marca, *supra* note 1, at 66.

ownership rights in order to exploit commercial data collected by IoT devices; however, through strong contractual agreements that properly allocate rights in data ownership, and through IP protection and policies, businesses can ensure exclusive ownership of IoT data.

Chapter 7

Consumer Protection Litigation

§ 7:1   Overview

This chapter examines harms to consumers caused by IoT devices, including physical injury and discrimination. In the context of product liability, the chapter explores theories of liability, causes of action, and standing. With respect to discrimination, this chapter discusses how both economic and non-economic discrimination can occur as the result of the collection of IoT data, as well as the efforts that can mitigate such effects.

§ 7:2   Theories of Liability

Consumer use of IoT devices grows substantially each year, with some experts predicting that more than 36 billion IoT products will be connected by the year 2021.[1] This exponential growth gives rise to questions about allocation of liability in relation to the risks associated with the safety of the products.[2] Traditionally, the United States has relied on the civil tort system and the codification of new laws and regulations to ensure product safety.[3] Such legal theories of product liability stemming from tort actions include (1) strict liability, (2) negligence, or (3) breach of warranty.[4] Currently, these theories of liability are still critical in the analysis of consumer rights in connection with IoT products.

§ 7:2.1   *Chain of Liability in Product Liability Cases*

Modern technologies require a reevaluation of the traditional chain of liability used to establish product defect claims. Historically, in order to hold a party liable for a product defect, the consumer first looked to the chain of distribution of that product.[5] Typically, the consumer would trace liability through each business in the chain from the retailer, distributor, or product manufacturer, to the providers of raw materials or component part manufacturers.[6] However, with modern technologies, product liability can attach to many additional businesses in the chain such as programmers, software developers, and sensor manufacturers. Although products relying on this extended chain of liability have existed among consumers for more than a generation, these once atypical objects and products, not commonly owned or interacted with by consumers, are now a regular part of a modern consumer's daily use and interaction.[7]

By way of example, when a defect in an x-ray machine's software emitted a deadly dose of radiation, patients treated by the device

---

1.   Erin Bosman, Julie Park & Benjamin Kage, *Connected Devices Bring New Product Liability Challenges*, LAW360 (Jan. 5, 2018), https://media2.mofo.com/documents/180105-connected-devices-liability-changes.pdf.

2.   Benjamin Powers, *Who Is Responsible When the Internet of Things Malfunctions?*, DAILY DOT (July 9, 2018), www.dailydot.com/layer8/internet-things-liability/.

3.   *Id.*

4.   Benjamin C. Dean, *Strict Products Liability and the Internet of Things: An Exploration of Strict Products Liability and the Internet of Things*, CTR. FOR DEMOCRACY & TECH. (Apr. 2018), https://cdt.org/files/2018/04/2018-04-16-IoT-Strict-Products-Liability-FNL.pdf.

5.   THE INTERNATIONAL COMPARATIVE LEGAL GUIDE TO PRODUCT LIABILITY 2018 (16th ed., Global Legal Grp.).

6.   *Id.*

7.   Powers, *supra* note 2.

brought a product liability suit involving an extended chain of distribution.[8] The victims initially brought suit against both the oncology center and the manufacturer of the x-ray machine because the true cause of the malfunction was still largely unknown at the introduction of the lawsuit.[9] Ultimately, each defendant settled out of court for an undisclosed amount.[10] In similar fashion, consumers today will undoubtedly utilize the extended chain-of-liability theory to hold businesses liable for IoT product defects.

Autonomous vehicles provide a noteworthy example of complications that arise in IoT product defect cases. Plaintiffs injured by products in the autonomous vehicle industry would most certainly need to make use of the extended chain of liability theory to hold businesses liable for defects.[11] Theoretically, although autonomous vehicles are touted to be safer than human-driven vehicles, accidents will still occur. In 2018, a woman was struck and killed by an Uber-owned self-driving car.[12] Uber settled the claim with the victim's estate and suspended testing of the autonomous cars until a full investigation into the cause of the accident could be completed.[13] Therefore, lingering questions remain surrounding how the legal system will apportion liability for injuries caused by autonomous cars in the future.[14]

---

8. *Id. See also* Adam Fabio, *Killed by a Machine: The Therac-25*, HACKADAY (Oct. 26, 2015), https://hackaday.com/2015/10/26/killed-by-a-machine-the-therac-25/.

9. *Fatal Radiation Dose in Therapy Attributed to Computer Mistake*, N.Y. TIMES, June 21, 1986, www.nytimes.com/1986/06/21/us/fatal-radiation-dose-in-therapy-attributed-to-computer-mistake.html.

10. Nancy Leveson & Clark Turner, *An Investigation of the Therac-25 Accidents*, IEEE COMP., vol. 26, no. 7 (July 1993), www.erenkrantz.com/Geeks/Therac-25/An%20Investigation%20of%20Therac-25%20Accidents.shtml.

11. Benjamin C. Dean, *Strict Products Liability and the Internet of Things: An Exploration of Strict Products Liability and the Internet of Things*, CTR. FOR DEMOCRACY & TECH. (Apr. 2018), https://cdt.org/files/2018/04/2018-04-16-IoT-Strict-Products-Liability-FNL.pdf.

12. Nathaniel Meyersohn & Matt McFarland, *Uber's Self-Driving Car Killed Someone. What Happened?*, CNN (Mar. 20, 2018), https://money.cnn.com/2018/03/20/news/companies/self-driving-uber-death/index.html; Paul J. Pearah, *Opening the Door to Self-Driving Cars: How Will This Change the Rules of the Road?*, 18 J. HIGH TECH. L. 38 (2017).

13. Scott Neuman, *Uber Reaches Settlement with Family of Arizona Woman Killed by Driverless Car*, NPR (Mar. 29, 2018), www.npr.org/sections/thetwo-way/2018/03/29/597850303/uber-reaches-settlement-with-family-of-arizona-woman-killed-by-driverless-car.

14. *Id.*

In accidents involving self-driving vehicles, establishing fault can be complicated.[15] In traditional vehicle product defect claims, liability for product defects may rest with the manufacturer, the parts manufacturer, or the dealership that sold the defective vehicle.[16] But, who should be liable when a fully autonomous car, capable of stopping at stop signs, traffic lights, and negotiating through traffic without human intervention, causes an accident?

Attorneys with experience in bringing lawsuits against car manufacturers indicate that liability may potentially rest with the vehicle's manufacturers, software providers, or the person behind the wheel at the time.[17] Some chief executive officers (CEOs) of autonomous car companies have suggested that liability for these fully self-driving cars must inherently fall on the manufacturer because the autonomous nature of the vehicle elicits no human intervention in its operation, leaving little room for defense lawyers to conscionably argue that the human passenger caused the accident.[18] Yet, Tesla's CEO, Elon Musk, who recently announced that its vehicles will soon be able to drive a pre-programmed route without any human input, was silent as to whether Tesla would assume liability for any accidents caused as a result of the new software. In fact, in the past, Musk has rejected the proposal that liability in these cases should lie with the manufacturer.[19]

Alternatively, liability may fall on vehicle owners if they cause the product to fail.[20] Further, owners may be targeted as an outlet for fault apportionment in the accident if the owner failed to update software, downloaded malware from unsecure sites, or assigned weak passwords that exposed the product at issue to hacking.[21] Still, others suggest that rather than searching for negligent parties in autonomous

---

15.   Ethan Baron, *Blame Game: Self-Driving Car Crash Highlights Tricky Legal Question*, SAN JOSE MERCURY NEWS (Jan. 23, 2018), www.mercurynews.com/2018/01/23/motorcyclist-hit-by-self-driving-car-in-s-f-sues-general-motors/.

16.   *Product Liability Claims Involving Defective Cars*, NOLO, www.nolo.com/legal-encyclopedia/product-liability-claims-defective-cars-29648.html.

17.   Sergei Lemberg is the quoted attorney. Tina Bellon, *Liability and Legal Questions Follow Uber Autonomous Car Fatal Accident*, INS. J. (Mar. 20, 2018), www.insurancejournal.com/news/national/2018/03/20/483981.htm.

18.   Jonathan M. Gitlin, *Elon Musk Promises Big New Tesla Autopilot Upgrade, but Is It Legal?*, ARS TECHNICA (Dec. 10, 2018), https://arstechnica.com/cars/2018/12/elon-musk-promises-autopilot-update-to-allow-for-no-driver-input-at-all/.

19.   *Id.*

20.   H. Michael O'Brien, *The Internet of Things: The Inevitable Collision with Product Liability*, JD SUPRA (July 16, 2015).

21.   *Id.*

car accidents, the legal system should instead apply strict liability theory with court-compelled insurance policies.[22] Another approach would be to hold each member of the autonomous car enterprise jointly and severally liable for actions of the group.[23] Here, the car would have its own legal personhood, so the car would be sued by the individual injured, and then the joint and severally liable insured group, including the owner of the car, would take part in the payout.[24] These possible scenarios represent the multitude of approaches that could develop for apportioning fault amongst the parties.

Due to the challenges in establishing liability, federal agencies are beginning to look at regulating the IoT market, as discussed in chapter 2. In May 2018, the Consumer Product Safety Commission (CPSC) held a hearing on IoT products to discuss emerging safety, privacy, and product liability issues arising from IoT technologies.[25] The hearing focused on concerns of industry leaders regarding developing standards for IoT device security and the suggestions for IoT-specific regulations.[26] During the hearing, both industry representatives and the CPSC expressed hesitancy to attempt to codify regulations and instead suggested the development of industry guidelines that would allow industry leaders to more thoroughly address quickly evolving IoT technologies.[27] Legislators are also interested in investigating the risks of IoT device security. In June 2018, the Smart IoT Act, discussed in chapter 2, called for a study and a report by the Secretary of Commerce on the state of IoT devices in the United States.[28]

Currently, a party can be held criminally liable for a defective product that causes serious harm or death when the party makes a misrepresentation to regulatory bodies or Congress regarding the product, destroys evidence, or fails to recall and replace products as

---

22. Benjamin C. Dean, *Strict Products Liability and the Internet of Things: An Exploration of Strict Products Liability and the Internet of Things*, CTR. FOR DEMOCRACY & TECH. (Apr. 2018), https://cdt.org/files/2018/04/2018-04-16-IoT-Strict-Products-Liability-FNL.pdf.

23. *Id.*

24. *Id.*

25. Heather Bramble & Thomasina E. Poirot, *The Internet of Things, Product Safety, and Product Liability: A Risky Combination* (May 23, 2018), www.allaboutadvertisinglaw.com/2018/05/the-internet-of-things-product-safety-and-product-liability-a-risky-combination.html.

26. Russell J. Chibe, *Regulating the Internet of Things: CPSC Holds Public Hearing to Address the Risk of Hazardization in Smart Products*, FAEGRE DRINKER BIDDLE & REATH LLP (July 10, 2018), www.lexology.com/library/detail.aspx?g=22581197-ad35-4814-9d72-16610f2e1177.

27. *Id.*

28. H.R. 6032, 115th Cong., State of Modern Application, Research, and Trends of IoT Act, www.govtrack.us/congress/bills/115/hr6032.

the law requires.[29] In some foreign jurisdictions, criminal liability attaches to companies when a product is outright unsafe rather than just defective.[30] In the future, there may be a point at which liability transfers from civil claims to criminal prosecution depending upon the severity of harm caused by the IoT object.[31] The evolution of this doctrine could eventually lead to criminal charges against companies when a known defect in their product poses a severe risk to the public.[32]

§ 7:3   Drafting Around Liability

In order to reduce their potential liability, manufactures of IoT products will need to craft terms of service agreements that are enforceable upon the end-users of their products.[33] Since IoT products may be shared, resold, or reused by consumers, problems will arise for companies attempting to ensure each consumer receives notice and subsequently consents to their terms of service, regardless of when or how they obtained the relevant IoT device.[34] If a company is unable to enforce their terms of service with each consumer within the chain of resale or usage, they will face a number of legal risks including class action lawsuits.[35] For example, when consumers with Nest smart thermostats experienced a malfunction that caused the temperatures in their homes to plummet, they were required to settle their claims for damages through arbitration, rather than in court, pursuant to the terms of service they had previously agreed to.[36]

---

29.   Frank Vandall, *Should Manufacturers and Sellers of Lethal Products Be Subject to Criminal Prosecution?*, 17 WIDENER L.J. 877, 888 (2008).

30.   *Criminal Liability for Defective Products: A Refresher*, HERBERT SMITH FREEHILLS (Dec. 3, 2015), https://sites-herbertsmithfreehills.vuturevx.com/20/8765/landing-pages/criminal-liability-for-defective-products-e-briefing.pdf.

31.   Michael Kassner, *IoT and Liability: Who Pays When Things Go Wrong?*, TECHREPUBLIC (Aug. 1, 2018), www.techrepublic.com/article/iot-and-liability-who-pays-when-things-go-wrong/. *See also* Vandall, *supra* note 29.

32.   For example, it has been suggested by some commentators that malfunctioning traffic lights could result in criminal liability due to the seriousness of the possible accident. *See id.*

33.   Mauricio Paez & Mike La Marca, *The Internet of Things: Emerging Legal Issues for Businesses*, 43 N. KY. L. REV. 29, 60 (2016).

34.   *Id.*

35.   Nick Belton, *Nest Thermostats Glitches Leaves Users in the Cold*, N.Y. TIMES, Jan. 13, 2016, www.nytimes.com/2016/01/14/fashion/nest-thermostat-glitch-battery-dies-software-freeze.html.

36.   *Id.* Buried deep in Nest's 8,000-word service agreement is a section called "Disputes and Arbitration" which prohibits customers from suing the company or joining a class action suit. Instead, disputes are settled through arbitration.

§ 7:3.1 *Shrinkwrap Contracts vs. Clickwrap Contracts*

Replacing shrinkwrap contracts with clickwrap contracts is one method of strengthening the enforceability of a company's terms of service agreement.[37] Shrinkwrap contracts are those terms of service agreements bound to a product within the packaging.[38] With traditional software products, courts have typically enforced these terms of service agreements even though they may be contracts of adhesion.[39] Yet, in the world of IoT, these shrinkwrap contracts containing the product's terms of service may be insufficient due to the fact that IoT devices are more likely to be resold, reused, or shared.[40] Thus, subsequent users may not have adequate notice of the terms of service. Some commentators recommend using electronic terms of service in the form of websites, apps, or the product's own interface to bind subsequent users to their terms.[41] This, however, requires IoT companies to find ways to incorporate their terms of service into the functionality of their devices.[42]

Another option is a clickwrap contract in which users must assent to the terms of service by clicking a box that indicates that the consumer agrees to those terms. Courts are more likely to uphold these types of contracts because consumers must expressly assent to the terms therein in order to use the service or device. Obtaining this express consent by way of a clickwrap contract will therefore likely become increasingly important for companies; it provides proof that an end user of an IoT product, despite the fact that they may not be the original purchaser, still consented to the company's terms of service.[43]

§ 7:4 Product Liability

Product liability includes holding a manufacturer, software company, distributor, or responsible seller liable for injuries caused by a defective product.[44] Typically, to recover under product liability,

---

37. Shrinkwrap and clickwrap contracts are also discussed in chapter 5.
38. Batya Goodman, *Honey, I Shrink-Wrapped the Consumer: The Shrink Wrap Agreement as an Adhesion Contract*, 21 CARDOZO L. REV. 319 (1999).
39. *Id.*
40. Paez & La Marca, *supra* note 33.
41. *Id.*
42. *Id.*
43. *Id.*
44. Benjamin C. Dean, *Strict Products Liability and the Internet of Things: An Exploration of Strict Products Liability and the Internet of Things*, CTR. FOR DEMOCRACY & TECH. (Apr. 2018), at 9, https://cdt.org/files/2018/04/2018-04-16-IoT-Strict-Products-Liability-FNL.pdf.

a product must cause harm to a person or property.[45] Under product liability, the imposed standard is categorized as negligence, strict liability, or breach of warranty.[46] Negligence occurs when a manufacturer breaches a duty of care owed to the consumer of the product. Strict liability arises when a failure caused by a product's design defect, manufacturing defect, or inadequate warnings of potential danger[47] and requires only that an unreasonably dangerous product caused the harm.[48] Further, liability attaches even when the manufacturer lacks knowledge of the risk of harm.[49] Finally, breach of warranty is a "violation of an agreement between a seller and a buyer as to the condition, quality, or title of real property or goods, or to an assurance about the quality of the item sold."[50]

§ 7:4.1   *Challenges Regarding Software Liability*

Unlike its application in contract law discussed in chapter 5, under tort law, software is not typically considered a "product." Instead, most courts consider software to be a "service," allowing software providers protection from traditional strict liability claims for defects. But, with the context of IoT, software is embedded in the product, rather than used on its own accord. Thus, the debate continues about whether a software vendor can be liable in the product defect chain for the software inherent in the IoT product itself.[51]

Inclusion would lead to a host of still unanswered questions, such as whether software should be considered a distinct component part of the IoT product or an altogether different product that is independent from the device itself. If the software is considered a component, then the provider of each component part is held strictly liable for defects in the IoT product together with the end-product manufacturer. Under this component part theory, software manufactures would be held strictly liable for their products regardless of negligence, even when these software suppliers have no control over how their components were used by the manufacturer.[52]

---

45.   *Id.* at 9; Michael L. Rusted & Thomas H. Koenig, *The Tort of Negligent Enablement of Cybercrime*, 20 BERKELEY TECH. L.J. 1553 (2005).

46.   *Id.*; defective warning is discussed *infra* section 7:4.2.

47.   Dean, *supra* note 44.

48.   *Id.* at 10. *See also* Wendy Knox Everette, Security Vulnerabilities, the Current State of Consumer Protection Law, & How IOT Might Change It, YouTube, www.youtube.com/watch?v=EFGcZwjw9Q4&index=4.

49.   *See* Failure to warn as basis of liability under doctrine of strict liability in tort, 53 A.L.R.3d 239, 2a.

50.   Breach of Warranty, LEGAL INFO, INST., CORNELL L. SCH., www.law.cornell.edu/wex/breach_of_warranty (last viewed Apr. 20, 2020).

51.   Paez & La Marca, *supra* note 33, at 57.

52.   *Id.*

Strict liability is especially threatening to software providers since it is nearly impossible "to guarantee that software of any complexity contains no errors."[53] As liability concerns surrounding software providers is further explored, it is likely that courts will choose to consider IoT software as property as opposed to a service. For this to occur, courts must continue to expand their ever-growing definition of tangible property to include software; to do otherwise would exclude software from product liability.[54]

Another factor contributing to the ability of software companies to escape product liability is that under current law, the product at issue must cause harm, death, or property damage.[55] For example, if a defective wireless router leaks a person's personal information, the harm caused would be largely economic, resulting in no actual physical harm or property damage. Breaches of this nature cause an invasion of privacy without leaving physical injury, making the existing framework for liability inapplicable.[56] Although harm caused by a defective router leaking personal information may not be perfectly analogous to harm caused by software in a defective coffee maker that causes a fire and damages a consumer's kitchen, the impact of personal data breaches can be as devastating and far reaching as identity theft. Furthermore, the software in IoT devices sense "the world around us and affect that world in a direct physical manner." Thus, in the case of IoT products like pacemakers, thermostats, or home security systems, information that is stolen or accidentally exposed could lead to destruction of property or—even worse—loss of life.[57] Therefore, advocates for consumer safety argue that security breaches, like other products susceptible to product liability claims, should be monitored by the U.S. Consumer Product Safety Commission (CPSC). The CPSC's mission is to "protect against unreasonable risk of injury and death associated

---

53. *Id.* at 59 (quoting Uniform Comp. Info. Transactions Act, § 403 cmt. 3(a) (2002)).

54. Benjamin C. Dean, *Strict Products Liability and the Internet of Things: An Exploration of Strict Products Liability and the Internet of Things*, CTR. FOR DEMOCRACY & TECH. (Apr. 2018), https://cdt.org/files/2018/04/2018-04-16-IoT-Strict-Products-Liability-FNL.pdf. Product liability has extended the definition of intangible property to include "(gas), naturals (pets), real estate (house), and writings (navigational charts)."

55. *Id.*

56. Erin Bosman, Julie Park & Benjamin Kagel, *Connected Devices Bring New Product Liability Challenges* (Jan. 5, 2018), https://media2.mofo.com/documents/180105-connected-devices-liability-changes.pdf.

57. Bruce Schneier, *We Need Stronger Cybersecurity Law for the Internet of Things*, CNN (Nov. 10, 2018), www.cnn.com/2018/11/09/opinions/cybersecurity-laws-internet-of-things-schneier/index.html.

with consumer products."[58] Thus, there is a continual push to include security harms into the product liability framework.

§ 7:4.2   Manufacturing Defect

Manufacturing defects are random defects that result from the manufacturing process and manifest "when a product departs from its intended design and is more dangerous than consumers expect the product to be."[59] To bring a manufacturing defect claim, a plaintiff typically must show: (1) the manufacturer distributed a product, (2) that contained a manufacturing defect, (3) from which the plaintiff was harmed, and (4) the defect was a substantial factor in causing that harm.[60] Contrary to design defects, discussed next, proof of unreasonable danger is not required in most manufacturing defects claims.[61] In a pre-IoT manufacturing system, corporations used quality control processes to check for defects, limiting inspections to a random sampling of the product line within any given time-frame.[62] Errors in IoT device manufacturing context could include "oversights in coding, random malfunctions or bugs in the system."[63] Analogous to traditional manufacturing, IoT companies should establish regular quality control checks to identify software bugs or malfunctions in their systems.[64] Also, companies should consider that IoT technology used for automation and integration during the manufacturing process of other products can also inadvertently introduce defects into those products as well.[65] Therefore, further quality control processes and risk management systems must be implemented by manufacturers.[66]

---

58. Bosman, Park & Kagel, *supra* note 56.
59. Gerald Tietz, *Strict Products Liability, Design Defects and Corporate Decision-Making: Greater Deterrence Through Stricter Process*, 38 VILL. L. REV. 1361 (1993); Manufacturing Defect, LEGAL INFO, INST., CORNELL L. SCH., www.law.cornell.edu/wex/manufacturing_defect.
60. Sample jury instructions, California, CACI No. 1201, Strict Liability—Manufacturing Defect—Essential Factual Elements.
61. John F. Vargo, *The Emperor's New Clothes: The American Law Institute Adorns a "New Cloth" for Section 402A Products Liability Design Defects—A Survey of the States Reveals a Different Weave*, 26 U. MEM. L. REV. 493 (1996).
62. Tietz, *supra* note 59.
63. Bosman, Park & Kagel, *supra* note 56.
64. *Id.*
65. Jon Minnick, *IoT Brings Great Potential, But Increases Risk for Manufacturers*, MANUFACTURING.NET (Aug. 8, 2018), www.manufacturing.net/blog/2018/08/iot-brings-great-potential-increases-risk-manufacturers.
66. *Id.*

§ 7:4.3   *Design Defect*

Whereas a manufacturing defect applies to an error that occurs in production of one copy of a product, design defects impact the entire product line. To bring an action regarding a defective design, the consumer must prove that an alternative design is safer than the original and is both as economically feasible and as practical as the original design.[67] Courts use two different tests to determine whether there is a design defect: (1) the consumer expectation test; and (2) the risk-utility test. The consumer expectation test involves determining whether a reasonable consumer would expect the product to behave in a certain way. If the product's behavior is unexpected under a reasonable consumer's standard, a design defect likely exists.[68] The risk-utility test then involves conducting a cost-benefit analysis, weighing the cost associated with removing the defect through a complete redesign of the product against the social benefit of the removal of the defect.[69] Theoretically, if the cost of removing the defect through an alternative design is less than the gravity of the social risk from the original design, then the manufacturer should be held liable under the risk-utility test.[70]

Currently, one of the few cases in active litigation that addresses software liability and design defect in an IoT product is *Flynn v. FCA U.S. LLC*. In this case, the plaintiffs brought a design defect suit claiming that a Chrysler vehicle contained cybersecurity defects in its software controls.[71] The complaint was brought after an article published in *Wired* magazine exposed how two white hat hackers were able to remotely gain control of certain benign functions of the Chrysler vehicle, such as air conditioning, radio controls, and windshield wiper functions.[72] The hackers also gained control of more critical functions such as turning off the car's transmission, engine, and brakes. In response to the publication, Chrysler encouraged consumers to manually install a patch to protect their vehicles from such hacks. Despite the admitted vulnerabilities, the defendants, FCA (Chrysler Group) and Harman International Industries

---

67. Benjamin C. Dean, *Strict Products Liability and the Internet of Things: An Exploration of Strict Products Liability and the Internet of Things*, CTR. FOR DEMOCRACY & TECH. (Apr. 2018), https://cdt.org/files/2018/04/2018-04-16-IoT-Strict-Products-Liability-FNL.pdf.

68. *Id.*

69. *Id.*

70. *Id.*

71. Flynn v. F.C.A. U.S., LLC, 327 F.R.D. 206, 214 (S.D. Ill. 2018).

72. *See* Andy Greenberg, *Hackers Remotely Kill a Jeep on the Highway—With Me in It*, WIRED (July 21, 2015), www.wired.com/2015/07/hackers-remotely-kill-jeep-highway/.

(the software manufacturer), maintained that the vehicles contained no design defect and were safe.

The plaintiffs however, claimed that the vehicle's design was defective since the software allowed remote hacking of various critical and non-critical systems. The allegations included design flaws relating to the "uConnect" system in Chrysler vehicles that had yet to be remedied by the company at the time the lawsuit was filed. The parties disputed whether it was possible to hack into the Jeep's controls through its "uConnect" software. When the defendants moved for summary judgment in the case, the court denied the motion, finding a genuine dispute of fact as to whether the alleged defects existed. Subsequently, the class action was partially certified by an Illinois district court as to vehicle owners in Illinois, Michigan, and Missouri. This class was certified despite the defendants' contention that plaintiffs' do not have standing under Article III because the cars were never actually hacked by someone intending to cause harm. The defendants petitioned the Supreme Court to appeal the certification of the class.[73]

In 2020, the federal district court hearing *Flynn v. FCA U.S. LLC* agreed with the defendants and dismissed the case finding that the plaintiffs lacked standing. Plaintiffs subsequently appealed to the Seventh Circuit Court of Appeals where the case currently rests as of the time of this publication.

§ 7:4.4   *Product Failure*

Product failure occurs when a product malfunctions and causes personal injury or property damage. In January 2016, users of the Nest smart thermostat experienced a malfunction that caused the entire line of Nest thermostats to go offline.[74] The error was caused by a bug within a prior update to the software system that did not manifest as a problem until a month after being offered to the consumer.[75] The flaw resulted in extremely low household temperatures and pipe damage in areas of the nation where outdoor temperatures had dropped below freezing.[76] In response to the media attention surrounding the product's failure, Nest announced publicly the remote

---

73. *See Fiat Chrysler Asks Justice to Review Car-Hacking Cert. Order*, LAW360 (Oct. 11, 2018), www.law360.com/articles/1091459/fiat-chrysler-asks-justices-to-review-car-hacking-cert-order.

74. Nick Belton, *Nest Thermostats Glitches Leaves Users in the Cold*, N.Y. TIMES, Jan. 13, 2016, www.nytimes.com/2016/01/14/fashion/nest-thermostat-glitch-battery-dies-software-freeze.html.

75. Dan Misener, *Nest Thermostat Outages Highlight Issues with Smart Home Technology*, CBC (Jan. 19, 2016), www.cbc.ca/news/technology/nest-smart-home-problems-1.3410143.

76. Belton, *supra* note 74.

restoration of control of the devices to the owners.[77] Pursuant to the agreed-upon terms of service, customers had to use arbitration as opposed to the court system in order to obtain recourse for damages caused by the malfunction.[78]

§ 7:4.5   *Failure to Warn*

Individuals can also bring a suit for harms caused by inadequate warnings of the potential risks that may arise with regular use of a particular product.[79] For example, product warnings on a child car seat can preemptively specify that the seat will not protect children over a certain weight, or labels on coffee cups can clearly warn that the liquid within the cup is hot. Within the IoT context, failure-to-warn principles might inspire software companies to create better policies and practices to inform consumers about potential vulnerabilities within their software.[80] Commentators in this area point out that any proposed failure-to-warn requirements imposed on software companies should focus on commercial sellers of software and products as opposed to software hobbyists.[81] If liability for failure to warn eventually extends to the IoT, additional questions regarding the unique aspects of the industry will arise. For example, should IoT companies include both risk reduction warnings and informed choice warnings? Should warnings clearly state the ways in which a consumer can reduce potential risks of harm, or should they provide additional information, so consumers can make an informed decision of whether or not to use the product? In the context of informed choice warnings, should companies be required to warn consumers about insecurities that do not, or will not, have a patch designed to remedy the insecurity?

§ 7:4.6   *Ransomware*

"Ransomware" is a type of malicious software installed on a computer or server that is designed to block access to a computer system

---

77.   Todd Haselton, *Nest Thermostats Offline in Massive Outage During U.S. Heatwave*, TECHNOBUFFALO (July 26, 2016), www.technobuffalo. com/2016/07/26/nest-thermostats-offline-in-massive-outage-during-u-s-heatwave/.

78.   Belton, *supra* note 74.

79.   Hildy Bowbeer, Wendy Lumish & Jeffrey Cohen, *Warning! Failure to Read This Article May Be Hazardous to Your Failure to Warn Defense*, 27 WM. MITCHELL L. REV. 439 (2000).

80.   *See* Wendy Knox Everette, *Security Vulnerabilities, the Current State of Consumer Protection Law, & How IOT Might Change It*, YOUTUBE, https://www.youtube.com/watch?v=EFGcZwjw9Q4&index=4.

81.   *Id.*

until a ransom is paid, usually in the form of bitcoin.[82] For example, in 2016, a hospital in California suffered a cybersecurity attack where its computer system was held hostage.[83] Hospital employees were unable to digitally access patient files during a period of ten days.[84] Under this pressure, the hospital paid $17,000 to the hackers to regain control of their computer system.[85] While the hospital attested that no patient information was stolen, that risk was certainly apparent. Furthermore, other institutions could also be vulnerable as indicated by figures in a 2010 report demonstrating that more than 150 medical institutions detected either hacking activity or technology issues that put patient records at risk.[86]

In May 2017, malware named "WannaCry" infected computers in 150 nations through a vulnerability in Microsoft operating systems.[87] During the attack, hard drives were encrypted by ransomware that required the owner to pay a ransom for decryption of the computer. The computers remained inoperable unless the $300 ransom was paid. More than a hundred thousand computers were infected, including devices in U.K. hospitals, Russian train stations, and U.S. car factories.[88] Two months prior to this attack, Microsoft had released a patch designed to fix the issue; however, not all users downloaded the patch.[89]

In subsequent litigation resulting from the WannaCry malware, establishing liability may be a challenge. Should Microsoft be liable because their software allowed the bug? Should the developer of WannaCry be liable? Or, should the people responsible for updating

---

82. Fed. Bureau of Investigation, FBI Public Service Announcement, Alert No. 1-091516-PSA: Ransomware Victims Urged to Report Infections to Federal Law Enforcement 1 (Sept. 15, 2016), www.ic3.gov/media/2016/160915.aspx.

83. Jeff Stone, *Hackers' Ransom Attack on California Hospital More Proof Healthcare Cybersecurity Is Floundering*, INT'L BUS. TIMES (Feb. 17, 2016), www.ibtimes.com/hackers-ransom-attack-california-hospital-more-proof-healthcare-cybersecurity-2309720.

84. *Id.*

85. Alex Dobuzinskis & Jim Finkle, *California Hospital Makes Rare Admission of Hack, Ransom Payment*, REUTERS (Feb. 18, 2016), www.reuters.com/article/us-california-hospital-cyberattack/california-hospital-makes-rare-admission-of-hack-ransom-payment-idUSKCN0VS05M.

86. Stone, *supra* note 83.

87. *Id.*

88. Agamani Ghosh & India Ashok, *WannaCry: List of Major Companies and Networks Hit by Ransomware Around the Globe*, INT'L BUS. TIMES (May 16, 2017), www.ibtimes.co.uk/wannacry-list-major-companies-networks-hit-by-deadly-ransomware-around-globe-1621587.

89. *Id.*

the computers be liable because a software patch was made available, and yet they never used it? The resolution of these questions might shed light on how similar software vulnerabilities in IoT devices will be dealt with by the courts.

Many commentators believe Microsoft will avoid liability for the WannaCry malware pursuant to its licensing agreement with users that protects the company from subsequent security breaches and misuse of their product.[90] Traditionally, courts have enforced these types of license agreements. With WannaCry, the vulnerability stemmed from the failure of users to update the software using patches offered by Microsoft.[91] Thus, the Federal Trade Commission may bring a complaint against companies in the United States that failed to incorporate the updates and patches.[92] Although no notable lawsuits have been brought by consumers in reaction to the hack, the Department of Justice filed a criminal complaint in September 2018 against a Korean hacker, Park Jin Hoyk, for participating in three hacking events, including the WannaCry hack, the Sony hack in 2014, and a Bangladesh cyber bank theft.[93]

§ 7:4.7 Negligence

In addition to strict liability claims, consumers can also bring product liability claims under the theory of negligence. Liability for negligence arises when a company breaches its duty to take reasonable care and its product thereby causes harm. Traditionally, negligence requires a duty of care, breach of that duty, causation, and damages or injury based on the breach.[94] A company's duty of care is typically based on the industry standard. Because the standard of care has not been established for many IoT products, imposing liability on IoT companies under a negligence theory may be difficult.[95] Furthermore, the duty of care varies for each link in the distribution chain: design, manufacturing, and distribution.[96]

---

90. Jan Wolfe, *Post WannaCry Risks: Lawsuits Over Lax Cyber Attack Protection*, CARRIER MGMT. (May 17, 2017), www.carriermanagement. com/news/2017/05/17/167261.htm.

91. *Id.*

92. *Id.*

93. Brian Barrett, *DOJ Charges North Korean Hacker for Sony, WannaCry, and More*, WIRED (Sept. 6, 2018), www.wired.com/story/doj-north-korea-hacker-sony-wannacry-complaint/.

94. Charles Gueli, *The 4 Elements of Negligence You Need to Win Your Injury Claim*, INJURY CLAIM COACH (June 28, 2019), www.injuryclaimcoach. com/elements-of-negligence.html.

95. *Id.*

96. *Id.*

In 2015, Toy Talk settled a suit regarding a negligence claim for its product, Hello Barbie.[97] In this case, Mattel partnered with software company, Toy Talk, to create a doll enabled with artificial intelligence. This doll was designed to interact with children by responding to questions. During these interactions, conversations with children were recorded and uploaded to an app and subsequently to the Internet to search for responses to questions. Experts claimed that the recordings could be hacked and ultimately, the doll could be used as a surveillance device that continuously records discussions. Hackers could also access user account information and the audio files corresponding to that doll's account.

Plaintiffs in the class action claimed that defendant, Toy Talk, was negligent in designing this product because the manufacturers knew or should have known that the toy collects, stores, uses, and shares audio recordings of children without parental consent. Further, plaintiffs attested that the defendants violated their duty of care to fully represent the extent of the collection of such recordings. This duty of care was owed to the plaintiffs because they were foreseeable victims of the inadequate protection practices. Defendants breached this duty by failing to prevent the collection, storage, or sharing of these non-consensual recordings of children. The cause of action claimed that as a result of the defendants' breach of their duty, the plaintiffs suffered emotional distress regarding the safety and privacy of their children and families. Before the court could rule on the dispositive motions or the merits of the case, the plaintiffs agreed to dismiss the case with prejudice. While this suit was not seen to fruition, similar disputes are likely to arise in the future that will require courts to determine the standard of care for IoT products.

§ 7:5   Standing

Due to the nature of IoT devices, many product liability claims are likely to involve stolen or compromised data. One of the major challenges with litigating data cases is demonstrating standing by the plaintiff.[98] A plaintiff has Article III standing to sue when the

---

97.   Archer Hayes v. Toy Talk, 2015 WL 8304161 (Cal. Super.) (Trial Pleading) (Dec. 7, 2015). *See also* Leta Gorman, *The Era of the Internet of Things: Can Product Liability Laws Keep Up?*, 84 DEF. COUNS. J. 1, 9 (2017), www.iadclaw.org/securedocument.aspx?file=DCJArticles/The_Era_of_the_Internet_of_Things.pdf; Stacy Liberatore, *Is Barbie Spying on Your Children? Top Toy Firms Fined $835,000 for Tracking Online Activity and Collecting Personal Data of Children Under 13*, DAILY MAIL (Sept. 16, 2016), www.dailymail.co.uk/sciencetech/article-3787859/NY-settles-4-companies-stop-tracking-children-online.html.

98.   Gorman, *supra* note 97.

complaint alleges an injury (1) in fact, (2) fairly traceable to the actions of the defendant, and (3) redressable by a favorable decision of the tribunal.[99] Courts further attest that when the harm is concrete, there is an injury in fact.[100] This injury can be either actual or imminent. When there is actual data misuse, such as identity theft, standing is established because the plaintiff has suffered an actual injury in fact.[101]

The more uncertain issue arises when parties experience potential future misuse or fear of misuse of their content when their data has been stolen or compromised. A security breach with no actual misuse of the underlying data in many cases would lead to dismissal of the civil claim due to a lack of standing.[102] However, a plaintiff may be able to establish standing if a data breach is so egregious as to make the heightened risk of misuse "certainly impending."[103] Additionally, even if allegations of misuse of stolen data are made, the causal connection between a particular security breach and a particular incident of misuse may be challenging for plaintiffs to prove.

The Supreme Court held in *Spokeo v. Robins* that to establish standing in a claimed statutory privacy violation, here the Fair Credit Reporting Act, the plaintiff must show a "real" and "not abstract" injury.[104] However, the injury suffered does not necessarily have to be "tangible."[105] In this case, the defendant, Spokeo, Inc., operated a people search engine that organized white-pages listings, public records, and social media information. The plaintiff discovered the company had a profile for him, which contained incorrect information. He claimed that Spokeo failed to follow the Fair Credit Reporting Act, which required reporting companies to adhere to procedures ensuring maximum accuracy of consumer reports. The plaintiff's profile contained inaccurate information regarding his marital and parental status, assets, age, and education. The plaintiff initiated a class action suit on behalf of himself and similarly situated individuals with reports containing false information.

Although the District Court of Central California originally dismissed the claim for lack of standing, the Ninth Circuit found that

---

99. Spokeo, Inc. v. Robins, 136 S. Ct. 1540 (2016).

100. Massachusetts v. EPA, 549 U.S. 497 (2007).

101. Nikole Davenport, *Smart Washers May Clean Your Clothes, But Hacks Can Clean Out Your Privacy, and Underdeveloped Regulations Could Leave You Hanging on a Line*, 32 J. MARSHALL J. INFO. TECH. & PRIVACY L. 259 (2016).

102. *See Spokeo*, 136 S. Ct. 1540; Clapper v. Amnesty Int'l USA, 568 U.S. 1138 (2013).

103. Reilly v. Ceridian Corp., 664 F.3d 38 (3d Cir. 2011).

104. *Spokeo*, 136 S. Ct. at 1556.

105. *Id.*

the plaintiff's complaint sufficiently conferred Article III standing to survive a motion to dismiss.[106] The court held that the plaintiff did suffer an injury in fact traceable to the defendant's conduct. Further, the court stated that because the injury was traceable to the defendant's violations of the Fair Credit Reporting Act, the injury could be remedied by the court. The defendants alternatively petitioned for review by the Supreme Court.

At the Supreme Court, the plaintiff's standing was challenged because the injury in fact was not both "concrete *and* particularized."[107] In determining that the injury needs to be concrete but not necessarily tangible, the Court held that the violation of the procedural requirements of the Fair Credit Reporting Act may not result in harm. Thus, the case was remanded, resulting in the conclusion by the District Court that the plaintiff's alleged injuries were sufficiently concrete for Article III standing.[108]

Since the *Spokeo* decision, jurisdictions are split on the issue of standing.[109] The Seventh and Ninth Circuits have found standing for victims of data theft based on the increased risk of identity theft.[110] However, in the majority of jurisdictions, this increased risk of identity theft does not rise to the level of injury in fact to confer standing.[111]

Although decided before *Spokeo*, the Supreme Court's decision in *Clapper v. Amnesty International USA*[112] suggests an alternative standard for determining standing—"substantial risk." The dispute in *Clapper* included a statute that allowed for surveillance of non–"United States persons" believed to be outside the United States. Attorneys and media organizations argued that this statute was unconstitutional because in their course of business they were often likely to communicate with the people subject to the surveillance. The plaintiffs claimed that they established injury in fact because at some point in the future, they would inevitably communicate with someone under surveillance and would have to go to extensive lengths to maintain the confidentiality of the communication.

---

106.   Robins v. Spokeo, Inc., 742 F.3d 409 (9th Cir. 2014).
107.   Spokeo, Inc. v. Robins, 136 S. Ct. 1540 (2016) (emphasis in original).
108.   *See* Robins v. Spokeo, Inc., 867 F.3d 1108, 1118 (9th Cir. 2017).
109.   Bradford C. Mank, *Data Breaches, Identity Theft, and Article III Standing: Will the Supreme Court Resolve the Split in the Circuits?*, 92 NOTRE DAME L. REV. 1323, 1327 (2017).
110.   *Id.* at 1338, 1351. *See* Lewert v. P.F. Chang's China Bistro, Inc., 819 F.3d 963 (7th Cir. 2016); Pisciotta v. Old Nat'l Bancorp, 499 F.3d 629, 634 (7th Cir. 2007); Ruiz v. Gap, Inc., 622 F. Supp. 2d 908, 913 (N.D. Cal. 2009).
111.   Mank, *supra* note 109.
112.   Clapper v. Amnesty Int'l USA, 568 U.S. 1138 (2013).

The specific question before the Court was whether the possibility of injury to the lawyers and media organizations was too attenuated to give them Article III standing. The Supreme Court held that this injury was too speculative to satisfy the "certainly impending" standard. Here, the Court concluded that the injury was not imminent due to the speculative chain of possibilities regarding whether the government would target the plaintiffs' communications, whether authorization would be approved for those communications, and whether the communications would actually be acquired and intercepted. In addition, the money spent to prevent injury to communications was in reaction to a hypothetical future harm, and thus was not a sufficient injury to confer standing.

In the text of the decision, the majority explicitly clarified that they were not creating a new standard; however, footnote five in the decision appeared to state the opposite. In the footnote, the Court stated that plaintiffs were not required to show that a harm is absolutely certain to occur. Further, the Court indicated that the plaintiffs had failed to reach even the "substantial risk" standard. The passage in footnote five highlights that the Court may be willing to accept a showing of substantial risk by a plaintiff. The dissenters in this case preferred a broader interpretation similar to a showing that the harm is "reasonably likely" to occur.

§ 7:6   Class Actions

Assuming representatives for a class satisfy the standing requirement, class action procedures for IoT products are similar to traditional class actions. Class actions appeal to plaintiffs for a variety of factors such as: 1) enhancing efficiency, 2) improving access to the legal system, and 3) serving the public's interests.[113] Federal Rule of Civil Procedure 23 governs the requirements for class actions in federal court. Subsection A states that one representative of a class may sue on behalf of the other member if: 1) the class is so numerous that joinder of all members is impracticable; 2) there are questions of law or fact common to the class; 3) the claims or defenses of the representative are typical of all members of the class; and 4) the representative parties will fairly and adequately protect the interests of the class. Some plaintiffs prepare alternative classes or subclasses within their complaints to be sure that the court will certify the class as a group; subclasses must each have their own representative spokesperson. After a complaint is served upon a defendant, the court will confirm the class only if the above requirements are fulfilled.

---

113.   *Id.*

Like other lawsuits, class actions often result in settlements; however, unlike lawsuits involving single plaintiffs or a small number of plaintiffs, class actions often lead to outsized attorney's fees but little in compensation for those actually harmed. The recent class action against Tesla serves as a striking example. In this case, the plaintiffs (car owners) paid $5,000 for an enhanced autopilot feature, which, at the time of filing the lawsuit, was still non-functional.[114] After the enhanced autopilot feature became functional, the car unnecessarily engaged the brakes upon sensing a bridge on the road in the distance. Further, the car did not recognize large vehicles like buses or trucks when they were immediately in front of the car, so, the car increased speed regardless of the position of the large vehicle, requiring drivers to take control and save themselves from certain injury. Consumer dependency on this feature resulted in car accidents, as the autopilot feature failed to function as advertised. More importantly, customers could not depend on the car to drive on its own as promised and paid for.

According to plaintiffs, Tesla promised its customers that additional safety features would be available to make driving more stress-free. In the complaint, plaintiffs brought four claims on behalf of the proposed nationwide class. First, the plaintiffs claimed Tesla violated the California Unfair Competition Act by marketing and selling vaporware and advertising and selling non-existent safety features.[115] Furthermore, plaintiffs attested that Tesla had admitted in an online article to be only in the testing phase with these features but failed to state this admission on the website and marketing materials when promoting the product. Additional claims against Tesla consisted of California Consumer Legal Remedies Act, California False Advertising Act, and California Fraud by Concealment. The proposed nationwide class action brought the claims under California law because all wrongful conduct allegedly took place from within the Tesla headquarters in California. The plaintiffs' alternative classes consisted of similar state claims from the state of domicile of each plaintiff as well as where the plaintiffs had purchased the cars.

Approximately one year after plaintiffs filed the complaint, a motion for settlement was filed with the court.[116] Reports indicate

---

114.   Sheikh v. Tesla, Inc., Amended Complaint, No. 5:2017cv02193, Document 71 (N.D. Cal. 2018). *See also* Matt Drange, *Lawsuit Takes Aim at Tesla's Autopilot*, The Info. (Sept. 5, 2018), www.theinformation.com/briefings/dbe84d.

115.   Vaporware is defined as "[c]omputer software that is advertised but still nonexistent," *see* Dictionary.com.

116.   Kyle Hyatt, *Tesla Owners Could See a $20 Check from Autopilot Settlement*, CNET (May 1, 2018), www.cnet.com/roadshow/news/tesla-enhanced-autopilot-settlement-20-dollars/.

that Tesla offered $5,032,530 for all members of the class of "U.S. residents who purchased Enhanced Autopilot in connection with their purchase or lease of a Tesla Hardware 2 Model S or Model X vehicle delivered to them on or before September 30, 2017."[117] This settlement would be distributed among attorneys and cover class representative fees, as required under the procedure of a class action.[118] After all fees are covered, it is estimated that qualifying Tesla owners will receive $20 to $280 as reimbursement for an add-on feature that originally cost them $5,000 when they purchased their new Tesla.[119]

Commentators liken this payout to interest that a company has to pay on a loan to develop software.[120] Under this reasoning, the consumers that purchased vehicles with the advanced autopilot feature were essentially loaning the company money to develop the product. By selling the feature for an additional $5,000, Tesla was able to accumulate enough capital through purchasers to develop the feature in a fashion similar to a loan from a bank.[121] Therefore, some may view this settlement payment as interest on a loan used toward developing the software.[122] Unfortunately for consumers, they were unaware that the product was incomplete when they purchased the vehicles or when they attempted to use unsafe and dangerous software on public roadways. Consumers did not agree to loan the company the capital to develop the promised software.[123] Regardless of Tesla's reasoning for this process, the payout per class member seems extraordinarily low for the potential harm to consumers who relied on a product not yet ready for the market.

§ 7:7   Mass Torts

Consumers who experience physical harm or significant property damage often turn to mass tort litigation.[124] Different from class actions, plaintiffs in mass torts are part of a larger group of affected individuals, but each member is treated as an individual, contrary to class actions, where one representative stands in the position of all

---

117.   *Id.*
118.   *Id.*
119.   Fred Lambert, *Tesla Agrees to Partially Reimburse People Who Bought Autopilot 2.0 in $5 Million Settlement of Class Action Lawsuit* (May 1, 2018), https://electrek.co/2018/05/01/tesla-autopilot-reimburse-delayed-features-settlement-class-action-lawsuit/.
120.   *Id.*
121.   *Id.*
122.   *Id.*
123.   *Id.*
124.   Mark Raffman & Amanda Russo, *Mitigating Transactional Risk in the Internet of Things*, 21 J. PRIVATE EQUITY 65 (2018).

members of the class.[125] Mass tort actions tend to occur when the qualifications for a class action are not met.[126] For example, when the specific incident among plaintiffs was too varied, the group of plaintiffs would fail to meet the requirements for a class action but could potentially litigate under a mass tort action.[127]

This type of litigation can be utilized by consumers experiencing a variety of IoT device defects.[128] The hallmark of a mass tort is that the claim of each plaintiff can be similar, but vary slightly, and the plaintiffs can aggregate claims.[129] For example, if an IoT device was used to manage a city dam and the device experienced a malfunction that released water causing flooding throughout the city, the plaintiffs might bring a mass tort against the company that manufactures the IoT device.[130] Because each plaintiff would be at an equal risk of harm resulting from the flood, the claims of each plaintiff would be similar, but unlike a class action suit, the claims would not be brought together.[131] Commentators indicate that as the value of damage to the plaintiffs increases, the plaintiffs would have no incentive to file class actions and instead would initiate mass tort claims in order to allow full recovery from damage caused by IoT devices.[132]

§ 7:8   Discrimination Based on IoT Data

With the development of new IoT technologies, certain companies accumulate vast amounts of consumer data and information. The use of this information by companies ranges from benevolent assumptions to discriminatory practices. Examples include: 1) collecting data that allow inferences to be made about a person; 2) linking datasets for consumer profiling purposes; and 3) data sharing with third parties who then combine information with other datasets.[133]

---

125.   Greg M. Zipes, *After Amchem and Ahearn: The Rise of Bankruptcy Over the Class Action Option for Resolving Mass Torts on a Nationwide Basis, and the Fall of Finality*, 1998 DET. C. L. REV. 7.

126.   *Id.*

127.   *Id.*

128.   Tarifa B. Laddon & Blake A. Angelino, *Medical Device Litigation the "Internet of Things" Is Coming*, 12 DRI IN-HOUSE DEF. Q. 26 (Summer 2017).

129.   Zipes, *supra* note 125.

130.   *Id.*

131.   *Id.*

132.   Sergio J. Campos & Howard M. Erichson, *The Future of Mass Torts*, 159 U. PA. L. REV. ONLINE 231 (2011).

133.   Sandra Wachter, *Normative Challenges of Identification in the Internet of Things: Privacy, Profiling, Discrimination, and the GDPR*, 34 COMPUT. L. & SEC. REV. 436 (2017), www.researchgate.net/publication/321959135_Normative_Challenges_of_Identification_in_the_Internet_of_Things_Privacy_Profiling_Discrimination_and_the_GDPR.

The sharing of data collected by the IoT opens consumers' personal information to anyone with access, which in turn permits inferences about the consumer. For example, data from a Fitbit can be used to make conclusions about an individual's impulsiveness in addition to an inability to delay gratification.[134] Both of these characteristics may be inferred from a consumer's physical exercise habits in relation to alcohol use, erratic eating behavior, cigarette smoking, high credit card debt, and low credit scores.[135] Fitbit trackers can also identify a lack of sleep, which is linked to poor psychological well-being, health-related issues, poor cognitive performance, and emotions such as anger, depression, fear, and sadness.[136]

The use of web users' information through monitoring purchasing history, tweets, demographics, and location, combined with data received from other sources, results in the creation of advanced profiles that an employer or landlord might use to deny someone a job or housing.[137] People in positions of power, such as potential employers, may reject candidates with undesirable traits. This type of arranging and selecting individuals based on certain characteristics is not protected under anti-discrimination laws, as there is no requirement that employers refrain from discriminating based on impulsivity or other similar features.[138]

Information collection is utilized more effectively when multiple IoT devices are combined and linked together. However, as consumers increasingly link their devices to one another, the risk of discrimination increases as a more detailed profile is created through all the information collected.[139] For example, by linking accounts, insurance companies have access to a fuller picture of an individual—to include information that the individual might never have previously disclosed.[140] This information includes, at times, sensitive facts like health data accumulated by linked IoT devices.[141]

Using such information may result in the loss of opportunities for consumers who are deemed unworthy due to the inferences made

---

134.   *Id.* at 442.
135.   *Id.*
136.   *Id.*
137.   David Talbot, *Data Discrimination Means the Poor May Experience a Different Internet*, MIT TECH. REV. (Oct. 9, 2013), www.technology review.com/s/520131/data-discrimination-means-the-poor-may-experience-a-different-internet/.
138.   Scott R. Peppet, *Regulating the Internet of Things: First Steps Toward Managing Discrimination, Privacy, Security, and Consent*, 93 TEX. L. REV. 85, 125 (2014).
139.   *Id.*
140.   Talbot, *supra* note 137.
141.   *Id.*

from their information.[142] For example, customers that share characteristics with other "bad" individuals may be wrongly denied opportunities.[143] For instance, credit card companies lowered the credit limits of customers because they shopped at the same stores as customers with poor repayment histories.[144] Other credit card companies flagged consumers as having a greater credit risk because their cards were used for payments for marriage counselling, therapy, or tire repairs because the company had credit issues with other customers who used the cards for similar payments.[145] Greater government scrutiny over credit companies may work to reduce these lost opportunities.[146] Also, consumers included incorrectly in a group of so-called "bad customers" could bring legal action to receive statutory damages from remedial torts.[147]

Companies that accumulate IoT data and use it to eliminate job applicants with undesirable characteristics may unintentionally walk the line toward illegal discrimination when that information relates to protected classes such as race, gender, and age.[148] For example, this foray into illegal discrimination may arise when an employer categorizes a person as "financially challenged," based upon assumptions about a person's race, employment status, smoking history, and parental status. Ultimately, these determinations will be in conflict with existing laws banning certain forms of discrimination.[149] Also, the algorithms used to determine whether someone is a "bad customer" may stem from discriminatory information indicating an individual's race, religion, age, or gender, all of which were collected from IoT device profiles and user habits.[150]

---

142.   Kate Crawford & Jason Schultz, *Big Data and Due Process: Toward a Framework to Redress Predictive Privacy Harms*, 55 B.C. L. REV. 93 (2014).

143.   Big Data: A Tool for Inclusion or Exclusion?, FTC Report (Jan. 2016), www.ftc.gov/system/files/documents/reports/big-data-tool-inclusion-or-exclusion-understanding-issues/160106big-data-rpt.pdf.

144.   *Id.*

145.   *Id.*

146.   Crawford & Schultz, *supra* note 142.

147.   *Id.*

148.   Peppet, *supra* note 138.

149.   Nikole Davenport, *Smart Washers May Clean Your Clothes, But Hacks Can Clean Out Your Privacy, and Underdeveloped Regulations Could Leave You Hanging on a Line*, 32 J. MARSHALL J. INFO. TECH. & PRIVACY L. 259 (2016). "For instance, algorithmic scores for 'financially challenged' may include data points that also indicate the person's race, whether she is a single-mom, employment status, smoking history, and more. An employer, insurance company, or an intended landlord could potentially use these assessments, built upon data gathered from IoT devices, in a way that interferes with existing law."

150.   *Id.*

§ 7:8.1   *Economic Discrimination*

Data from IoT devices can also facilitate economic discrimination. For example, some car insurance companies provide lower rates to consumers that allow a tracking device to monitor their driving. The companies require that an app or plug-in device be used to monitor driving. Rates then may be charged based on a variety of factors such as time of day of driving, amount of driving, and any sudden changes in speed while driving.

It is not difficult to imagine an antidiscrimination law that effectively banned this practice of evaluating risk.[151] Currently, insurers are permitted to charge different rates to different customers depending upon the expected risk and whether a customer will be expensive to insure. Lenders can also charge more interest for questionable debtors. The level of detail provided by IoT devices will allow differentiation that is so distinct, it may begin to resemble the illegal forms of discrimination previously addressed herein.[152]

§ 7:8.2   *Application and Mitigation of Discrimination*

One challenge with preventing unintentional discrimination in the context of the IoT arises from the increased reliance on Artificial Intelligence (AI) software that uses both traditional information, such as work experience and education, and information obtained from IoT devices to make decisions.[153] A system set to prefer certain characteristics for a position may run afoul of antidiscrimination laws.[154] Left unchecked or unmonitored, the software may inadvertently make discriminatory decisions via its programs.[155]

In reaction to this discovery, commentators suggest multiple ways to implement checks on the process. First, systems should be monitored by an individual to ensure the ultimate decisions are legal and not discriminatory.[156] In addition, the decisions made by the program

---

151. *See* James C. Cooper, *Separation Anxiety*, 21 VA. J.L. & TECH. 1, 40 (2017). See *supra* section 3:4.1 for a list of states that have enacted laws regulating access to event data recorders located in cars.

152. Insurers are permitted to discriminate among customers in these ways because, unlike most goods, the value of insurance coverage is entirely dependent on the identity of the purchaser. *See* Peppet, *supra* note 138; Max N. Helveston, *Consumer Protection in the Age of Big Data*, 93 WASH. U. L. REV. 859, 863 (2016).

153. Charlotte A. Tschider, *Regulating the IoT: Discrimination, Privacy, and Cybersecurity in the Artificial Intelligence Age*, 96 DENV. U. L. REV. 87 (2018).

154. *Id.*

155. *Id.*

156. Matthew Scherer, *AI in HR: Civil Rights Implications of Employers Use of Artificial Intelligence and Big Data*, SCITECH LAW. (Winter 2017).

should be cross-checked with internal company policies and regulations.[157] If problems are discovered, the AI instructions should be revised.[158]

Alternatively, scholars believe the best way to protect consumers is to confront the situation with notice and procedural due process considerations consistent with the Fourteenth Amendment.[159] The idea is that consumers should be made aware of automated decisions that impact consumers, thus, giving them an opportunity to adjust their behavior to alter the outcome of the automated decision.[160] There is a relatively large group of scholars who believe in this process because it reflects the E.U.'s General Data Protection Regulation (GDPR), discussed in chapter 10.[161] Pursuant to GDPR, the consumer would have notice of the source of data or notice reflecting the data used to make a decision.[162] For example, landlords should notify all applicants for an apartment of the specific characteristics or profiles that they are looking for in renters.[163] This notice allows consumers to challenge the fairness of the AI or predictions used against the consumer.[164] With a neutral decision-maker, the data and algorithm can be examined to allow the consumer to be heard and the decision process of the AI to be analyzed.[165]

§ 7:9   Conclusion

IoT devices—like other products—will unfortunately cause harm to consumers in certain instances. At present, it is not entirely clear how courts will define the harm or assess liability attributed to the IoT. Similar to other advancements in technology, courts will most likely evolve to ensure that consumers have the ability to seek redress for any IoT-related injury regardless of whether it results in a physical or non-physical harm or comes in the form of unlawful discrimination.

---

157.   *Id.*
158.   *Id.*
159.   Tschider, *supra* note 153.
160.   *Id.*
161.   *Id.*
162.   Kate Crawford & Jason Schultz, *Big Data and Due Process: Toward a Framework to Redress Predictive Privacy Harms*, 55 B.C. L. REV. 93 (2014).
163.   *Id.*
164.   *Id.*
165.   *Id.*

Chapter 8

Civil Discovery

---

§ 8:1   Overview

This chapter examines the discovery issues that arise when attorneys attempt to use content derived from IoT objects in civil litigation. The chapter begins with a brief explanation of e-discovery, including the importance of metadata within the discovery process. The chapter then explores the best methods for identifying, locating, and obtaining IoT-related content, followed by an examination of data preservation and spoliation during litigation.

§ 8:2   Background

IoT objects—including wearable devices—are everywhere, collecting information and becoming more sophisticated, accessible, and shareable every day.[1] As a result, attorneys are increasingly seeking ways to use the content created and stored by these devices as evidence during litigation. One of the first known uses of content from

---

1.   Antigone Peyton, *A Litigator's Guide to the Internet of Things*, 22 RICH. J.L. & TECH. 9 (2016).

an IoT device in court occurred in Canada.[2] In this personal injury case, the plaintiff relied on data from her Fitbit to show that her physical activity levels had decreased after her accident. The plaintiff, who prevailed on her claims, presented data to the court pertaining to her activity levels, location, sleep patterns, and quality of life both pre- and post-accident. With the help of a Fitbit, the plaintiff was able to demonstrate that her level of physical activity was less than an average woman of her age and profession.

§ 8:2.1   E-Discovery

"Electronic discovery . . . is the electronic aspect of identifying, collecting, and producing electronically stored information (ESI) in response to a request for production in a lawsuit or investigation. ESI includes, but is not limited to, emails, documents, presentations, databases, voicemail, audio and video files, social media, and web sites."[3] Put more succinctly, electronic discovery (e-discovery) is a set of processes that involve linked actions of obtaining and reading, and parsing through information in preparation for litigation. An integral part of the discovery process, e-discovery came about due to the shift in the nature of evidence from traditional paper and offline materials to pervasive online content and electronic data.

When triggered by the anticipation of litigation, the e-discovery process creates a legal duty to preserve all potentially relevant ESI.[4] The attorneys involved in the case determine the scope of e-discovery, identify and preserve the relevant ESI, and make requests and challenges for e-discovery.[5] To determine the scope, the legal team examines the:

(1)   list of custodians responsible for the data;

(2)   types of data;

(3)   forms of production of the data; and

(4)   relevant timeframe to produce the data.[6]

---

2.   *See* Parmy Olson, *Fitbit Data Now Being Used in the Courtroom*, FORBES (Nov. 16, 2014).

3.   The Basics: What Is e-Discovery?, Complete Discovery Source, https://cdslegal.com/knowledge/the-basics-what-is-e-discovery (last visited May 28, 2020).

4.   *Id.*

5.   *Id.*

6.   Processing: Scoping Electronic Discovery Projects, FINDLAW, https://technology.findlaw.com/ediscovery-guide/processing-scoping-electronic-discovery-projects.html (last visited May 28, 2020).

Historically, e-discovery was fairly straightforward.[7] It was created for obtaining human communication that occurred electronically and online.[8] Thus, e-discovery was helpful for locating evidence on social media platforms. However, the IoT primarily involves machine-to-machine communication, which makes e-discovery a bit more challenging. According to one practitioner working in IoT discovery, "[c]omputers talk to each other in code, and . . . e-discovery is not set up to analyze that. E-discovery is set up to analyze human communication; it's not set up to analyze computer communication. And computer communication is what the internet of things will thrive on."[9] E-discovery of machine-to-machine communication is exacerbated by the billions of IoT devices currently in use that operate without a standard format. At present, there is no uniform "standard for interoperable IoT data."[10] Furthermore, IoT manufacturers use their own unique methods to collect data, which in turn makes it difficult to create standard procedures for preserving, collecting, reviewing, and producing information.[11] Today's e-discovery world has become increasingly more complex.

§ 8:2.2 *Metadata*

Federal Civil Rule of Procedure 26(f) defines metadata as "information describing the history, tracking, or management of an electronic file [that] is usually not apparent to the reader viewing a hard copy or screen image." Metadata may also be described as the history of the file that persists from medium to medium.[12] Prior to the explosion of IoT devices on the market, metadata was fairly uniform.[13] The metadata for the average digital file consisted of the name of the author, the date, and change history information. Thus, identifying an email or Word document was uncomplicated because of the easily accessible information located in the file's metadata or text.

Today, many believe that the definition of "metadata" must be expanded to include "contextual information about IoT sensors such

---

7.   Christopher Suarez, *Forensics and Electronic Discovery in an IoT Era*, AM. BAR ASS'N (Jan. 1, 2018), www.americanbar.org/groups/young_lawyers/publications/tyl/topics/resources-technology/forensics-and-electronic-discovery-an-iot-era/.

8.   Ian Lopez, *The Internet of Things Means a Big Dilemma for Big Law Discovery*, LAW.COM (Feb. 7, 2017).

9.   *Id.*

10. Suarez, *supra* note 7.

11. Peyton, *supra* note 1.

12. Blake Klinkner, *Metadata: What Is It? How Can It Get Me into Trouble? What Can I Do About It?*, THE WY. LAW., at 18 (Apr. 2014).

13. Suarez, *supra* note 7.

as their calibration, type, and locations."[14] This metadata, in addition to the sensor readings themselves, may be required in order to fully understand the scope of IoT content that must be turned over in discovery. By way of example, the NEST thermostat could, in addition to revealing temperature readings, let attorneys know through metadata how many people were in a house at any given time. Another benefit of metadata is proving chain of custody, which can become increasingly challenging in the IoT world where content regularly travels from device to the cloud. For example, it might be difficult to identify who actually spoke to Alexa or "whose movements a particular fitness wearable is tracking at [a] particular" time.

§ 8:3   Identifying IoT Content

The first challenge with IoT discovery is identifying the scope and nature of potentially pertinent content. Here, the practitioner must determine which devices a witness might have interacted with or might contain information relevant to potential litigation. Early identification of IoT content (pre-litigation) helps everyone in the process to understand their legal risks and obligations to secure and produce information.

Like other forms of discovery, information from the IoT device must be "relevant to any party's claim or defense."[15] For example, the Fitbit, which monitors sleep patterns, compares the wearer to the average sleeper. This comparison may or may not be relevant to a particular issue in dispute. In the Canadian personal injury case referred to above in section 8:2, this information was very relevant to the plaintiff's claims.

§ 8:4   Locating IoT Content

After identification, IoT content must next be located. IoT content will generally be found in one of two places, either on an IoT device or in the cloud. Upon locating the content, the practitioner must find the key custodians or systems that host the relevant data. The difficulty here lies in determining who exactly has custody, possession, and control of the data. This in turn may require practitioners to examine applicable privacy policies. While some policies allow the device owner to determine how information is shared or released, there are certain exceptions, such as a subpoena or warrant, which ensure compliance with applicable laws. After the relevant data is found and custodians identified, practitioners should send out litigation

---

14.   *Id.*
15.   FED. R. CIV. P. 26(b)(1).

hold letters. At a minimum, litigation hold letters should have specific instructions on preserving IoT data.

In addition to litigators, judges will also be asked to analyze the complex issues unique to the IoT, including possession and custody. For example, judges might have to determine who is responsible for producing data inside of a wearable device. Is it the owner who can produce the data after "jailbreaking" the device and having an expert collect the data, or the manufacturer that can easily export and collect the same data with ease? Also, how will access, control, privacy restrictions, and contractual obligations impact discovery obligations?

§ 8:5 Obtaining IoT Content

Regardless of where the content is found, obtaining IoT data raises a number of challenges even for the most sophisticated litigator. First, as a general rule, proper legal methods of IoT data collection rarely (if ever) keep up with the latest devices and technology.[16] Second, extracting IoT content from a device can be difficult even for skilled e-discovery vendors.[17] Third, both security and encryption make it difficult to "crack" IoT devices to access content.[18] If the content has been uploaded to the cloud and is no longer on the device, obtaining such information poses a challenge. The content may have been aggregated with other content, typically in some type of structured database where discovery may prove problematic. IoT databases are no different. The situation gets more muddled once the different IoT devices and APIs (application program interfaces) are factored in. Finally, if the cloud location is controlled by a third party, then the person requesting the content must still address possession, custody, and control issues that may arise with the third party.

While Federal Rule of Civil Procedure 26 requires attorneys to disclose certain information prior to receiving a formal discovery request, attorneys should nonetheless remember to reference IoT devices and content in any formal discovery request. For example, an attorney might include the following language in a discovery request to opposing counsel:

> Produce the location data for your smartphone or other wearable device, including FitBit, Android Wear, Apple iWatch, or other similar device, from [date of data] to present.[19]

---

16. Maureen O'Neill, *E-Discovery and the Internet of Things*, DISCOVERREADY.COM (Nov. 14, 2014).
17. *Id.*
18. *Id.*
19. Jeff Taylor, *Your Next Discovery Request: Defendant's FitBit Data*, THEDROIDLAWYER.COM (Nov. 17, 2014).

If opposing counsel objects to the release of IoT content, the requesting attorney may file a motion to compel. In deciding whether to release IoT content pursuant to a motion to compel, the court may look at prior decisions involving content derived from social media for guidance.[20] While this may provide some benefit, it should be remembered that social media data may be more public than IoT data.[21] In deciding a motion to compel, most courts will employ a balancing test, weighing the probative value of the data against an individual's reasonable expectation of privacy.[22] This may become a non-issue if the individual keeps most of their data in the public view.[23]

§ 8:6   Preservation of IoT Content

The preservation of IoT content and metadata is exceedingly important because it decreases the likelihood of chain of custody and spoliation issues.[24] As a general rule, a party's need to preserve content arises when it is reasonable for that party to anticipate litigation. With respect to Electronically Stored Information (ESI), which includes IoT content, Federal Rule of Civil Procedure 26(b)(2)(b) states: "[while] a party need not provide discovery of electronically stored information from sources that the party identifies as not reasonably accessible because of undue burden or cost . . . the court may nonetheless order discovery from such sources if the requesting party shows good cause." The rule in the notes section then goes on to say that "a party's identification of sources of Electronically Stored Information as not reasonably accessible does not relieve the party of its common-law or statutory duties to preserve evidence." Therefore, just because it is difficult and challenging to retrieve IoT content, a party may still be required to produce it.

At present, there are established procedures in place to capture digital evidence before it becomes unavailable.[25] For example, first responders can create memory dumps of electronic devices prior to

---

20.   Ryan Garcia & Thaddeus Hoffmeister, *Social Media Law in a Nutshell*, at 330–34 (West 2017). *See, e.g.*, Romano v. Steelcase, Inc., 907 N.Y.S.2d 650 (App. Div. 2010); McMillen v. Hummingbird Speedway, Inc., No. 113-2010 CD, 2010 WL 4403285 (Pa. Ct. Com. Pl. Sept. 9, 2010); EEOC v. Simply Storage, 270 F.R.D. 430 (S.D. Ind. 2010).

21.   *Id.*

22.   Forman v. Henkin, 30 N.Y.3d 656 (2018).

23.   *Id.*

24.   The Basics: What Is e-Discovery?, *supra* note 3.

25.   R. C. Hegarty, D. J. Lamb & A. Attwood, *Digital Evidence Challenges in the Internet of Things*, Proceedings of the 10th International Network Conference, at 163–72 ch. 2 (2014), https://pdfs.semanticscholar.org/b789/f84ef58d5963996e134aa51fd9d01613b922.pdf.

the devices getting shut down at the scene. However, there are a number of issues that arise with preserving IoT content. First, some IoT data was not envisioned to be stored for future use or accessed after being collected and used. Second, data might be stored locally on the device which means it needs to be pulled before it gets overwritten. Another option is to have the device connect to the cloud and upload the data there. But with this option, the chain of custody will become more difficult to establish, which makes metadata even more important. Third, data may be shared amongst multiple devices.[26]

Another major issue with preservation is the method by which content is preserved. Generally speaking, ESI should be preserved in the same manner it is normally maintained. This means that printing information or converting the file type are not necessarily proper methods of preservation and could be considered unusable. Rule 34(b)(i) states that "a party who produces documents for inspection shall produce them as they are kept in the usual course of business." The committee responsible for drafting Rule 34(b)(i) also stated that "the responding party must produce ESI either in a form or forms in which it is ordinarily maintained or in a form or forms that are reasonably usable."[27]

Companies that store data from IoT devices will need to develop methods for the preservation, collection, and production of this information when litigation calls for its use. However, the question of who has the responsibility for production, the user or the entity storing the data, remains.

§ 8:7   Spoliation

Spoliation arises when a "party fails to preserve evidence."[28] One of the first litigated cases involving IoT content and spoliation is *Below v. Yokohama Tires Corp.*[29] In this case, the plaintiff was driving his 2005 GMC Sierra truck when he lost control and crashed. As a result of the accident, the plaintiff was deemed incapacitated and his wife subsequently brought a products liability lawsuit on behalf of both herself and her husband. The plaintiffs based their lawsuit on both negligence and strict liability, claiming that the tire on the truck was defective.

Prior to trial, the truck in question was destroyed at the salvage yard save for the defective tire. This in turn led the defendants to

---

26.   *Id.*
27.   *Id.*
28.   Garcia & Hoffmeister, *supra* note 20, at 334–35.
29.   Below v. Yokohama Tires Corp., 2017 WL 764824 (W.D. Wis. Feb. 27, 2017).

file a motion for relief due to spoliation of evidence. The defendants argued that the destruction of the truck was done in bad faith because they needed to evaluate the truck and the electronic data recorder within it.[30] Plaintiffs, who had hired a fairly sophisticated personal injury firm, argued that there was no intent on their part to destroy evidence.[31] Ultimately, the court determined that a spoliation instruction is appropriate when there is "an intentional act or bad faith by the party in possession of the destroyed evidence."[32] Here, the court found that plaintiffs' conduct was not done in bad faith and fell "somewhere between negligence and gross negligence."[33] It held that in light of plaintiffs' actions they were "preclud[ed] from using [Below's truck] as a sword, even if defendants [couldn't] use it as a shield,"[34] but that the defendants could "explore how information from an inspection of Below's truck could have affected the experts' opinion at trial."[35] The court also prohibited the plaintiffs from arguing that the defendants "failed to explore or prove something if they were prevented from doing so by the negligence in preserving evidence."[36]

One of the major takeaways from this case is that practitioners should try early on to identify what evidence may contain IoT related content—even when it comes in the form of a 2005 pickup truck.

§ 8:8   Conclusion

As this chapter illustrates, the injection of the IoT into e-discovery has not only greatly increased the amount of content that attorneys must review in preparation for litigation, it has also raised a number of unique legal challenges that courts are now only starting to confront. Similar to the early days of social media, courts need to provide further guidance as more IoT-related cases work their way through the legal system. As for the voluminous amount of IoT data that continues to grow daily, a few attorneys are starting tackle this problem through leveraging predictive coding and artificial intelligence to review and collect content.[37]

---

30.   David Horrigan, *E-Discovery Spoliation in Unusual Places: Preserve Your Pickup Truck*, IDS10 (Mar. 2, 2017).
31.   *Id.*
32.   *Below*, 2017 WL 764824, at *2.
33.   *Id.*
34.   *Id.*
35.   Horrigan, *supra* note 30.
36.   *Id.*
37.   Suarez, *supra* note 7.

Chapter 9

Criminal Law and Procedure

---

§ 9:1   Overview

This chapter will explore the impact of the IoT on criminal law and procedure, beginning with how IoT is used as a vehicle for criminal activity. The bulk of the chapter, however, discusses the role of the IoT in criminal investigations and adjudications: police use of data collected by IoT devices in investigations; constitutional limitations on the government's use of the IoT to monitor, investigate, and apprehend suspects; and defenses raised to a criminal prosecution based primarily on IoT-related evidence.

§ 9:2   IoT As a Vehicle for Crime

Criminals are discovering ways to exploit the IoT. Generally speaking, criminals use the IoT in one of three ways, all of which involve either gaining access or control of an IoT device:

1.   Preventing access by others;

2.   Causing a malfunction; and

3.   Weaponizing.

§ 9:2.1   *Preventing Access by Others*

In January 2017, there was an incident at a four-star hotel in Austria, the Seehotel Jagerwirt, that provides a useful illustration of the IoT and criminal activity based on denying access to a device.[1] During the attack, hackers took control of the hotel's smart locks and prevented hotel management from issuing key cards to new guests.[2] The hotel had no back-up system, like traditional keys, to gain entry into the rooms, and thus, rather than physically break into every room to regain access, the hotel owners paid the two-bitcoin ransom ($1,800) demanded by the hackers.

Had such an incident occurred in the United States, the smart lock hackers could be charged under a generic theft statute because they prevented the hotel owners from accessing property, i.e., their hotel rooms. A typical state theft statute in the United States reads:

(A)   No person, with purpose to deprive the owner of property or services, shall knowingly obtain or exert control over either the property or services in any of the following ways:

   (1)   Without the consent of the owner or person authorized to give consent;

   (2)   Beyond the scope of the express or implied consent of the owner or person authorized to give consent;

   (3)   By deception;

   (4)   By threat;

   (5)   By intimidation.

(B)   (1)   Whoever violates this section is guilty of theft.[3]

---

1.   Josephine Wolff, *The Ransomware Attack That Locked Hotel Guests Out of Their Rooms*, SLATE (Feb. 1, 2017), www.slate.com/articles/technology/future_tense/2017/02/the_ransomware_attack_that_locked_hotel_guests_out_of_their_rooms.html.

2.   James Vincent, *Don't Believe the Story About Hackers Locking Guests in Their Rooms at a Luxury Hotel*, THE VERGE (Jan. 30, 2017), www.theverge.com/2017/1/30/14438226/hackers-austrian-hotel-bitcoin-ransom-ransomware.

3.   OHIO REV. CODE § 2913.02.

As a general rule, criminal statutes, like theft, are written with method-neutral terminology. As a result, the laws are equally applicable to criminal conduct regardless of whether or not an IoT device is used.[4] In addition, new laws have been enacted as gap fillers for online criminal conduct that may not have a true offline counterpart. For example, the Computer Fraud Abuse Act, discussed in greater detail later in this chapter, could cover the criminal conduct that occurred at the Seehotel Jagerwirt.

§ 9:2.2   *Causing the IoT Device to Malfunction*

Individuals have caused malfunctions in IoT devices ranging from an insulin pump[5] to an automobile[6] with varying degrees of success. At present, a number of criminal statutes would cover the act of causing an IoT device to malfunction. At the low end would be criminal damaging, which can be defined as "caus[ing], or creat[ing] a substantial risk of physical harm to any property of another without the other person's consent."[7] The criminal charges, however, could quickly escalate depending upon the subsequent harm caused. In the case of modifying an IoT insulin pump, possible charges could begin as an assault but turn into manslaughter or murder if the victim died as a result.

Domestic violence abusers have also used IoT devices to inflict abuse on their victims. Recently, there has been an increase in reports by domestic violence victims that involve malfunctioning IoT devices, e.g., air conditioners switching off, digital locks changing, and unattended doorbells ringing.[8] According to one intake specialist at the National Domestic Violence Hotline, "[c]allers have said the abusers were monitoring and controlling them remotely through the smart home appliances and the smart home system."[9] IoT devices are ripe for abuse because they are inexpensive and may be under the control of one person—the abuser.[10] While courts and attorneys are just

---

4. Matthew Ashton, *Debugging the Real World Robust Criminal Prosecution in the Internet of Things*, 59 ARIZ. L. REV. 805 (2017).
5. FTC STAFF, INTERNET OF THINGS: PRIVACY & SECURITY IN A CONNECTED WORLD (Jan. 2015), www.ftc.gov/system/files/documents/reports/federal-trade-commission-staff-report-november-2013-workshop-entitled-internet-things-privacy/150127iotrpt.pdf.
6. *See, e.g.*, Andy Greenberg, *Hackers Remotely Kill a Jeep on the Highway—With Me in It*, WIRED (July 21, 2015), www.wired.com/2015/07/hackers-remotely-kill-jeep-highway/.
7. OHIO REV. CODE § 2913.02.
8. Nellie Bowles, *Thermostats, Locks and Lights: Digital Tools of Domestic Abuse*, N.Y. TIMES, June 23, 2018.
9. *Id.*
10. *Id.*

getting up to speed on this recent phenomenon, they are starting to expressly include IoT devices when requesting and issuing domestic violence protection orders.[11]

§ 9:2.3   *Weaponizing*

When criminals gain control of IoT devices, they can restrict access or cause the devices to malfunction. In addition, a criminal can weaponize a device, employing the device for some harmful purpose.[12] To date, the most common use for a weaponized IoT device has been the "distributed denial-of-services" (DDoS) attack.

DDoS attacks involve individuals, or so-called masters, taking over compromised systems. Since the only requirement to take over a compromised system is connectivity to the Internet, these systems can be located anywhere in the world—thus the term "distributed." These compromised systems, often called zombies, are organized into "botnets," groups of computers infected with malicious software.[13] In a typical DDoS attack, botnets, operating without the original owner's knowledge or permission, direct thousands—if not millions—of requests to a targeted website. This targeting takes the website offline, making it unavailable to others—thus the term "denial of services."[14] While traditional botnets consisted of compromised computers programmed by masters to complete a set of repetitive tasks, today's botnets also include IoT devices.[15]

In some ways, botnets are more problematic than the worms or viruses that arose in the early stages of the Internet, especially when they involve IoT devices.[16] Unlike a worm or virus, being part of a botnet does not necessarily impact the performance of the device.[17] Thus, owners may never even know that their devices have been compromised.[18] If owners learn that their computers have been corrupted,

---

11.   *Id.*
12.   Adam Levin, *How Cyber Criminals Will Weaponize the Internet of Things in 2017*, INC. (Nov. 30, 2016), www.inc.com/adam-levin/how-cyber-criminals-will-weaponize-the-internet-of-things-in-2017.html.
13.   Sam Zeitlin, *Botnet Takedowns and the Fourth Amendment*, 90 N.Y.U. L. REV. 764 (2015).
14.   *Id.*
15.   Michael Kassner, *Internet of Things Botnet May Include TVs and a Fridge*, TECHREPUBLIC (Jan. 21, 2014), www.techrepublic.com/blog/it-security/internet-of-things-botnet-may-include-tvs-and-a-fridge/.
16.   Lily Hay Newman, *The Botnet That Broke the Internet Isn't Going Away*, WIRED (Dec. 9, 2016), www.wired.com/2016/12/botnet-broke-internet-isnt-going-away/.
17.   *Id.*
18.   *Id.*

there are usually steps they can take to fix the problem.[19] However, the same cannot be said for an IoT device, especially if that device lacks a direct interface.[20]

The Mirai botnet is one example of how IoT devices can be used in a DDoS attack.[21] Here, an unknown master used Mirai malware to search for Internet-connected devices that had default administrative passwords such as "123456," "password," "admin," etc.[22] Upon discovering these devices, the malware logged in and infected them.[23] Within the first twenty hours of its release, the Mirai botnet had infected approximately 65,000 IoT devices.[24] It is estimated that between 200,000–300,000 endpoints from poorly connected IoT devices—such as routers, security cameras, and baby monitors—were compromised.[25] The master then organized these devices into botnets to flood Dyn, an Internet infrastructure company, with data.[26]

Dyn was hit with 1.2 terabytes per second of nuisance signals, nearly twice the volume of any previously recorded DDoS attack.[27] The nuisance signals prevented Dyn from routing Internet traffic.[28] As a result, several websites such as Paypal, Twitter, Reddit, GitHub, Amazon, Netflix, and Spotify were unavailable to users in the United States and Europe for several hours, resulting in a loss of revenue for those companies.[29]

There are various motivations for DDoS attacks. Some attacks are politically motivated and occur in order to make a statement to the entity attacked or the world as a whole.[30] This is more likely to happen when the attack is state-sponsored. However, as DDoS attacks rise in popularity, non-state actors like Anonymous have also used them for political purposes. Some groups have even claimed that

---

19.   *Id.*
20.   *Id.*
21.   Stephen A. Riga, *Two Breaches, Two Enforcement Actions, and a DDOS Attack: Data Security and the Rise of the Internet of Things*, 20 J. INTERNET L. 3 (2017).
22.   *Id.*
23.   *Id.*
24.   Robert S. Metzger, *Security and the Internet*, SCITECH LAW. (Spring 2018).
25.   *Id.*
26.   *Id.*
27.   Adam Levin, *How Cyber Criminals Will Weaponize the Internet of Things in 2017*, INC. (Nov. 30, 2016), www.inc.com/adam-levin/how-cyber-criminals-will-weaponize-the-internet-of-things-in-2017.html.
28.   *Id.*
29.   *Id.*
30.   W. Cagney McCormick, *The Computer Fraud & Abuse Act: Failing to Evolve with the Digital Age*, 16 SMU SCI. & TECH. L. REV. 481 (2013).

a DDoS attack is a form of civil disobedience as opposed to a criminal act.[31]

Other DDoS attacks are motivated by financial gain.[32] These attacks often involve ransomware, where the attacker holds the website or information on the site hostage until a monetary sum, usually in bitcoin, is paid.[33] That said, all DDoS attackers have the same ultimate goal—to prevent the operation of a specific website or to make it unavailable to others.

At present, the most common criminal statute relied upon by law enforcement to address DDoS attacks is the Computer Fraud and Abuse Act (CFAA).[34] This statute is broad enough to cover the various ways in which someone might conduct a DDoS attack. The CFAA targets anyone who knowingly and intentionally:

accesses exclusive government computers or classified information without authorization;

1. obtains information from computers through unauthorized access;

2. commits fraud through unauthorized access;

3. threatens to engage in cybercrime through extortion; and

4. causes "damage" to protected computers.[35]

Most DDoS prosecutions fall under the damage to protected computers category section 1030(a)(5) which reads:

Knowingly caus[ing] the transmission of a program, information, code, or command, and as result of such conduct, intentionally caus[ing] damage without authorization, to a protected computer [ ].

While a DDoS attack may or may not physically harm the zombie computer or IoT device, the broad definition of "damage" and "loss" will bring the attack under the CFAA so long as the government proves at least $5,000 in damages and the intent to cause harm. The CFAA defines "damage" as "any impairment to the integrity or availability of data, a program, a system, or information." Arguably, the hacker damages the IoT device when forcing it to "behave in a manner not

31. Xiang Li, *Hacktivism and the First Amendment: Drawing the Line Between Cyber Protests and Crime*, 27 HARV. J. L. & TECH. 301 (2013).

32. *Id.*

33. Ben Dickson, *Are We Ready to Face the Coming Wave of IoT Ransomware Attacks?*, THE DAILY DOT (Dec. 7, 2016), www.dailydot.com/layer8/iot-ransomware-attacks/.

34. 18 U.S.C. § 1030.

35. *Id.*

intended by the user."[36] Further "adverse actions [include those] that alter, encrypt, encipher, transmit, or delete data or exhaust system resources" because these actions, among other things, impact the IoT device's availability.[37] The CFAA also covers situations where a master recklessly or negligently causes damage through an IoT device.[38]

DDoS attacks that involve ransomware can also be successfully prosecuted under the CFAA. Subsection 1030(a)(7) prohibits "any communication containing any threat to cause damage to a protected computer" with the "intent to extort from any person any money or other thing of value" in interstate or foreign commerce.[39] Although this subsection requires the intent to extort something "of value," unlike section 1030(a)(4)–(5), the statute does not specify any dollar threshold.[40] The CFAA can also be used in conjunction with the Hobbs Act in situations when the DDoS attack contains a threat of "physical violence to any person or property."[41] If the potential harm contains a threat to injure property or reputation, prosecutors can invoke 18 U.S.C. § 875.[42]

In addition to DDoS attacks, IoT devices can be weaponized to influence electrical demand and actually take down an electrical grid.[43] According to one study which simulated a Manipulation of Demand Internet of Things (MaDIoT) attack, high wattage IoT devices like air conditioners, ovens, and electric heating systems could, if controlled through malware, cause havoc within the electrical grid.[44] For example, if an attacker had access to 90,000 air conditioners or 18,000 electric water heaters within a targeted geographical area, the attacker could cause all of the generators in the grid to go offline by modifying the electrical demand.[45]

---

36. Sara Sun Beale & Peter Berris, *Hacking the Internet of Things: Vulnerabilities, Dangers, and Legal Responses*, 16 DUKE L. & TECH. 161 (2018).

37. Ioana Vasiu & Lucian Vasiu, *Break on Through: An Analysis of Computer Damage Cases*, 14 U. PITT. J. TECH. L. POL'Y 158 (2014).

38. 18 U.S.C. § 1030(a)(5)(A)(i) (2006).

39. *Id.* § 1030(a)(5)(7).

40. *Id.*

41. *Id.* § 1951.

42. *Id.* § 875.

43. Sean Gallagher, *Just Say No: Wi-Fi-Enabled Appliance Botnet Could Bring Power Grid to Its Knees*, ARS TECHNICA (Aug. 17, 2018), https://arstechnica.com/information-technology/2018/08/just-say-no-wi-fi-enabled-appliance-botnet-could-bring-power-grid-to-its-knees/.

44. *Id.*

45. *Id.*

§ 9:3   Role of IoT in Criminal Investigations

With the growing volume of IoT content and variety of applications, law enforcement has increasingly sought IoT-related data to assist with criminal investigations and the apprehension of suspects. Like with other forms of technology, some law enforcement agencies have been early adopters of the IoT while others have simply ignored it. In the UK, detectives are being trained to find IoT devices that could contain evidence or data about the circumstances surrounding the crime scene.[46] Adoption has been slow, however, in those agencies that do not truly understand how the IoT works and the variety of data types available. To counter this IoT knowledge gap, a number of police departments around the United States are taking active steps to offer additional training to their work force. As the IoT continues to develop and proliferate, it is highly likely that searching a victim's or defendant's Fitbit or smart thermostat will become as second nature to police as dusting for fingerprints or swabbing for DNA.

§ 9:3.1   *Illustrative Cases*

Amazon Echo recordings. An Arkansas case, *State v. Bates*, illustrates how one law enforcement agency proactively sought out and leveraged IoT content to assist with an ongoing murder investigation.[47] In this case, the defendant called the police to report the death of an overnight guest. The defendant told police that, after watching a football game with friends in his home, he told his two remaining guests they could spend the night if they wanted to and then went to bed. Upon waking the next morning, the defendant found one of the guests unresponsive and the other guest was gone. In looking around the house, which was now a crime scene, the police found several smart devices including a Nest thermostat, Honeywell alarm, and an Amazon Echo. The police took possession of the Echo and sent a preservation letter to Amazon for all records associated with it.

Approximately two months later, police served Amazon an extension of the warrant. Both the original warrant and the extension requested that Amazon turn over "audio recordings, transcribed records, or other text records related to communications and transactions" between the Echo in the defendant's house and Amazon's servers for the dates on which the events at issue took place. Amazon challenged the warrant's constitutionality. However, the constitutionality of the government's warrant was never put to the test; the defendant

---

46.   Jimmy McCloskey, *CSI Alexa: The Smart Home Has Become the New Crime Scene Witness*, THE AMBIENT (2018), www.the-ambient.com/features/smart-home-crime-scene-264.

47.   State v. Bates, CR-2016-370-2 (Ark. Cir. Ct. Mar. 6, 2017).

ultimately consented to the disclosure of the content and therefore the trial court never had to rule on Amazon's motion. Nonetheless, this case serves as an early illustration of how law enforcement can enlist IoT devices to assist with criminal investigations.

Pacemaker data. In a case involving data from a pacemaker, the defendant was charged with aggravated arson and insurance fraud, stemming from a fire in his own house.[48] The defendant told police that when he saw the fire he quickly gathered some belongings, busted a bedroom window with his cane, threw his items out of the window, and took them to his car.[49] In light of the defendant's medical state at the time, the police were skeptical of his story. After obtaining a warrant, police collected data from the defendant's pacemaker covering the time prior to, during, and after the fire.[50] Police then gave this data to a cardiologist who determined that, based on the heart rate and cardiac rhythms from the defendant's pacemaker, his version of the events during the fire were "highly improbable."[51]

Emergency Assistance feature on automobile. While police in the two prior examples were required to seek out and uncover content from a defendant's device, sometimes the information comes directly to law enforcement without the need for a search warrant. In a hit-and-run case, a motorist's car automatically called the police after striking another car.[52] The motorist had previously enabled the Ford Emergency Assistance feature on the vehicle, which contacts the police anytime airbags deploy.[53] Immediately after the accident, a 9-1-1 emergency dispatcher reached out to the motorist to enquire about her well-being. The motorist claimed that nothing had happened and that her car had not been in an accident. The police nonetheless went to the motorist's home where her car, which had front-end damage and a deployed airbag, told a different story. When confronted with this information, the defendant admitted to being involved in an earlier accident.

---

48. Amanda Watts, *Pacemaker Could Hold Key in Arson Case*, CNN (Feb. 8, 2017), www.cnn.com/2017/02/08/us/pacemaker-arson---trnd/index.html.

49. Beth Mole, *Ohio Man's Pacemaker Data May Betray Him in Arson, Insurance Fraud Case*, ARS TECHNICA (Feb. 8, 2017), https://arstechnica.com/science/2017/02/ohio-mans-pacemaker-data-betrays-him-in-arson-insurance-fraud-case/.

50. Don Reisinger, *Pacemaker Data Led Police to Accuse Someone of Arson*, FORTUNE (Feb. 7, 2017), https://fortune.com/2017/02/07/pacemaker-arson-charges/.

51. *Id.*

52. Kashmir Hill, *Florida Woman's Car Calls Police After She Flees the Scene of an Accident*, FUSION (Dec. 7, 2015).

53. Charlie Osborne, *Car Calls 911 After Alleged Hit-and-Run, Driver Arrested*, ZDNET (Dec. 7, 2015), www.zdnet.com/article/car-calls-911-after-alleged-hit-and-run-driver-arrested/.

Fitbit data. Law enforcement not only seeks out IoT data that is under the control of a defendant, but also seeks out information from crime victims. In one case, the defendant alleged that his wife was killed by an intruder, but her Fitbit indicated otherwise and ultimately led to the defendant being charged in her death.[54] He claimed that on the day in question, he left his house in the morning to go to work but returned home sometime between 8:45–9:00 a.m. because he had forgotten his laptop. He stated that once inside his home, he encountered an intruder who assaulted him and, when his wife returned home from the gym immediately thereafter, the intruder killed her. The defendant stated that the intruder burned him with a blowtorch, but that he was able to turn the blowtorch on the intruder, causing him to flee. The defendant then allegedly called 9-1-1 at approximately 10:11 a.m.[55] The defendant's description of the attack and subsequent death of his wife, however, could not be reconciled with data from her Fitbit. The defendant claimed that his wife returned home around 9:00 a.m. and was immediately killed; however, her Fitbit showed movement of 1,217 steps between 9:18 a.m. and 10:05 a.m. on the morning of her death.[56] The distance between her car and the basement of the house was only 125 feet. The Fitbit provided strong proof that the defendant's description of the murder was fabricated.[57]

In another case, a woman's status changed from victim to defendant after police discovered that data from her Fitbit contradicted her statement to them.[58] The woman had called 9-1-1 and claimed she had been sexually assaulted. When police arrived at her home, she stated that she had been asleep in bed when she awoke to find a man on top of her; the man assaulted and then raped her at knifepoint in the bathroom.[59] The woman told police she had been wearing a Fitbit at the time of her attack but had lost it during the struggle. When police were able to locate the Fitbit in an adjoining hallway, they requested her Fitbit username and password and she obliged. According to the Fitbit data, the woman had not been asleep that night as she had claimed, but had instead been walking around. She was ultimately convicted of making false statements to law enforcement.

---

54.   Tracy Connor, *Fitbit Murder Case: Richard Dabate Pleads Not Guilty in Wife's Death*, NBC NEWS (Apr. 29, 2017).

55.   Steve Helling, *5 Things to Know About the Killing that Police Say Was Solved with Victim's Fitbit*, PEOPLE.COM (Apr. 27, 2017), https://people.com/crime/fitbit-murder-case-richard-dabate-5-things/.

56.   *Id.*

57.   *Id.*

58.   Commonwealth v. Risley, Criminal Docket: CP-36-CR-0002937-2015 (C.P. Pa. Nov. 16, 2015).

59.   *Id.*

GPS device. Two bicyclists were run off the road by a driver who passed the bicyclists and then suddenly braked in front of them, forcing them to take evasive action.[60] The driver claimed that the bicyclists were at fault for riding dangerously. However, prosecutors were able to refute the driver's testimony based on the bicyclists' GPS devices which showed that they were travelling at approximately 30 mph; thus, the driver could have passed them without incident. The driver was convicted of assaulting the bicyclists and was given a five-year prison sentence.

§ 9:3.2   *Role of Business in IoT Criminal Investigations*

In light of the growing role of IoT in criminal investigations, companies that manufacture IoT devices and store IoT content should plan for how to respond to data requests by law enforcement.[61] These considerations may be somewhat complicated if the companies are not in privity, e.g., signed a terms of use agreement, with the individual whose information is requested by law enforcement.[62] Another issue for companies is the location and storage of data. Pursuant to the CLOUD Act, law enforcement has authorization to obtain electronic data regardless of whether it is kept in the United States or abroad.[63] However, as noted in chapter 10, these same companies may have to still adhere to the privacy policies of the country where that information is stored. Furthermore, foreign law enforcement may also seek information held by a U.S. company.[64] Finally, in developing policies to respond to government requests for information, companies should consider the following:

1. the nature of the stored consumer and public data and the location of the data;

2. ability to explain the data possessed and the process for obtaining that data to the government;

3. enforcement of terms of service and privacy policies;

4. interaction with foreign governments;

---

60. Stephanie Francis Ward, *How Much Evidence Can You Get from Wearable Devices, and Is It Reliable?*, ABA J. (Mar. 17, 2017).
61. Wiley Rein LLP, *Internet of Things Cos. Must Prepare for Law Enforcement*, LAW360 (Aug. 16, 2018), www.wileyrein.com/newsroom-articles-Internet-Of-Things-Cos-Must-Prepare-For-Law-Enforcement.html.
62. *Id.*
63. 18 U.S.C. § 2713.
64. Wiley Rein LLP, *supra* note 61.

5. information to consumers about interaction with law enforcement;

6. notification to the public;

7. dealing with gag orders under 18 USC § 2705 or orders to seal;

8. potential litigation with the government; and

9. data in civil proceedings.[65]

§ 9:4   Constitutional Limitations on Government Use of IoT

As law enforcement increasingly turns to the IoT to assist with monitoring, investigating, and apprehending individuals, there is a heightened concern about government encroachment on civil liberties. This naturally raises the question of what constraints, if any, can be placed upon government conduct in this area. To answer that question, this section will examine IoT content (a) in the home, (b) on the person, (c) in the car, and (d) with a third party, to determine the limitations that can be placed on government access and acquisition of IoT information.[66] A number of legal issues involving the IoT have yet to work their way through the courts; therefore, some of the conclusions drawn in this section are unavoidably speculative in nature.

Since the IoT is still fairly new, there are few laws in place to regulate or restrict government behavior. Therefore, the greatest source of protection from overreaching police conduct in this realm is the Constitution. This chapter focuses on the U.S. Constitution, but some state constitutions may provide their citizens with greater protections. For example, both Arizona and Washington guarantee the right to privacy in their respective state constitutions.[67] The section of the U.S. Constitution most likely to be invoked to curb police power with respect to the IoT is the Fourth Amendment,[68] which provides: "the right of the people to be secure in their persons, houses, papers, and effects, against unreasonable searches and seizures, shall not be violated."

---

65. *Id.*
66. This configuration of "(a) in the home, (b) on the person, (3) in the car, and (4) with a third party" is based on Andrew Guthrie Ferguson, *The Internet of Things and the Fourth Amendment of Effects*, 104 CAL. L. REV. 805 (2016).
67. ARIZ. CONST. sec. 8, and WASH. CONST. sec. 7.
68. It should be noted that the First Amendment, although less likely to be raised, also offers protections against overreaching government conduct, *see, e.g., State v. Bates, infra* note 79.

In a nutshell, the Fourth Amendment prohibits unreasonable searches and seizures, and a search or seizure is reasonable if accompanied by a warrant or if an exception to the warrant requirement exists.[69]

A seizure is "some meaningful interference with an individual's possessory interest in [the individual's] property."[70] A search occurs when law enforcement physically trespasses on persons, houses, papers and effects[71] or violates an individual's "reasonable expectation of privacy."[72] An individual's reasonable expectation of privacy arises when (1) a person demonstrates an actual expectation of privacy and (2) that expectation of privacy is one that society is prepared to recognize as reasonable.[73] Pursuant to the third-party doctrine, a person does not have a reasonable expectation of privacy in information voluntarily disclosed to a third party.[74]

§ 9:4.1   *In the Home*

At present, there are a number of ways by which law enforcement might obtain information from an IoT device located within a home. First, police may attempt to physically enter a home and seize the device. In order for police to lawfully enter an individual's home, the police must either have a warrant to do so or, an exception to the warrant requirement must apply.[75]

If the police find themselves, for some reason, lawfully in a home, they may observe any IoT device in plain view and note any information displayed on that device;[76] however, they may not manipulate the device nor gain access to any information within it without a warrant or an exception to the warrant requirement.[77] This is because most IoT devices are likely to be viewed as closed containers in which the owner has a reasonable expectation of privacy.[78] As previously discussed, the police in *State v. Bates* sought and received an extension of their warrant to access and obtain content from the defendant's Echo.[79]

---

69.   Akhil R. Amar, *Fourth Amendment First Principles*, 107 HARV. L. REV. 757 (1994).

70.   United States v. Jacobsen, 466 U.S. 109 (1984).

71.   United States v. Jones, 132 S. Ct. 945 (2012).

72.   Smith v. Maryland, 442 U.S. 735 (1979).

73.   Katz v. United States, 389 U.S. 347 (1967).

74.   *Smith, supra* note 72.

75.   Payton v. New York, 445 U.S. 573 (1980).

76.   Washington v. Chrisman, 455 U.S. 1 (1982).

77.   Arizona v. Hicks, 480 U.S. 321 (1987).

78.   United States v. Chadwick, 433 U.S. 1 (1977).

79.   State v. Bates, CR-2016-370-2 (Ark. Cir. Ct. Mar. 6, 2017).

Second, police may attempt to access the IoT device remotely, i.e., without physically entering the house. The crucial issue brought into question in these circumstances is the purpose behind the government's conduct. If law enforcement remotely accesses an IoT device in order to destroy malware on the device, (e.g., the device has become part of a botnet as discussed in section 9:2) it is unlikely that a Fourth Amendment violation has occurred, because the owner of the device does not have a possessory interest in the malware itself.[80] The government may also remotely patch or update a device without violating the Fourth Amendment, so long as it did not "materially interfere" with the device.[81] In contrast, if the government remotely accesses an IoT device in order to investigate or gather information about the individual owner, a warrant or an exception to the warrant requirement is needed.[82]

In light of the unique challenges that arise with conducting remote searches of computers and IoT devices, Federal Rule of Criminal Procedure 41 was amended in 2016 to make it easier for the government to obtain warrants. Pursuant to the modified version of Rule 41, any "magistrate judge with authority in any district where activities related to the crime may have occurred" may issue a warrant if technological means have been used to hide the location of the media or information. Also, when the government is conducting an investigation pursuant to 18 U.S.C. § 1030(a)(5), such as investigating a botnet attack, it can seek a single warrant if protected computers have been damaged in five or more districts. Changes have also been made to the notice provision for remote searches conducted under Federal Rule 41. These modifications to Federal Rule 41 have been both praised and criticized.[83]

In addition to conducting remote searches, police may attempt to intercept the IoT signals emanating from an individual's home. Here, the police neither enter the house physically nor remotely. Instead, they remain outside the home and capture the electronic signals that the IoT device sends out. Based on the decision in *United States v. Kyllo*, courts are likely to require a warrant or an exception to the warrant requirement in order to capture the electronic signals from

---

80. Sam Zeitlin, *Botnet Takedowns and the Fourth Amendment*, 90 N.Y.U. L. REV. 746 (2015).
81. *Id.*
82. *Id.*
83. Leslie R. Caldwell, *Ensuring Tech-Savvy Criminals Do Not Have Immunity from Investigation*, U.S. Dep't of Justice (Nov. 21, 2016), and Markus Rauschecker, *Rule 41 Amendments Provide for a Drastic Expansion of Government Authority to Conduct Computer Searches and Should Not Have Been Adopted by the Supreme Court*, 76 MD. L. REV. 1085 (2017).

the IoT device.[84] In *Kyllo*, law enforcement suspected that the defendant, Danny Kyllo, was growing cannabis in his house. In order to gather evidence to support a search warrant to enter Kyllo's house, law enforcement, while in a police car, employed a thermal imager to record unusual heat patterns emanating from the home. With the thermal imager, police discovered "that the roof over the garage and a side wall" of Kyllo's home were hotter than the rest of his house and much warmer than other homes in the triplex.

Based upon the information from the thermal imager, the police obtained and executed a search warrant of Kyllo's home and discovered numerous cannabis plants. Kyllo was convicted of drug-related offenses and his case eventually reached the Supreme Court, which overturned the decision of the lower court, finding that the use of the thermal imager constituted a search within the meaning of the Fourth Amendment. According to the Court,

> obtaining by sense-enhancing technology any information regarding the interior of the home that could not otherwise have been obtained without physical 'intrusion into a constitutionally protected area'. . . constitutes a search—at least where (as here) the technology in question is not in general public use.[85]

Following the holding in *Kyllo*, it appears that the data signals from an IoT device, even after they leave the house, may be protected under a reasonable expectation of privacy depending on the type of information transmitted by the IoT device and the method used by law enforcement to obtain the signal. Encryption, although not present in the *Kyllo* case, may be another factor for the courts to consider.

In *Kyllo*, the Court was bothered by the fact that the thermal imager employed by law enforcement was "not in general public use." Another concern was the information the thermal imager revealed about what was occurring inside the house. According to one justice, by employing a thermal imager, law enforcement could determine "what hour each night the lady of the house takes her daily sauna and bath." Arguably, if the information collected from the IoT device was innocuous in nature and done using a tool generally in public use, the courts might be less inclined to find a search unlawful under the Fourth Amendment.

§ 9:4.2   On the Person

Similar to the home, there are a number of ways by which law enforcement might obtain information from an IoT device located

---

84.   United States v. Kyllo, 533 U.S. 27 (2001).
85.   *Id.* at 34.

on an individual. First, police may attempt to briefly stop or detain an individual and enquire about an IoT device. This type of police activity in and of itself does not raise Fourth Amendment concerns so long as the individual detained feels free to leave.[86] During this brief detention, a law enforcement officer may observe information visually displayed on the individual's IoT device (e.g., the number of steps on a Fitbit).

The protections change, however, when law enforcement wants to conduct a search of an individual in order to gain access to the data on an IoT device, as searches of this nature raise Fourth Amendment implications.[87] Assuming law enforcement has grounds to search an individual, e.g., the person is under arrest, law enforcement may take control and custody of any IoT device discovered; however, based upon the ruling in *Riley v. California*, they most likely may not access content from within the device.[88] In *Riley*, the defendant was initially stopped by police for a traffic violation. He was subsequently arrested on weapons charges and searched. A police officer found a cell phone in the defendant's pocket and, without a warrant, accessed data on the phone. Based upon the information found within the phone, the defendant was also charged with a prior gang-related shooting. The defendant was convicted and his case eventually made it to the Supreme Court, which held that warrantless searches of cell phones incident to an arrest violate the Fourth Amendment.

The Supreme Court based its *Riley* decision upon the vast amount of information held within the smartphone. According to the Court,

> cell phone search[es] would typically expose to the government far more than the most exhaustive search of a house: A phone not only contains in digital form many sensitive records previously found in the home; it also contains a broad array of private information never found in any form.[89]

With *Riley* as precedent, it is highly likely that searching an IoT device without a warrant will raise Fourth Amendment protections. Arguably, if the IoT device contained only very limited content similar to a beeper, the court might be less inclined to find a Fourth Amendment violation.[90]

When IoT signals are transmitted from the person, it is less clear whether intercepting those signals will raise Fourth Amendment

---

86. United States v. Mendenhall, 466 U.S. 544 (1980).
87. Wyoming v. Houghton, 526 U.S. 295 (1999).
88. Riley v. California, 134 S. Ct. 2473 (2014).
89. *Id.* at 2491.
90. United States v. Ortiz, 84 F.3d 977 (7th Cir.), *cert. denied*, 519 U.S. 900 (1996).

protections. This is because the *Kyllo* decision was based, in large part, on the high regard that the Court places on protecting privacy in the home.[91] The same cannot be said for someone walking around in public with an IoT device. To answer that question, courts are most likely to turn to *United States v. Carpenter.*[92]

In *Carpenter*, several individuals allegedly conspired to rob cell phone stores in Michigan and Ohio. The police apprehended four of the alleged conspirators, one of whom confessed and identified fifteen accomplices. This individual also turned over his phone to law enforcement, which enabled them to identify additional telephone numbers that the conspirator called around the time of the robberies. Using the information obtained from the phone, law enforcement applied for U.S.C. § 2703(d) court orders under the Stored Communications Act to obtain cell phone records for Tim Carpenter.[93] The judge granted the government's request and ordered MetroPCS and Sprint to turn over cell-site location[94] information for Carpenter's telephone "at call origination and at call termination for incoming and outgoing calls" for the four-month period when the robberies occurred.

At trial, the government argued that Carpenter was the leader of the robbery ring. Furthermore, the government introduced evidence placing Carpenter's phone near four of the charged robberies. Carpenter was convicted and subsequently appealed arguing, among other things, that his Fourth Amendment rights were violated because the government relied on 18 U.S.C. § 2703(d) court orders rather than search warrants to obtain his cell-site location information. In a narrow 5-4 decision, the U.S. Supreme Court sided with Carpenter. The Court, relying on *Kyllo, Knotts, Jones,* and *Riley,* found that Carpenter

---

91. *Id.*
92. Carpenter v. United States, 138 S. Ct. 2206 (2018).
93. The government obtained 127 days of records placing Carpenter's cell phone at more than 12,000 locations.
94. "A cell phone's location can be detected through cell site location information (CSLI) or global positioning system (GPS) data. CSLI refers to the information collected as a cell phone identifies its location to nearby cell towers. CSLI from nearby cell towers can indicate a cell phone's approximate location. With information from multiple cell towers, a technique called 'triangulation' is used to locate a cell phone with greater precision. A cell phone's GPS capabilities allow it to be tracked to within five to ten 10 feet. Cell phone location information can be 'historical' or 'prospective.' In addition to the location information cell phones ordinarily generate, a cell phone may be 'pinged' to force it to reveal its location." Cell Phone Location Tracking, A National Association of Criminal Defense Lawyers (NACDL) Primer, www.law.berkeley.edu/wp-content/uploads/2015/04/2016-06-07_Cell-Tracking-Primer_Final.pdf.

did have a reasonable expectation of privacy in his physical location and movements. Writing for the majority, Chief Justice Roberts wrote:

> [the] deeply revealing nature of CSLI[cell site location information], its depth, breadth, and comprehensive reach, and the inescapable and automatic nature of its collection, the fact that such information is gathered by a third party does not make it any less deserving of Fourth Amendment protection.[95]

The Court went on to cite Justice Alito's concurring opinion in *Jones*, in which he wrote that, "long term GPS monitoring in investigations of most offenses impinges on expectations of privacy."

The Court then addressed the third-party doctrine, distinguishing *Smith* and *Miller* from *Carpenter*. The Court stated, "while the third-party doctrine applies to telephone numbers and bank records, it is not clear whether its logic extends to the qualitatively different category of cell-site records." The Court continued that it was not extending "*Smith* and *Miller* to cover these [cell site information] novel circumstances."

Due to the recency of *Carpenter*, lower courts have not had much opportunity to test its holding. However, the Supreme Court appears to be directing law enforcement to obtain a warrant when conducting long-term surveillance of a person, even if that surveillance occurs in public. The *Carpenter* Court held that the defendant had a reasonable expectation of privacy in the information communicated from his phone to cell-site towers. Thus, it is likely that an individual with an IoT device that communicates with the cloud has an expectation of privacy in that information, especially if the information sought covers an extensive period of time. Second, deviating from past precedent, the *Carpenter* Court found that individuals do not forego their Fourth Amendment protections by venturing in the public sphere. Therefore, an IoT device that communicates information about the person in a public place may still be protected.

§ 9:4.3   *In the Car*

At present, there are a number of ways by which law enforcement might obtain IoT-related information from a vehicle. First, the police may place an IoT device on an individual's car in order to track and monitor the movement of the vehicle. For example, some police departments when in "hot pursuit" of a suspected criminal will forego the high-speed chase and instead launch a small projectile onto the

---

95.   Carpenter v. United States, 138 S. Ct. 2206, 2223 (2018).

suspect's car.[96] This so-called "lojack spitball" attaches itself to the car and provides police with a method of following the suspect without engaging in dangerous and oftentimes lethal chases.[97] This type of police conduct does not require a warrant because the police are in hot pursuit of a suspect.[98] In contrast, if the police were not facing exigent circumstances, but still desire to place an IoT device on a vehicle in order to monitor it, they most likely need a warrant or an exception to the warrant requirement based on *United States v. Jones*.[99]

In *Jones*, police suspected that the defendant was trafficking drugs and obtained a warrant to attach a GPS tracking device to the defendant's car. However, the government exceeded the scope of the warrant's geographic and duration limitations, and the U.S. Supreme Court unanimously found that the police conduct constituted an unlawful search. Importantly, there was a split among the justices on which test to apply in determining whether an unreasonable search had occurred. A majority found that physically installing a GPS tracking device on the defendant's car was a trespass against his "personal effects" and thus constituted a search. The concurrence, while reaching the same conclusion as the majority, relied on a reasonable expectation of privacy as established by *Katz v. United States*.[100]

If, instead of putting an object on a vehicle, the police monitor a suspect's car with a device already in the car, e.g., OnStar,[101] police would still need a warrant or an exception to the warrant requirement.[102] For example, in one case where the police suspected that a certain vehicle was being used in a criminal enterprise, the police requested and obtained a warrant directing Sirius XM "to activate and monitor as a tracking device the SIRIUS XM Satellite Radio installed on the Target Vehicle for a period of 10 days."[103]

---

96.   Andy Meek, *Body Cams, Smart Guns and Tracking Darts: Policing and the Internet of Things*, THE GUARDIAN (Oct. 16, 2015), www.theguardian.com/technology/2015/oct/16/police-law-enforcement-body-cams-tracking-internet-of-things.

97.   *Id.*

98.   Warden v. Hayden, 387 U.S. 294 (1967).

99.   United States v. Jones, 132 S. Ct. 945 (2012).

100.   Katz v. United States, 389 U.S. 347 (1967).

101.   The OnStar service allows motorists to contact OnStar call centers during an emergency. In the event of a collision, detected by airbag deployment or other sensors, Advanced Automatic Collision Notification features can automatically send information about the vehicle's condition and GPS location to OnStar call centers. All OnStar-equipped vehicles have Stolen Vehicle Tracking, which can provide the police with the vehicle's exact location, speed, and direction of movement.

102.   United States v. Dantzler, No. 3:10-cr-00024 (W.D. La. Mar. 31, 2010).

103.   *In re* Activation of the Sirius XM, 14-MJ-4098 (June 27, 2014).

If law enforcement goes beyond just tracking a car and instead actually uses a device within the car to listen in on the passengers' conversations, it would again need a warrant or an exception to the warrant requirement. The situation changes, however, if those inside the vehicle initiate the contact. For example, in one case, passengers accidentally pushed the emergency button in their car, which connected them to OnStar.[104] This, in turn, allowed an OnStar employee to listen in on the conversation in the vehicle, which included a discussion about a possible drug transaction. This information was passed on to law enforcement, who subsequently located, stopped, and searched the car, where they found cannabis and the passengers were criminally charged. The passengers were not afforded the protections of the Fourth Amendment because they exposed, albeit accidentally, their conversation to OnStar.

In addition to monitoring the whereabouts of a vehicle, police may want to stop or seize the vehicle in order to obtain IoT-related content within it. Unlike the home, which the court has traditionally given a higher level of privacy protection, there are a number of automobile exceptions to the Fourth Amendment that allow law enforcement to stop a vehicle and search it.[105] Assuming police lawfully stop a vehicle, they may observe information visually displayed on any IoT device within the car. In addition, pursuant to the Supreme Court's decision in *California v. Acevedo*, police "may search an automobile and the containers within it where they have probable cause to believe contraband or evidence is contained."[106] If police have grounds to impound the car, they can also conduct an inventory search, which includes searching closed containers.[107]

It is less clear whether police can search an IoT device within the car without a warrant or an exception to the warrant requirement. The confusion here stems from two distinct issues. First, it is highly unlikely that the Supreme Court, in deciding *Acevedo*, considered the twenty-first century smart car and all the information it could hold. Thus, courts may choose to rethink or redefine what constitutes a closed container with respect to an automobile. Second, courts have not been entirely consistent with how they treat black boxes

---

104.   Thomas Fox-Brewster, *Cartapping: How Feds Have Spied on Connected Cars for 15 Years*, FORBES (Jan. 15, 2017), www.forbes.com/sites/thomasbrewster/2017/01/15/police-spying-on-car-conversations-location-siriusxm-gm-chevrolet-toyota-privacy/#30dbdda22ef8.

105.   Andrew Guthrie Ferguson, *The Internet of Things and the Fourth Amendment of Effects*, 104 CAL. L. REV. 805 (2016); California v. Carney, 471 U.S. 386 (1985).

106.   California v. Acevedo, 500 U.S. 565 (1991). In *Acevedo*, the police searched a brown paper bag in the defendant's trunk.

107.   Colorado v. Bertine, 479 U.S. 367 (1987).

or event data recorders (EDRs) which can be IoT devices, depending upon how such devices are used. Most cars sold in the last twenty years in the United States are equipped with an EDR. Pursuant to the requirements imposed by the National Highway Traffic Safety Administration (NHTSA), EDRs must at a minimum capture fifteen different types of information including braking status, vehicle speed, accelerator position, engine revolutions per minute, safety belt usage, air-bag deployment, and number and timing of crash events.[108] NHTSA places no limitations on the collection of additional data, thus manufacturers can equip EDRs to obtain other types of information.[109] Also, according to the Driver Privacy Act of 2015, information "retained by an event data recorder . . . is property of the [car] owner, or . . . lessee."[110] Lastly, the Data Privacy Act of 2015 limits, who besides the owner and lessee, may access EDR data.

One of the first cases to address the question of whether a search of the black box in a defendant's car raises Fourth Amendment protections was *People v. Christmann*.[111] In *Christmann*, the defendant was involved in a fatal accident. The initial police officers who responded to the scene requested the assistance of an accident re-constructionist. Upon arriving at the scene, the re-constructionist accessed the black box in the defendant's car and downloaded data from it without a warrant. The data retrieved from the black box included acceleration and deceleration, vehicle speed, engine RPM, throttle percentage and brake data, change in velocity (or delta V) and seat belt usage. The defendant unsuccessfully challenged the warrantless downloading of data from the black box, arguing that it violated his Fourth Amendment rights. In upholding the actions of law enforcement, the court determined:

> Because of this extensive regulation of vehicular safety equipment, there is only a diminished expectation of privacy in the mechanical areas of the vehicle . . . [which] must yield to the overwhelming state interest in investigating fatal accidents. . . . In the area of automobile safety, there is a high degree of governmental regulation, and a search conducted to carry out this regulation has a lower threshold of reasonableness. Since the testing done of the SDM records data regarding the performance of the vehicle during the incident such testing is a reasonable extension of Quackenbush. The downloading of the information is not analogous to a container search, nor does it extend to the private areas

---

108.   49 C.F.R. §§ 563.6–.7.
109.   *Id.*
110.   49 U.S.C. § 30101 (Driver Privacy Act of 2015).
111.   People v. Christmann, 776 N.Y.S.2d 437 (N.Y. J. Ct. 2004).

of the vehicle. There is also no opportunity for a police officer to select only the desired data or to manipulate it. . . .

While a pure 'automobile exception' does not apply since the officer had no probable cause to believe that evidence of a crime was contained within the car, courts have upheld warrantless searches of automobiles based upon exigency. . . . Here, however, real exigency exists. Evidence regarding the preaccident conditions within defendant's automobile could easily be destroyed, either purposely or accidently, if the automobile was moved from the scene under its own power.[112]

In contrast to *Christmann*, which has been followed by other courts, is a recent opinion out of Florida, *State v. Worsham*.[113] In *Worsham*, the defendant was involved in a fatal accident, and his car was impounded. Twelve days after the accident, the police, without a warrant, downloaded data from the black box in the defendant's car, which was used in the defendant's subsequent trial for drunk driving and vehicular homicide. After being convicted, the defendant appealed, arguing that law enforcement should have obtained a warrant before searching the black box in his car. The appellate court agreed with him, stating:

A car's black box is analogous to other electronic storage devices for which courts have recognized a reasonable expectation of privacy. Modern technology facilitates the storage of large quantities of information on small, portable devices. The emerging trend is to require a warrant to search these devices. See *Riley v. California*, 134 S. Ct. 2473 (2014) (requiring warrant to search cell phone seized incident to arrest).

. . .

Extracting and interpreting the information from a car's black box is not like putting a car on a lift and examining the brakes or tires. Because the recorded data is not exposed to the public, and because the stored data is so difficult to extract and interpret, we hold there is a reasonable expectation of privacy in that information, protected by the Fourth Amendment, which required law enforcement in the absence of exigent circumstances to obtain a warrant before extracting the information from an impounded vehicle.

Although electronic data recorders do not yet store the same quantity of information as a cell phone, nor is it of the same personal nature, the rationale for requiring a warrant to search a cell phone

---

112.   *Id.* at 441.
113.   Florida v. Worsham, 227 So. 3d 602 (2017) (Fla. Dist. Ct. App. 2017).

is informative in determining whether a warrant is necessary to search an immobilized vehicle's data recorder. These recorders document more than what is voluntarily conveyed to the public and the information is inherently different from the tangible "mechanical" parts of a vehicle. Just as cell phones evolved to contain more and more personal information, as the electronic systems in cars have gotten more complex, the data recorders are able to record more information. The difficulty in extracting such information buttresses an expectation of privacy.[114]

While it is not entirely clear whether courts will require law enforcement to obtain a warrant to search an IoT device within a car, it appears that a strong argument exists for requiring a warrant. This is largely due to the amount of information stored on an IoT device and the growing trend of courts to afford individuals privacy in matters relating to their portable devices. Another factor for courts to consider is that unlike personal devices such as a Fitbit, EDRs and similar devices installed in automobiles are not necessarily optional; they are mandated for almost all cars. Thus, failing to protect this information provides the government with a wealth information about individuals. Finally, as in *Carpenter*, it appears that IoT signals transmitted from the car are protected, especially if they include data collected over a prolonged period of time.

§ 9:4.4 With a Third Party

Sometimes the IoT data that law enforcement seeks is held by a third party, such as Amazon or a local utility company. Prior to *Carpenter v. United States*, if the third party did not fall under the Stored Communications Act, law enforcement could typically obtain IoT non-content data with little more than a subpoena or court order based upon the third-party doctrine.[115] According to the Supreme Court in *Smith v. Maryland*, "a person has no legitimate expectation of privacy in information he voluntarily turns over to third parties."[116] In *Smith*, the defendant robbed a woman and subsequently began harassing her by phone in order to prevent her from testifying against him. In an effort to stop the harassment and to collect evidence for the pending robbery charge, the police, without first obtaining a warrant, requested that the phone company set up a pen register to record

---

114. *Id.* at 606.
115. "Non-content" generally refers to information that would be found on the outside of an envelope, e.g., the "to" and "from." In contrast, "content" refers to the information normally found inside the envelope. This offline analogy does not always hold up online.
116. Smith v. Maryland, 442 U.S. 735, 744 (1979).

numbers dialed from the defendant's home. The pen register did not record phone conversations, which would have required a warrant.[117] Shortly after installation, the registry recorded a call from the defendant's home to the victim's home. Based on this evidence, the police obtained a search warrant for defendant's home, where they discovered evidence from the robbery.

The defendant was convicted and his appeal eventually wound up before the U.S. Supreme Court. In affirming the lower court's decision to permit the warrant and subsequent search of the defendant's home, the Supreme Court found that the defendant's Fourth Amendment rights had not been violated by the pen register. The Court stated:

> [w]hen [petitioner Smith] used his phone, petitioner voluntarily conveyed numerical information to the telephone company and "exposed" that information to its equipment in the ordinary course of business. In so doing, petitioner assumed the risk that the company would reveal to police the numbers he dialed.[118]

Nevertheless, third-party doctrine does have some limitations. In *United States v. Carpenter*, the Supreme Court refused to apply the third-party doctrine to long-term surveillance by cell sites.

There have also been efforts by third parties to place limitations on the accessibility of IoT content by law enforcement. For example, in *State v. Bates*, discussed previously, Amazon did not willingly turn over the IoT content from the defendant's Echo, despite the fact that the government obtained a warrant for it.[119] Instead, Amazon claimed First Amendment protections for not only the defendant's online requests to his Echo, but also for the search results the Echo provided to him. Amazon argued that the government's warrant "should be quashed unless the Court finds that the State has met its heightened burden for compelled production of such materials," and that the government had to demonstrate:

1. a compelling need for the information sought, including that it is not available from other sources; and

2. a sufficient nexus between the information and the subject of the criminal investigation.[120]

---

117.   The Pen Register Act, 18 U.S.C. ch. 206, prohibits the installation or use of pen register or trap and trace device without a court order obtained under 18 U.S.C. § 2523. A government agency authorized to install such a device must use technology reasonably available to restrict use so as not to include the contents of any wire or electronic communication.
118.   *Id.*
119.   State v. Bates, CR-2016-370-2 Warrant Affidavit.
120.   *Id.*

Unfortunately, the court never had the opportunity to decide Amazon's First Amendment challenge because the defendant consented to the release of the IoT content from his Echo to the police.[121]

Other attempts at limiting government access to IoT content held by third parties involved so-called "smart meters." Based upon the *Smith* decision and subsequent cases, courts have held that individuals do not have a reasonable expectation of privacy in their utility records.[122] Nonetheless, some have argued, unsuccessfully to date, that today's smart meters reveal so much about their users that the court should not treat them like meters of the past.

In *NSMA v. City of Naperville*, plaintiffs brought suit to prevent the city of Naperville, Illinois, from installing smart meters.[123] The court described the smart meters as follows:

> Like analog meters, smart meters can measure customers' total residential usage for monthly billing purposes. Unlike analog meters, smart meters are also equipped with wireless radio transmitters that, when activated, send usage data via radio-frequency waves to nearby neighborhood "network access points," which then relay usage data to Naperville's Department of Public Utilities-Electric. While analog meters are capable of measuring only total accumulated consumption of energy ("total kilowatt hours used over a month"), smart meters measure aggregate electricity usage much more frequently—in intervals of fifteen minutes that "include real power in kWH and reactive power in kVARh." Smart meters have the ability to collect data consisting of "granular, fine-grained, high-frequency type of energy usage measurements" (so-called "Interval Data") totaling to "over thousands of intervals per month."[124]

Plaintiffs argued that the smart meters invaded their privacy in violation of Article I, section 6 of the Illinois Constitution, and violated the Fourth Amendment rights of Naperville's citizens because they "collected detailed electricity usage data that can reveal intimate information about residents' personal lives within their homes." For example, the smart meters can indicate whether a home has a refrigerator, television, indoor grow light, or respirator, and can monitor

---

121. Ben Fox Rubin, *Amazon Hands Over Echo Data in Murder Case*, CNET (Mar. 7, 2017), www.cnet.com/news/amazon-echo-alexa-agrees-to-hand-over-data-in-murder-case/.

122. *See, e.g.*, United States v. McIntyre, 646 F.3d 1107, 1111–12 (8th Cir. 2011).

123. Naperville Smart Meter Awareness v. City of Naperville, 114 F. Supp. 3d 606 (N.D. Ill. 2015).

124. *Id.* at 609.

whether or not any such device is currently in use.[125] Furthermore, while some cities that adopt smart readers allow residents to opt out, Naperville did not. Ultimately, the federal district court dismissed the plaintiffs' complaint, stating:

> [b]ecause NSMA has failed to allege that smart meters are relaying detailed information beyond aggregate data about members' electricity usage to the City and that the City is disaggregating the data to analyze the private lives of its residents, there is no cognizable claim upon which relief can be granted.[126]

Some privacy organizations like the Electronic Frontier Foundation (EFF) have questioned the district court's ruling in *City of Naperville*.[127] According to the EFF, the information collected by smart meters is far more intrusive than what is collected by traditional meters:

> a single monthly read of cumulative household energy use does not reveal how energy is being used throughout the course of a day. But smart meter data does. And its time granularity tells a story about what is going on inside the home for anyone who wishes to read it.[128]

On appeal, the Seventh Circuit found that the information gathered by the smart readers was more invasive than the information collected by the thermal imagers in *Kyllo*.[129] Contrary to the argument put forward by Naperville, the Seventh Circuit declined to apply the third-party doctrine. The court said that it was inapplicable because the residents were challenging information within the control of the energy company. Furthermore, in applying *Carpenter v. United States*, the court determined that one does not "assume the risk of near constant monitoring by choosing to have electricity in her home."[130] Even with this finding, however, the Seventh Circuit, sided with the City of Naperville. The court stated that even if it assumed that the information collected by smart readers constituted a search,

---

125. *Id.*
126. *Id.* at 613.
127. Jamie Williams & Karen Gullo, *An Illinois Court Just Didn't Get It: We Are Entitled to Expect Privacy in Our Smart Meter Data, Which Reveals What's Going on Inside Our Homes*, ELEC. FRONTIER FOUND. (Mar. 1, 2017), www.eff.org/deeplinks/2017/03/illinois-court-just-didnt-get-it-we-are-entitled-expect-privacy-our-smart.
128. *Id.*
129. Naperville Smart Meter Awareness v. City of Naperville, 900 F.3d 521 (7th Cir. 2018).
130. *Id.*

the "significant government interests in the program, and the diminished privacy interests at stake [make] the search . . . reasonable."[131]

§ 9:5 Possible Defenses in IoT-Related Prosecutions

As discussed throughout this chapter, law enforcement has increasingly explored the use of IoT devices to gather evidence against criminal defendants, and the practice will likely becoming more and more common in the future. Therefore, defense attorneys will need to learn how to formulate defenses to content derived from the IoT.[132] The challenge here is that few cases involving IoT content have been litigated. Thus, to examine what potential defenses might be employed, it is helpful to turn to other areas of criminal law where law enforcement relies heavily on machines to obtain convictions. To date, the most common use of machine-generated criminal evidence arises in the area of traffic offenses. While it can be difficult to challenge, cross-examine, or raise questions of reasonable doubt for inanimate objects, like red-light cameras and breathalyzers, a few defendants have nonetheless been successful doing so.[133]

Defendants challenging machine-generated evidence make several different arguments. Some raise Sixth Amendment claims, asserting that, by introducing evidence derived from machines, defendants are denied their right to confront and cross-examine.[134] Unfortunately for defendants, most courts have determined that "forensic machines speak with a voice of their own, and those statements—the raw data of a machine—invoke no Confrontation Clause right."[135] Courts reach this conclusion because the machines, not those operating them, make the statements in question; therefore, the machines are not "witnesses" within the meaning of the Confrontation Clause.[136]

---

131.   *Id.*
132.   *See* Antigone Peyton, *A Litigator's Guide to the Internet of Things*, RICH. J.L. & TECH. (Apr. 1, 2016), http://jolt.richmond. edu/2016/04/01/a-litigators-guide-to-the-internet-of-things/.
133.   As of January 2016, 439 communities in the United States have red light cameras and 139 had speed cameras. *See* Printable List of Cities with Red Light and Speed Cameras, INS. INST. FOR HIGHWAY SAFETY, HIGHWAY LOSS DATA INST., https://perma.cc/H4AG-RH44 (last visited Jan. 27, 2016).
134.   Gary Biller, *Motorists vs. Cameras: Four Winning Defenses*, NAT'L MOTORISTS ASS'N BLOG (Mar. 27, 2012), www.motorists.org/blog/four-winning-defenses/.
135.   Brian Sites, *Rise of the Machines: Machine Generated Data and the Confrontation Clause*, 16 COLUM. SCI. & TECH. L. REV. 36 (2014).
136.   *Id.*

Defendants also argue that the presumption of innocence guaranteed to all criminal defendants is destroyed when the prosecution introduces so-called infallible evidence created or collected by an impartial, error-free device.[137] It remains to be seen how judges and juries will treat machine-generated evidence and what weight and credibility will be given when such evidence is introduced. For instance, if there is conflicting testimony between a parent and an IoT refrigerator regarding whether there was sufficient food in the house to feed the children living there, which witness will the jury give more credence to?[138] Both the "human" witness and the IoT witness "are fallible."[139]

If IoT data-driven evidence is prioritized over eyewitness statements or expert analysis, then the algorithms used to analyze IoT data need to be understood and disclosure of the imperfections within the devices should be explained.[140] While the prospect of having devices available to provide ironclad alibis is promising, the fact remains that data can be manipulated.[141] The manipulation does not even have to be digital; for example, one might create a false alibi based upon IoT data of another.[142] For example, a wife could wear her husband's Fitbit to sleep while the husband goes off to commit a crime.[143] The data from the Fitbit, if used, would show that he was asleep at the time of the crime, and if the wife corroborated the story, or did not testify, then the testimony of the Fitbit would be the "perfect alibi" with nothing in the story to contradict it. Any evidence relating to the husband's presence at the scene of the crime would have to be strong enough to counteract the Fitbit.

Finally, defendants may call into question the scientific reliability of the device and whether content derived from it should be admitted into evidence.[144] In order to admit IoT data as evidence, practitioners must demonstrate that it is objective and unbiased.[145] To do that, IoT evidence must adhere to the same requirements imposed on scientific or forensic evidence in order to be introduced in the courtroom.[146] Even when admitted, issues will still arise when IoT device

---

137.   Biller, *supra* note 134.
138.   *Id.*
139.   *Id.*
140.   *Id.*
141.   *Id.*
142.   *Id.*
143.   Antigone Peyton, *A Litigator's Guide to the Internet of Things*, RICH. J.L. & TECH. (Apr. 1, 2016), http://jolt.richmond.edu/2016/04/01/a-litigators-guide-to-the-internet-of-things/.
144.   *Id.*
145.   *Id.*
146.   *Id.*

evidence is given far more weight despite the known limitations that these devices have.[147] The questions pertaining to how these issues will be resolved depends upon the courts that first address IoT device evidence.[148]

On a final note, one growing area of concern with respect to challenging IoT-related evidence is the law surrounding trade secrets. Some criminal defendants have been stymied with respect to obtaining the algorithm or source code used by a specific IoT device that was responsible for producing incriminating content.[149] Merely requesting that information through discovery may not be sufficient to receive it from the government.[150] Instead, the defendant may be required to make a "prima facie showing of the relevance and necessity of the trade secret before disclosure occurs."[151]

---

147. *Id.*
148. *Id.*
149. Rebecca Wexler, *When a Computer Program Keeps You in Jail*, N.Y. TIMES, June 13, 2017, www.nytimes.com/2017/06/13/opinion/how-computers-are-harming-criminal-justice.html.
150. Rebecca Wexler, *Life, Liberty, and Trade Secrets: Intellectual Property in the Criminal Justice System*, 70 STAN. L. REV. 1343 (2018).
151. People v. Chubbs, 2015 WL 139069 (Cal. Ct. App. Jan. 9, 2015).

Chapter 10

International Law

---

§ 10:1   Overview

This chapter examines the various methods employed by countries around the globe to protect personal information. Since many of the laws concerning the protection of an individual's private data were written before IoT devices became so widely used, most countries do not specifically mention IoT devices in their general privacy laws. As demonstrated herein, the rules and regulations surrounding data security and privacy vary widely. Differing among the nations, these variations create challenges for businesses and organizations in the global market that collect and store personal information about individuals. As the complexities of the different national data protection laws continue to shift and change, it will be increasingly important for businesses to alter their data collection methods to stay in-step with the growing legislation. The constantly evolving landscape of data regulation may require companies and organizations in the global market to retain privacy and compliance officers, lawyers, and other professionals specializing in foreign and international laws of cybersecurity and data protection in order to keep their companies up-to-date with regulations.

§ 10:2   European Union

§ 10:2.1   *EU Data Protection Directive*

The 1995 European Union (EU) Data Protection Directive ("the Directive") was developed before the Internet and social media transformed personal and professional ways of life across the globe.[1] It has since been replaced by the General Data Protection Regulation.

In the Directive, EU member countries established a regulatory framework to secure personal data across national borders and to set a security baseline pertaining to the storage, transmission, and processing of personal information. The Directive "define[d] the basic elements of data protection that member states must transpose into national law."[2] Each of the EU member states managed the regulation

---

1.   EPIC-EU Data Protection Directive, ELEC. PRIVACY INFO. CTR., https://epic.org/privacy/intl/eu_data_protection_directive.html#introduction (last visited Dec. 11, 2018).
2.   *Id.*

of data protection and enforcement within their own jurisdiction, with data protection commissioners from the states participating in working groups at the community level.[3] The Directive required that data controllers ensure compliance with the law relating to data quality and the obligation to provide legitimate reasons for data processing when necessary.[4] Personal data was defined as "any information that relate[d] to an 'identified or identifiable natural person.'"[5] When the data controller directly collected or otherwise obtained personal data information from an individual, a duty was owed to that individual. A data controller was further required to implement technical and organizational measures to enforce laws against the unlawful destruction, accidental loss or unauthorized alteration, disclosure or access of personal data, when appropriate.

The Directive also outlined a data subject's individual rights, which were:

1. to know who the data controller is, the identity of the recipient of the data, and the purpose of the processing;

2. to ensure inaccurate data is rectified;

3. to seek recourse in the event of unlawful processing; and

4. to withhold permission to use data in certain circumstances.

The Directive contained stronger protections concerning the use of sensitive personal data relating to a person's health, sex life, or religious or philosophical beliefs.[6]

Enforcing the regulatory framework for the processing of personal data was accomplished through administrative proceedings of the supervisory authority or by judicial remedies. The supervisory authorities maintained the investigatory power and effective powers of intervention, such as order blocking, erasure and destruction of data, or imposition of a temporary or definite ban on processing. An individual who had suffered damage as a result of unlawful processing was entitled to receive compensation from the data controller who errantly handled the data. Finally, the Directive included a stipulation

---

3. *Id.*
4. Under the Directive, a data controller is any "natural or legal person, public authority, agency or any other body which alone or jointly with others determines the purposes and means of the processing of personal data." *See* Directive 95/46/EC of the European Parliament and of the Council of 24 October 1995 on the Protection of Individuals with Regard to the Processing of Personal Data and on the Free Movement of Such Data, 1995 O.J. (L 281), c. 1, art. 2(e) [hereinafter Directive].
5. *Id.* at c. 1, art. 2(a).
6. *Id.*

that transferring personal data outside the EU had to meet a level of processing that was "adequate" to the processing prescribed by the Directive's provisions.[7]

§ 10:2.2   *General Data Protection Regulation (GDPR)*

The GDPR is the culmination of four years of research conducted by the EU.[8] The EU embarked on this research in order to update the 1995 EU Data Protection Directive, which was repealed upon the effective date of the GDPR. The GDPR introduced tougher fines for noncompliance and breaches than those stipulated in the Directive and provided individuals with more autonomy in determining what companies do with their data.[9]

There are two major reasons why the GDPR was drafted. First, the EU wanted to give people more control over the use of their personal data. The EU crafted this regulation with companies that swap access to personal data for use of their services in mind, such as Facebook and Google. Since the Directive was enacted prior to widespread use of the Internet and development of cloud technology, the hope behind enacting the data protection legislation of the GDPR was to improve trust in the emerging digital economy. Second, the GDPR was enacted to allow businesses to operate within a simpler, clearer legal environment by making data protection regulation identical throughout the single market, collectively saving approximately €2.3 billion a year.[10]

On May 24, 2016, member states agreed to the final text of the GDPR legislation. However, the regulations within the GDPR did not apply immediately. Also, they did not come into effect until May 25, 2018. This delay in application was to allow companies sufficient time to ensure their policies and procedures complied with the GDPR.[11] After the May 25, 2018, deadline, the GDPR continues to apply to all organizations that control or process the personal data of EU residents.

---

7.   *Id.* at c. 4, art. 25.
8.   REGULATION 2016/679 OF THE EUROPEAN PARLIAMENT AND OF THE COUNCIL OF 27 APRIL 2016 ON THE PROTECTION OF NATURAL PERSONS WITH REGARD TO THE PROCESSING OF PERSONAL DATA AND ON THE FREE MOVEMENT OF SUCH DATA, AND REPEALING DIRECTIVE 95/46/EC (GENERAL DATA PROTECTION REGULATION), 2016 O.J. (L 119) 1 [hereinafter GDPR].
9.   *What Is GDPR? Everything You Need to Know Before the 2018 Deadline*, IT PRO (Mar. 11, 2020), www.itpro.co.uk/it-legislation/27814/what-is-gdpr-everything-you-need-to-know.
10.   *Id.*
11.   *Id.*

Both data controllers and data processors must abide by the GDPR.[12] A data controller is defined as an entity that programs the reasons and methods by which an individual's personal data is processed, while a data processor[13] is the third party conducting the actual processing.[14] A controller could encompass a variety of types of organizations ranging anywhere from a profit-seeking company to a charity or government. The processors could encompass I.T. firms that actually carry out the data processing. Under the GDPR, the data controller is responsible for ensuring processors abide by data protection rules, while the data processors themselves must adhere to those rules regarding the maintenance of processing activities records.

> Where processing is to be carried out on behalf of a controller, the controller shall use only processors providing sufficient guarantees to implement appropriate technical and organisational measures in such a manner that processing will meet the requirements of this Regulation and ensure the protection of the rights of the data subject.[15]

One significant aspect of this legislation is that the GDPR applies to every controller and processor of personal data, inside or outside the EU, so long as the data handled belongs to EU residents. The GDPR protects any individual who currently resides inside the territory of the EU. This protection of privacy extends to everything that occurs within the conglomerate of countries. The GDPR does not protect the privacy of an EU citizen if they are visiting a country outside of the EU jurisdiction.[16]

As the GDPR regulations are now in effect, a controller must ensure that personal data is processed "lawfully, fairly and in a transparent manner . . . for specified, explicit and legitimate purposes" and then subsequently deleted.[17] In order for data to be processed lawfully, the subject must consent to having their data processed. Additionally, data can be lawfully processed if it is necessary to do so: to maintain compliance with a contract; in protection of an interest "essential for the life of" the subject; in the public interest; or in the

---

12.   *See, e.g.,* GDPR, 2016 O.J. (L 119) 1; *see also* Data Protection Act 2018, c. 12, § 4 (Eng.).

13.   Under the GDPR, data processors are defined as any "natural or legal person, public authority, agency or other body which processes personal data on behalf of the controller." GDPR, art. 4, 2016 O.J. (L 119) 8.

14.   GDPR, 2016 O.J. (L 119) 1.

15.   *Id.* at c. 4, § 1, art. 28, 1.

16.   *Does GDPR Apply to EU Citizens Living in the US?,* HIPAA J. (May 11, 2018), www.hipaajournal.com/does-gdpr-apply-to-eu-citizens-living-in-the-us/.

17.   *Id.* at c. 2, art. 5, 1(b)–(c).

controller's legitimate interest—such as to prevent fraud.[18] Under the GDPR, consent must be an affirmative action by the subject, rather than pre-ticked boxes or opt-outs. A subject is also able to withdraw consent at any time. Controllers must keep a record of how and when the subject consented. If the current collection method for obtaining consent does not meet GDPR rules, controllers must either bring it up to the current standard or stop collecting data.[19]

Additionally, the GDPR allows for individuals to access their stored data at "reasonable intervals." An individual can request access to their data, and controllers must respond to the request within one month. When possible, a data controller must provide secure, direct access to allow people to review the personal information that a controller stores. The controllers and processors must be transparent about the collection of data, what is done with the data, and how the data is processed. This explanation must be provided in clear, plain language. The GDPR further gives people the right to: (1) access any information that a company holds about them; (2) know why the data is being processed; (3) know how long the data has been stored for; and (4) know who has access to it. Also, an individual has the right to ask for data to be corrected if it is incorrect or incomplete.[20]

The GDPR also allows people the right to be forgotten.[21] Under this right, an individual can demand that their data be deleted if it is no longer necessary to serve the purpose for which it was originally collected. Data subjects can also demand that their data be erased if they withdraw their consent for data collection or if they object to the way it is being processed. When the right to be forgotten is invoked, the controller is responsible for telling organizations to delete copies of the data as well as any links to copies of the data.[22]

In the event of a data breach, prior to calling the data protection authority, the organization must notify the individuals affected by the breach and must notify the data protection authority within seventy-two hours of discovering the breach. The GDPR provides a penalty of up to 2% of the organization's annual worldwide revenue, or €10 million, if they fail to meet the seventy-two-hour deadline.[23] In the initial contact with the data protection authority, the organization should outline the nature of the data breached, the approximate number of individuals impacted, the possible consequences of the breach for affected individuals, and the measures that the organization has

---

18.   *Id.* at 8, (44)–(47).
19.   *Id.* at 6, (32)–(33).
20.   *Id.*
21.   GDPR, art. 17.
22.   *Id.*
23.   *Id.* arts. 83 & 33.

actioned or is planning to action in response to the breach.[24] If the organization fails to follow the basic principles for processing data, ignores individuals' rights over their data, or transfers data to another country, the penalty can be up to €20 million or 4% of their global annual turnover, whichever is greater. The fines will be proportionate to the manner of the breach.[25]

§ 10:2.3 Cybersecurity Act

In the summer of 2018, the EU's parliamentary committee on Industry, Research and Energy (ITRE) advanced a proposal called the Cybersecurity Act, which would impose new rules on cybersecurity certifications and cooperation between EU nations.[26] The proposal set out regulations regarding the objectives, tasks and organizational aspects of the European Union Agency for Cybersecurity (ENISA) and proposed a framework for the establishment of EU certification schemes to assure adequate cybersecurity of IoT products within the EU.[27] The proposal was supported by the European Parliament, which desired to create mandatory certifications for high security risk IoT products and services like the technology involved in energy infrastructure. But, the proposal did not include mandatory security certifications for connected consumer products such as smartwatches and other smart home devices that are used by the general public on a day-to-day basis. Although Parliament wanted tough rules in the high security risk sectors, the European Commission and the Council of the EU, which represent the bloc's member states, wanted such certifications to be entirely voluntary.[28]

Yet, various consumer groups were unhappy with the proposed text of the Cybersecurity Act, which left connected consumer products, a major consumer vector, open to attack. These consumer organizations were concerned that Parliament, the European Commission,

24. *Id.* art. 33.
25. Danny Palmer, *What Is GDPR? Everything You Need to Know About the New General Data Protection Regulations* (May 17, 2019), www.zdnet.com/article/gdpr-an-executive-guide-to-what-you-need-to-know/.
26. David Meyer, *Smart Home Gadgets Are Open to Attack: So Time for IoT Security Laws? No, Says Europe*, THE GERMAN VIEW (July 11, 2018), www.zdnet.com/article/smart-home-gadgets-are-open-to-attack-so-time-for-iot-security-laws-no-says-europe/.
27. Proposal for a Regulation of the European Parliament and of the Council on ENISA, the "EU Cybersecurity Agency," and repealing Regulation (EU) 526/2013, and on Information and Communication Technology cybersecurity certification ("Cybersecurity Act") Eur. Parl. Doc. (COM 2017/0225(COD) 477 final (Sept. 13, 2017), http://data.consilium.europa.eu/doc/document/ST-9350-2018-INIT/en/pdf.
28. *Id.*

and Council of the EU were "missing the severity of the threat posed by insecure connected devices of the more everyday variety." The consumer organizations were advocating for European institutions to mandate cybersecurity requirements, such as security updates, strong passwords, or encryption for smartwatches and smart fridges. The director general of the European Consumer Organisation (BEUC[29]), Monique Goyens, stated: "It is very disappointing that the EU institutions still seem to underestimate the dimension of the problem and are unwilling to address it by mandating security by design and default."[30]

On March 12, 2019, the Cybersecurity Act passed in a plenary vote of the full European Parliament. Its passage followed various stages of political negotiations and compromises reached at the end of 2018 and the beginning of 2019, between the European Commission, the Parliament, and the Council of the European Union.[31] The legislation enhances the security of IoT devices together with critical infrastructure, incorporating security features such as security by design in the early stages of design and development. Users may ascertain assurances about the level of security through security features that are independently verified.[32]

§ 10:3   United Kingdom

§ 10:3.1   *Data Protection Act*

In Europe, the United Kingdom was at the forefront of protecting personal information. The U.K.'s Data Protection Act of 1998 (Data Protection Act)[33] defined personal data[34] as:

---

29.   An acronym coming from the French name of the organization: Bureau Européen des Unions de Consommateurs.
30.   Meyer, *supra* note 26.
31.   Eur. Comm'n News, *The Cybersecurity Act Strengthens Europe's Cybersecurity* (Mar. 19, 2019), https://ec.europa.eu/digital-single-market/en/news/cybersecurity-act-strengthens-europes-cybersecurity.
32.   Eur. Comm'n News, *Cybersecurity Act* (Dec. 11, 2018), https://ec.europa.eu/commission/news/cybersecurity-act-2018-dec-11_en.
33.   Data Protection Act 2018, c. 12, § 4 (Eng.).
34.   This language was updated in the Data Protection Act of 2018 to read: "'Personal data' means any information relating to an identified or identifiable living individual who can be identified, directly or indirectly, in particular by reference to (a) an identifier such as a name, an identification number, location data or an online identifier, or (b) one or more factors specific to the physical, physiological, genetic, mental, economic, cultural or social identity of the individual." C. 12, § 3.

[D]ata which relate to a living individual who can be identified—

(a) from those data, or

(b) from those data and other information which is in the possession of, or is likely to come into the possession of, the data controller, and includes any expression of opinion and the individual and any indication of the intentions of the data controller or any other person in respect of the individual.[35]

The Data Protection Act further defined "sensitive personal data" to mean:

[P]ersonal data consisting of information as to the data subject's—

(a) racial or ethnic origin,

(b) political opinions,

(c) religious beliefs or other beliefs of a similar nature,

(d) status as a member of a trade union . . .

(e) physical or mental health or condition,

(f) sexual life,

(g) commission or alleged commission of any offence, or

(h) proceedings of any offence committed or alleged to have been committed, and the disposal of or the sentence of any court in such proceedings.[36]

The GDPR added to this definition of personal data by including: online identifiers, such as IP addresses; economic, cultural, or mental health information; and pseudonymization of personal data, depending upon the level of difficulty involved in identifying the individual.[37]

§ 10:3.2   *U.K. Code of Practice*

The government of the United Kingdom, through its Department for Digital, Culture, Media and Sport and the National Cyber Security Centre, launched the U.K. Code of Practice ("Code") in October of 2018. The Code established new guidelines which encourage companies to incorporate "security by design"—the idea that strong security measures are incorporated into the product and technology from the

---

35.   DATA PROTECTION ACT OF 1998, c. 29, pt. I, § 1.

36.   *Id.* at c. 29, pt. I, § 2.

37.   *See What Is GDPR? Everything You Need to Know Before the 2018 Deadline*, IT PRO (Mar. 11, 2020), www.itpro.co.uk/it-legislation/27814/what-is-gdpr-everything-you-need-to-know.

beginning of its design—for all IoT products.[38] The Code contains the following thirteen guidelines for IoT companies:

(1) IoT devices should not have default passwords;

(2) companies should implement policies for disclosure of vulnerabilities;

(3) device software should be consistently updated;

(4) security-sensitive data and "credentials should be stored securely within services and on devices";

(5) "devices should communicate securely";

(6) devices should "[minimize] exposed attack surfaces";

(7) the integrity of device software should be verified through secure boot mechanisms;

(8) devices that process personal data should ensure that personal data is protected;

(9) systems should be resilient to network and power outages;

(10) "telemetry data . . . such as usage and measurement data . . . should be monitored for security anomalies";

(11) personal data should be easy for consumers to delete;

(12) installation and maintenance should be easy with minimal steps; and

(13) "data input via user interfaces . . . should be validated."[39]

The Code's recommendations are voluntary and therefore not binding on IoT companies.[40] Several large companies such as HP, Inc. and Centrica Hive, have already agreed to implement the Code's new rules.[41] But, some critics have suggested that because the Code is voluntary, small manufacturers will inevitably avoid implementation of the Code's rules, as there are no consequences in place for those who choose not to follow it.[42]

---

38. Tom Allen, *UK Gov Launches "World's First" Code of Practice for IoT Security*, THE INQUIRER (Oct. 15, 2018), www.theinquirer.net/inquirer/news/3064548/uk-gov-launches-worlds-first-code-of-practice-for-iot-security.

39. Chris Middleton, *IoT Security: Government Unveils Code of Practice—But It's Voluntary*, INTERNET OF BUS. (Oct. 15, 2018), https://internetofbusiness.com/iot-security-uk-unveils-new-code-of-conduct-but-its-voluntary/.

40. Allen, *supra* note 38.

41. Middleton, *supra* note 39.

42. *Id.*

§ 10:4   Australia

§ 10:4.1   *The Privacy Act 1988*

Australia has regulated personal privacy since 1988. The law defines personal information as: "information or an opinion, whether true or not, and whether recorded in a material form or not, about an identified individual, or an individual who is reasonably identifiable."[43] The Privacy Act contains thirteen Australian Privacy Principles (APPs) that apply to private sector organizations and Australian/Norfolk Island government agencies.[44]

§ 10:4.2   *Australian Privacy Principles (APPs)*

Schedule 1 of the Privacy Act 1988 outlines the content of the APPs. The APP entities discussed above are required to follow the same guidelines and principles for handling, using, and managing personal information. While the APPs are not regulations per se, the APP entities must follow the principles when their situation necessitates it.[45] The APPs encompass:

- the management of personal information in an open and transparent manner;

- privacy policies;

- individual options of transacting anonymously or under a pseudonym when practicable;

- collection of solicited personal information;

- the receipt of unsolicited personal information;

- concerns about notices regarding the collection of personal information;

- the use and disclosure of personal information;

- the use and disclosure of personal information overseas;

- maintenance of the quality of personal information;

- the security of personal information; and

---

43.   OFFICE OF THE AUSTL. INFO. COMM'R, PRIVACY ACT 1988, www.oaic.gov. au/privacy-law/privacy-act/ (last visited June 15, 2020).
44.   *Id.*
45.   OFFICE OF THE AUSTL. INFO. COMM'R, AUSTRALIAN PRIVACY PRINCIPLES, www.oaic.gov.au/privacy-law/privacy-act/australian-privacy-principles (last visited Dec. 13, 2018).

- the right for individuals to access and correct their personal information.[46]

The regulations for the APPs become increasingly strict when the information collected and handled is "sensitive information." The APPs define sensitive information as: health information, predictive genetic information, racial or ethnic origin, political opinions, membership in a union or political association, religious beliefs or affiliations, philosophical beliefs, sexual orientation or practices, criminal record, biometric information, and biometric templates.[47]

§ 10:4.3   *Notifiable Data Breaches (NDB)*

The Privacy Act 1988 also outlines requirements for responses when entities experience a data breach.[48] If a data breach is likely to result in serious harm, the APP requires notification to any individual whose personal information was involved in the breach. The Privacy Act also requires entities to notify all impacted individuals and the Australian Information Commissioner (Commissioner). The notification must include: the identity and contact information of the organization, a description of the breach, a description of the information that might have been obtained, and recommended steps that individuals should take in response to the breach. Not only does the Privacy Act include notification requirements, it also contains information pertaining to an organization's preparation for a data breach and their response procedures, including methods for securing personal information.[49]

§ 10:5   Japan

§ 10:5.1   *Basic Act on Cybersecurity*

Japan's Basic Act on Cybersecurity ("Basic Act"), passed in 2014, defines the roles of the national and local governments and other relevant stakeholders in the protection of personal data.[50] The Basic Act was developed as a first step in response to the growing threats in the sphere of cybercrime including theft of personal, business, and organizational information as well as threats to national security and governments across the world. The Basic Act created the Cybersecurity

---

46.   *Id.*
47.   *Id.*
48.   AUSTRALIAN PRIVACY PRINCIPLES, *supra* note 45.
49.   *Id.*
50.   Cabinet Order, Cybersecurity Strategy 14 [2015 Japan Cybersecurity Strategy] (Japan) (Jan. 27, 2018), www.nisc.go.jp/eng/pdf/cs-strategy-en.pdf.

Strategic Headquarters of Japan and formalized the role of the National Center of Incident Readiness and Strategy for Cybersecurity (NISC) Cabinet office within Japanese government, which is responsible for the development and implementation of national strategies and cybersecurity policies including security concerns surrounding the IoT.[51] Since NISC's authorization under the Basic Act, the Cabinet has developed two important planning and implementation documents: the 2015 Japan Cybersecurity Strategy and the General Framework for Secure IoT Systems of 2016.[52]

§ 10:5.2   2015 Japan Cybersecurity Strategy

The 2015 Japan Cybersecurity Strategy ("2015 Strategy") focuses on a commitment to involve a collaborative, yet completely voluntary, cross-sector approach to cybersecurity policy-making.[53] In this manner, Japan's Cybersecurity policy is similar to the U.S. NIST framework, acknowledging that the security risks relating to the regulation of the IoT and other cyber-platforms are best handled through a cross-sector development of IoT cybersecurity standards.[54]

The 2015 Strategy focuses on allowing innovation for safety and security measures to come from all stakeholders including users, civil society, critical information companies, and businesses alike, without the direct interference of strict regulation on behalf of government.[55] Instead, under the 2015 Strategy, the Japanese government seeks to support companies that aggressively address cybersecurity issues through recognition incentives and the creation of financial benefits for these security innovators.[56] The Japanese government will also incentivize companies that create their products under the principle of "Security by Design," which incorporates security assurances and protections in the initial development, planning, and design phases of IoT devices.[57] In adopting this cross-sector approach, the

---

51.   Hiroyuki Arie, *Japan's Approach to Tackling Cybersecurity Challenges*, *TÜV Rheinland Japan*, JAPAN INDUS. NEWS (Jan. 17, 2017), www.japanindustrynews.com/2017/01/japans-approach-tackling-cybersecurity-challenges/.

52.   Mihoko Matsubara, *Assessing Japan's Internet of Things (IoT) Security Strategy for Tokyo 2020*, PALO ALTO: BLOG HOME/CSO PERSPECTIVE (Sept. 16, 2016), https://researchcenter.paloaltonetworks.com/2016/09/cso-assessing-japans-internet-of-things-iot-security-strategy-for-tokyo-2020/.

53.   Scott J. Shackelford, *When Toasters Attack: A Polycentric Approach to Enhancing the "Security of Things"*, 2017 U. ILL. L. REV. 415, 459 (2017).

54.   *Id.*

55.   Matsubara, *supra* note 52.

56.   Arie, *supra* note 51.

57.   2015 Japan Cybersecurity Strategy, *supra* note 50, at 13.

Japanese government acknowledges the impracticality and bulkiness of government control and regulation over IoT systems and instead opts for collaborative efforts from various stakeholders. This holistic approach facilitates the creation of dynamic responses to new threats and interactive, coordinated relationships among private and public sector stakeholders.[58]

§ 10:5.3   *General Framework for Secure IoT Systems*

In August 2016, the government of Japan, through NISC, further defined strategies and policies for collaboration between stakeholders through effectuation of the General Framework for Secure IoT Systems ("General Framework"). This document defined Japan's two-step approach to ensure that IoT systems are developed under the principle of "Security by Design."[59] These steps include: (1) the development and implementation of comprehensive security requirements for the "design, development, and operation of all IoT systems"; and (2) requirements for "sector-specific" usage and operation of IoT systems.[60]

In developing safety and security in IoT systems, the General Framework recognizes that IoT systems are often interconnected. This interconnectedness creates potential vulnerabilities in aggregated IoT systems when one IoT system fails to adhere to proper safety requirements. Aggregated IoT systems require four elements under the General Framework: safety, confidentiality, integrity, and information availability in order to allow prompt recovery of service after a cyber attack.[61] The General Framework plans on accomplishing this resiliency in aggregated IoT systems through the implementation of the principle of "Security by Design," which in turn mandates close reliance upon mutual understanding and trust among stakeholders, close partnerships between public and private sectors, and collaboration among industry, academia, and the government.[62] Due to this emphasis on the idea of "Security by Design," manufacturers of IoT products have been included as part of the critical infrastructure of IoT systems in Japan's General Framework, allowing manufacturers of IoT products to help shape cybersecurity strategy within Japan's

---

58.   *Id.* at 9.
59.   NAT'L CTR. OF INCIDENT READINESS & STRATEGY FOR CYBERSECURITY (NISC), General Framework for Secure IoT Systems (Japan) (Aug. 26, 2016), www.nisc.go.jp/eng/pdf/iot_framework2016_eng.pdf.
60.   *Id.* at 1.
61.   *Id.* at 1–2.
62.   *Id.* at 3–4.

borders and in the global marketplace.[63] NISC's multi-stakeholder approach extends to the international marketplace in that the document places a high emphasis on its periodic revision and modification in order to continuously maintain alignment with both domestic and international advancements, innovations, and guidelines.[64]

§ 10:6   South Korea

§ 10:6.1   *Personal Information Protection Act (PIPA)*

The Personal Information Protection Act (PIPA), enacted in South Korea on September 30, 2011, is one of the world's strictest privacy policy regulation regimes.[65] Historically, South Korea's approach has included more governmental control than either the governments of the United States, Japan, or Australia. South Korean cybersecurity policies take a more hardline regulatory approach by "[combining] strong broad-spectrum legislation protecting [personal identifiable information] with sector-specific regulations governing other aspects of cybersecurity."[66]

As the single most important cybersecurity regulation of South Korea, the PIPA protects privacy rights of individual data subjects and applies to businesses, organizations and government entities.[67] Much like the GDPR, PIPA regulates the actions of data controllers and data processors engaged in the collection and use of this personal data information and provides for the protection of South Korean resident registration numbers.[68] Under PIPA, businesses must take certain minimum cybersecurity precautions and data controllers and processors must follow certain notification requirements in case of a breach of information.[69] The penalties under PIPA are enforced by

---

63.   Mihoko Matsubara, *Assessing Japan's Internet of Things (IoT) Security Strategy for Tokyo 2020*, PALO ALTO: BLOG HOME/CSO PERSPECTIVE (Sept. 16, 2016), https://researchcenter.paloaltonetworks.com/2016/09/cso-assessing-japans-internet-of-things-iot-security-strategy-for-tokyo-2020/.

64.   NAT'L CTR. OF INCIDENT READINESS AND STRATEGY FOR CYBERSECURITY (NISC), General Framework for Secure IoT Systems (Japan) at 5 (Aug. 26, 2016), www.nisc.go.jp/eng/pdf/iot_framework2016_eng.pdf.

65.   Alex Wall, *GDPR Matchup: South Korea's Personal Information Protection Act*, IAPP (Jan. 8, 2018), https://iapp.org/news/a/gdpr-matchup-south-koreas-personal-information-protection-act/.

66.   Scott J. Shackelford, *When Toasters Attack: A Polycentric Approach to Enhancing the "Security of Things"*, 2017 U. ILL. L. REV. 415, 459 (2017).

67.   Wall, *supra* note 65; *see also* Scott J. Shackelford, Scott Russell & Jeffrey Haut, *Bottoms Up: A Comparison of "Voluntary" Cybersecurity Frameworks*, 16 U.C. DAVIS BUS. L.J. 217 (2016).

68.   Shackelford, Russell & Haut, *supra* note 67.

69.   *Id.*

the Ministry of the Interior (MOI) and can include regulatory fines, criminal charges, and even imprisonment.[70]

§ 10:6.2   Master Plan for Building the Internet of Things

South Korea's highly regulated approach to cybersecurity has faced much criticism from stakeholders who claim that strict regulation makes it difficult to adapt to new cyber threats.[71] These critics argue that this type of government regulation is less mobile than the private-sector driven approach.[72] Yet, when considering the frequency of cybersecurity events in the country, paired with the fear of North Korean cyber attacks, these issues may have contributed to the South Korean government's slower, more cautious movement from the centralized, regulatory scheme to the adoption of the more private-sector approach seen in other countries.[73] Despite this reluctance, there has been some attempt by the South Korean government to address these concerns; in 2014, the South Korean government released the Master Plan for Building the Internet of Things ("Master Plan") which provides government agencies such as the MOI with a roadmap and guidance for the development of cybersecurity standards and best practices.[74]

Components of the Master Plan aim to increase domestic IoT markets, use IoT to advance public administration, further industrial productivity and efficiency, and improve the safety and quality of life of South Korean individuals. These domestic improvements in IoT accessibility and security will be accomplished, according to the Master Plan, through a collaboration between the South Korean government and the private IoT sector. This collaboration will focus on the development of an open IoT ecosystem to "improve interoperability, reduce costs through economies of scale and scope, and enable flexible responses to environmental changes. The ecosystem will support startups to transform ideas into businesses, using tools

---

70.   Wall, *supra* note 65; *see also* Daniel Lee, *Data Protection Laws of the World: South Korea*, DLA PIPER (Jan. 27, 2017), www.dlapiperdataprotection.com/index.html?t=law&c=KR.

71.   Shackelford, Russell & Haut, *supra* note 67, at 247–49; *see also* Shackelford, *supra* note 66.

72.   *Id.*

73.   Shackelford, Russell & Haut, *supra* note 67, at 247–49.

74.   Sachin Mittal, Tsz Wang Tam & Chris Ko, *Internet of Things: The Pillar of Artificial Intelligence*, DBS ASIAN INSIGHTS: SECTOR BRIEFING 63 (June 2018), www.dbs.com/aics/templatedata/article/generic/data/en/GR/062018/180625_insights_internet_of_things_the_pillar_of_artificial_intelligence.xml.

including open source hardware (circuit diagrams, board plans, and specifications required for hardware development) and software, and DIY open labs." As part of the step toward greater collaboration, the MOI created a public-private joint council in 2015 called the IoT Security Alliance, to further promote more private-sector involvement.[75]

Since the South Korean domestic market is relatively small, other components of the Master Plan aim to expand this market. This will be accomplished by focusing efforts on cooperation with global businesses and promotion of joint research projects with the Trans-Eurasia Information Network that consists of nineteen Asian and thirty-four European countries. This global focus is meant to position South Korea as a global leader in development of IoT products and services through the use of South Korea's information, communications, and technology (ICT) infrastructure and manufacturing capacities. In order to better align itself in the IoT global marketplace and to promote "security by design" in IoT systems, the South Korean government also established an information-sharing and analysis framework with U.S., Japanese, and E.U. governing bodies through the creation of the IoT Innovation Center of Korea.[76]

As of May 2016, the South Korean Ministry of Science, ICT, and Future Planning announced further plans to ease regulations on the ICT sector as part of an aggressive governmental deregulation drive. This deregulation focuses on "lowering the barrier for companies to launch businesses in the Internet of Things (IoT) industry and prompting an early establishment of IoT-only networks nationwide."[77]

South Korea is also creating more incentives for businesses that show a propensity for enhancing cybersecurity readiness. Furthermore, in an effort to allow IoT security systems to better adapt as new cybersecurity issues arise, the government's Telecommunications Strategy Council has been given responsibility to modify existing laws and regulations to ensure a liberal and competitive industrial environment for the IoT. If the Council finds regulations that hinder ICT convergence, it can request improvement of these regulations by the MOI or other relevant agencies. Additionally, the Council will focus its attention on prompt processing and interim licensing for new products and services to facilitate the implementation of "security

---

75.   Ian Brown, *GSR Discussion Paper: Regulation and the Internet of Things*, ITU (2015), www.itu.int/en/ITU-D/Conferences/GSR/Documents/GSR2015/Discussion_papers_and_Presentations/GSR_DiscussionPaper_IoT.pdf.

76.   Brown, *supra* note 75.

77.   *Regulations on IoT Industry Will Be Eased*, Yonhap News Agency (May 18, 2016), https://en.yna.co.kr/view/AEN20160518006700320?section=search.

by design."[78] These actions, among other factors, suggest that South Korea is showing a willingness to move into a more private-sector driven approach in order to increase its participation and position in the global IoT marketplace.[79]

§ 10:7   Thailand

§ 10:7.1   Leading Up to a Digital Economy Plan

Thailand's digital economy and the data protection plans employed to protect it has been an ongoing effort over a period of time. From 2000 through 2011, Thailand reportedly had very few cybersecurity regulations in place, and the regulations in existence were enforced irregularly by several agencies including the Royal Thai Police, the Department of Special Investigation, and the Central Institute of Forensic Science.[80] In 2014, a Master Plan for cybersecurity was proposed but not enacted because of a military coup that year which caused Thailand's economic growth to slow considerably. After this initial disruption, the Thai government developed an ambitious set of priorities and goals to revitalize Thai society and become a leader in the international technology and cyber sector through the Digital Economy Plan or Thailand 4.0.[81]

§ 10:7.2   Digital Economy Plan: Thailand 4.0

The Digital Economy Plan of Thailand, otherwise called Thailand 4.0, is a plan announced by the Thai government in 2014 that focuses on strategies and initiatives meant to bring the country out of the "middle-income trap"[82] and transform Thailand into a "value-based economy."[83] Thailand 4.0 seeks: (1) to transform production

---

78.   *Id.*

79.   Scott J. Shackelford, *When Toasters Attack: A Polycentric Approach to Enhancing the "Security of Things"*, 2017 U. ILL. L. REV. 415, 459 (2017).

80.   *Id.* at 460.

81.   Deanna Despodova Pajkovski, *The Future of Competition is Collaboration: Interview with Dr. Suvit Maesincee*, 1 THAI-AM. BUS. 10, 10–12 (2017).

82.   A middle-income trap is commonly defined as a situation where a country, which is successful in lifting its economy from the status of being a least-developed or low-income country to a middle-income one, then remains at that level without much prospect of becoming an advanced, rich country. Somchai Jitsuchon, *Thailand in a Middle-Income Trap*, TDRI Q. REV., at 13 (June 2012), https://tdri.or.th/wp-content/uploads/2012/12/t5j2012-somchai.pdf.

83.   Rumana Bukht & Richard Heeks, *Digital Economy Policy: The Case Example of Thailand*, 7 DEV. IMPLICATIONS OF DIG. ECONS. 1, 2 (2018),

from "commodities" into "innovative products"; (2) to convert industry-driven activities into technology, creativity, and innovation driven activities; and (3) to change the focus from product production to providing services.[84] In other words, the plan aims to transform the country's industry-driven economy into an economy driven by technology.[85] Thailand 4.0 envisions a country of smart cities, smart industries, and technology-savvy people.[86]

In building the "Digital Economy and Society," Thailand seeks to become a competitive leader within the ASEAN[87] economic community.[88] The ambitious goals of Thailand 4.0 aim to place Thailand "[within] the top 40 countries in the global ICT Development Index ("IDI") [ ] and the top 15 [countries] in the World Competitiveness Index."[89] Due to the importance of the Digital Economy Plan, it has been placed under the direct leadership of Thailand's Deputy Prime Minister.[90]

Thailand 4.0 involves four phases of development: (1) investing and building a digital foundation, (2) driving the country with digital technology and innovation, (3) ensuring that all residents of Thailand can access and use digital technology, and (4) leading the global digital technology and innovation sectors while becoming a developed country.[91] Strategies to accomplishing these phases include: (1) the construction of high-capacity digital infrastructures in Thailand, (2) the use of digital technology to boost the economy, (3) the creation of a knowledge-driven digital society, (4) the conversion to a completely digital government, (5) the development of the digital-era

---

https://diodeweb.files.wordpress.com/2018/03/digital-economy-policy-diode-paper.pdf.

84. *Id.*

85. Paulius Kuncinas, *Thailand 4.0: Systems Upgrade*, 1 THAI-AM. BUS. 14, 14–15 (2017), www.amchamthailand.com/wp-content/uploads/2018/11/T-AB1-2017_FINAL.pdf.

86. *Id.*

87. The Association of Southeast Asian Nations (ASEAN) promotes the economic growth of ten member countries located south of China including: the two largest economies and founding members, Indonesia and Thailand; and the eight other countries of Brunei, Cambodia, Laos, Malaysia, Myanmar, Philippines, Vietnam, and Singapore. The purpose of ASEAN is to form a common market based off the model of the European Union. Kimberly Amadeo, *ASEAN, Its Members, Purpose, and History: How Does It Affect China, the U.S. and You?*, THE BALANCE (June 15, 2018), www.thebalance.com/what-is-asean-3305810.

88. Bukht & Heeks, *supra* note 83, at 2.

89. *Id.*

90. *Id.* at 2–3.

91. *Id.* at 3.

workforce, and (6) increasing trust and confidence in digital technologies by updating laws and regulations that ensure data security.[92]

From 2015 through 2017, several agencies or commissions were established to help address various aspects of the plan including the: Ministry of Digital Economy and Society (MDES); National Digital Economy and Society Committee (Digital Economy Committee); and the Digital Economy Promotion Agency (DEPA 2017). Furthermore, thirteen committees or working groups are devoted to tackling a variety of issues ranging from "innovation and digitization, the new S-curve, and promoting infrastructure to grass-roots development, modernizing agriculture, education reform, as well as how to enhance the competitiveness of [their] labor force." In order to accomplish such lofty goals, the architects of Thailand 4.0 have stressed the need for collaboration among government agencies, the public and private sectors, and even "the people sector, or the civil society, by empowering citizens to solve local issues and concerns."[93]

As Thailand moves from an economy based in heavy industry to a digital economy, the governmental structures and agencies currently in place have proven to be too large, cumbersome and bureaucratic for the country's needs.[94] Hence, government officials stated that they would focus their efforts on reforming both administrative and regulatory agencies, as well as on relaxing regulatory constraints on the private sector and businesses in order to facilitate easier business practices in Thailand.[95] In 2016, some of these governmental bureaucracies were restructured and the MDES was formed.[96]

§ 10:7.3   *Digital Laws 4.0*

Along with maintaining a commitment to de-regulation and implementing incentives for innovative technologies in the private sector, the Thai government proposed eight drafts of various laws to guide the implementation of the new Digital Economy policy in technology, cybersecurity, computer crimes, personal data protection, and telecommunications sectors in 2015.[97] These acts include a newly

---

92.   *Id.* at 3–4.
93.   Deanna Despodova Pajkovski, *The Future of Competition is Collaboration: Interview with Dr. Suvit Maesincee*, 1 THAI-AM. BUS. 10, 10–12 (2017).
94.   Kuncinas, *supra* note 85, at 14–15.
95.   *Id.*
96.   *Id.*
97.   John Fotiadis & Panagiotis Fotiadis, *Thailand's Digital Law Landscape and What We Can Expect from the New Digital Economy Laws*, 1 THAI-AM. BUS. 22, 22–25 (2017), www.amchamthailand.com/wp-content/uploads/2018/11/T-AB1-2017_FINAL.pdf.

drafted Personal Data Protection Act, a revision of the Computer Crimes Act (CCA), and amendments to the Electronic Transactions Act (ETA).[98] These bills, referred to as Digital Laws 4.0, were intended to support the development of the digital economy and were drafted in response to constant cybersecurity threats which placed Thailand as the eleventh most frequently attacked nation in the world by cyber criminals.[99] The ETA and the CCA focus on providing security recommendations for organizations so that they may securely conduct electronic transactions and combat cybercrime.[100]

The Personal Data Protection Act was modeled after the GDPR and contains similar specifications requiring written legal consent for data collection, regulations regarding what information can be collected by data controllers and data processors, notices of breach requirements, and the rights of individuals to withdraw consent to the collection of their personal data. Any data controller in violation of the provisions within the Personal Data Protection Act could be subject to both civil and criminal penalties. The draft version of the Personal Data Protection Act was passed by the Thai Cabinet on May 22, 2018, and was unanimously approved by the military-appointed parliament on February 28, 2019.[101]

As a developing country, Thailand lags behind in the legislation needed to support the digital economy.[102] Thailand faces many hurdles in the pursuit of accomplishing the lofty goals of Thailand 4.0, and the country will need to work to catch up with neighboring developed countries further ahead on the path toward comprehensive IoT and cybersecurity policies.[103] Furthermore, Thailand has a historical legacy of reformist governments that have laid plans to resolve societal problems—at much cost and considerable effort—only for those plans to be forgotten or replaced by new aspirations. Some debate exists about whether Thailand can accomplish Thailand 4.0. In light

---

98.   *Id.*
99.   Scott J. Shackelford, *When Toasters Attack: A Polycentric Approach to Enhancing the "Security of Things"*, 2017 U. ILL. L. REV. 415, 459 (2017).
100. *Id.*
101. Patpicha Tanakasempipat, *Thailand Passes Internet Security Law Decried as "Cyber Martial Law"*, REUTERS (Feb. 28, 2019), http://news.trust.org/item/20190228122102-etufn/.
102. Rumana Bukht & Richard Heeks, *Digital Economy Policy: The Case Example of Thailand*, 7 DEV. IMPLICATIONS OF DIG. ECONS. 1, 16 (2018), https://diodeweb.files.wordpress.com/2018/03/digital-economy-policy-diode-paper.pdf.
103. Christopher F. Bruton, *Human Factor in Thailand 4.0*, 1 THAI-AM. BUS. 16, 16–18 (2017), www.amchamthailand.com/wp-content/uploads/2018/11/T-AB1-2017_FINAL.pdf.

of actions taken by the Thai government to date, international part-
ners and businesses are watching the progression of Thailand 4.0
closely. Despite these challenges, there is potential for Thailand to
become a leading nation among the ASEAN countries and for Thai
society to be pushed forward into the digital future if the government
truly commits to aggressively implementing Thailand 4.0.[104]

§ 10:8　　Canada

§ 10:8.1　　*General Development of IoT Privacy in Canada*

Canada's current framework of privacy laws were first developed
during the 1980s by Organization for Economic Cooperation and
Development (OECD) Guidelines. The OECD Guidelines established
eight principles encompassing the collection of personal information
including: "collection limitation, data quality, purpose specification,
use limitation, security safeguards, openness, individual participation and accountability."[105] The OECD Guidelines were voluntary in
nature. Therefore, businesses could choose to self-regulate their data
collection activities. Also, the OECD created no effective enforcement
authority to monitor compliance.[106]

This self-regulatory scheme continued through the mid-1990s
when the Canadian Standards Association (CSA) adopted a similar
measure to the OECD Guidelines of self-regulation called the CSA
Model Code for the Protection of Personal Information. The adopting committee of the CSA consisted of forty-five representatives from
sectors including the Canadian government, corporations, academics,
consumers, and experts in information technology and security. The
CSA Model Code encompassed all eight principles given in the OECD
Guidelines and added two more core principles to the ranks: consent,
and an individual's ability to challenge compliance. Yet, due to the
creation of the EU Data Protection Directive during the same time
period, there was a growing call for more robust legislative regulations
to enable Canadian businesses to remain in compliance with data
collection regulations from nations within the European Union.[107]

This need eventually led to the passage of Canada's two most
important federal data and privacy laws: the Personal Information
Protection and Electronic Documents Act (PIPEDA) and the Privacy

---

104.　*Id.*
105.　Samuel E. Trosow et al., *The Internet of Things: Implications for Consumer Privacy Under Canadian Law* (Working Paper 2017), https://samtrosow.files.wordpress.com/2017/10/the-internet-of-things-implications-for-consumer-privacy-under-canadian-law.pdf.
106.　*Id.*
107.　*Id.*

Act.[108] The Canadian federal law governing privacy of a citizen's personal data, PIPEDA, was enacted in 2000. PIPEDA set guidelines and rules on the collection of personal data by private companies.[109] In addition, some provinces in Canada adopted legislation regarding privacy and cybersecurity that supersede this federal rule.[110]

§ 10:8.2 Territorial Legislation in the Provinces

The privacy laws of Canada are organized around either the public or private sector.[111] The public sector refers to public bodies or organizations that are owned and operated by the federal or provincial governments. The private sector includes organizations that are privately owned such as corporations, partnerships, trade unions, and non-profit organizations.[112] These sector designations are significant because, in addition to federal PIPEDA legislation, there are some Canadian provinces that have enacted separate privacy laws that supersede the federal regulation. This is permissible so long as the provincial laws are substantially similar to PIPEDA, much like legislation that exists in individual states within the United States.[113] For example, three provinces, including Alberta, British Columbia, and Quebec, created private sector privacy legislation that applies to their individual provinces. Furthermore, each province developed its own laws regarding personal health information and public sector privacy.[114]

§ 10:8.3 Personal Information Protection and Electronic Documents Act (PIPEDA)

The legal framework of the PIPEDA applies in the IoT context for private sector organizations only.[115] This federal legislation sets rules

---

108. Adam Kardash & Patricia Kosseim, *Canada, in* THE INT'L COMPARATIVE LEGAL GUIDE TO: DATA PROT. 2018 54, 54–64 (Glob. Legal Grp. Ltd., 5th ed. 2018).
109. Trosow et al., *supra* note 105, at 2.
110. Wendy J. Wagner & Christopher Oates, *Privacy in Canada: Overview*, THOMSON REUTERS PRACTICAL LAW: COUNTRY Q&A (July 1, 2018), https://ca.practicallaw.thomsonreuters.com/3-589-4795/.
111. Kardash & Kosseim, *supra* note 108, at 54–64.
112. *Id.*
113. Amy Talbott, *Privacy Laws: How the US, EU and Others Protect IoT Data (or Don't): Rules About Data Security Can Vary Widely. Here's a Look at Laws in Place in the US, the EU, Canada, APAC, and More*, ZDNET (Mar. 7, 2016), www.zdnet.com/article/privacy-laws-how-the-us-eu-and-others-protect-iot-data-or-dont/.
114. *Id.*
115. Lyndsay Wasser et al., *Cybersecurity and the Internet of Things*, 13 CAN. PRIVACY L. REV. 47, 48 (May 2016).

for companies regarding: limitations on the collection, use, and storage of personal data; the creation of a privacy management program;
and the provision of systems in which user complaints can be filed.[116]
The most important statutory obligations for private sector organizations under PIPEDA include: the protection of personal information from loss or theft; the level of safeguards afforded based on the
sensitivity of the information; the methods of protection including
physical, organizational, and technological measures; and the responsibility of organizations to ensure compliance to the regulations from
third party processors.[117]

Under PIPEDA, the term "personally identifiable" information is
defined broadly to include any "information about an identifiable individual."[118] The Ontario Court of Appeals found that personal information "has an elastic definition and should be interpreted accord-
ingly."[119] Furthermore, due to the interconnectivity of IoT devices, the
collection of a detailed range of information creates a "profile of the
individual's lifestyle, habits, health, etc. which would undoubtedly
qualify as personal information."[120] Because of the interconnectivity of IoT technology, the Federal Privacy Commissioner has stated
that, in the context of IoT, individual pieces of data should not be
considered in isolation but instead by what the data communicates
when paired with other interconnected devices.[121] Once an organization meets the threshold for whether the information they collect is
personally identifiable, the PIPEDA requires compliance with the ten
obligations that correspond to those set by the CSA in the 1990s.[122]

One of the most important aspects of PIPEDA is the consent
requirement that precedes the collection of sensitive personal data.
To determine the level of consent needed from individuals and the
level of safeguards for the data protection, a determination of the
information's degree of sensitivity must be made. The designation
of sensitive verses non-sensitive data has been criticized in the IoT
context given the dynamic nature of IoT devices. Consent requires
that individuals also have knowledge about the type of information
collected, how that information is used, and who has access to the
collected information. These consent considerations must be defined
in the Privacy Policy and Terms of Service agreement and be easy for
individuals to locate.[123]

---

116.   Talbott, *supra* note 113.
117.   Wasser, *supra* note 115, at 24.
118.   Trosow et al., *supra* note 105, at 24.
119.   Wasser, *supra* note 115, at 48.
120.   *Id.*
121.   *Id.*
122.   Trosow et al., *supra* note 105, at 27.
123.   *Id.*

Although the PIPEDA was deemed satisfactory under the requirements of the EU's Directive prior to the enactment of the GDPR,
PIPEDA now falls short under the GDPR in the EU.[124] The PIPEDA
receives only "partial" adequacy under the GDPR standards as some
of the directives do not meet the high bar created by the GDPR. One
such directive relates to obtaining consent to the gathering of personal information and stands as a notable difference between the
PIPEDA and the GDPR.[125]

Under PIPEDA, consent is generally necessary in order to gain
permission to collect, use, and disclose personal information of
an individual, but that consent can be either express or implied.[126]
Under the GDPR, consent must be specific, and there should be an
informed indication of permission either through a statement or by
clear affirmative action which shows an unambiguous agreement
to the processing of an individual's personal data. Hence, under the
GDPR, there is no such concept as implied consent, consent must
be freely given, and the consent cannot be written into a contract.[127]
Additionally, whereas PIPEDA does not enumerate a minimum age
for consent, the GDPR sets the minimum age for consent at sixteen
years, with the option that countries may seek to lower that age to
thirteen years.

Other rights granted to individuals that vary between the PIPEDA
and GDPR include provisions in the GDPR allowing for data portability. These provisions enable individuals to receive their stored
personal data from one data controller in a machine-readable format
in order to be able to send that data to another data controller.[128] The
PIPEDA does not include this right.[129] Another significant difference
lies in the robust provision under the GDPR to the right to be forgotten, which, under the GDPR, includes: (1) the right for individuals
to require that companies erase their personal information if that
information is no longer necessary for the purposes for which it was
collected, (2) the right to compel data erasure if consent is withdrawn,
or (3) in cases where the data was made public, such as through social
media, the controller must inform others who received the information

---

124.   Timothy M. Banks, *GDPR Matchup: Canada's Personal Information
         Protection and Electronic Documents Act*, IAPP (May 2, 2017), https://
         iapp.org/news/a/matchup-canadas-pipeda-and-the-gdpr/.
125.   *Id.*
126.   Sebastien A. Gittens et al., *Understanding the GDPR: A Comparison
         Between the GDPR, PIPEDA and PIPA*, BENNETT JONES BLOG (May 14,
         2018), www.bennettjones.com/en/BloBl-Section/Understanding-the-GDPR;
         see also Banks, *supra* note 124.
127.   Banks, *supra* note 124.
128.   *Id.*
129.   Gittens, *supra* note 126.

that consent was withdrawn.[130] Although the PIPEDA does contain the basic right for an individual's data to be forgotten, this right is limited to the first two situations mentioned previously and companies are therefore not required to contact other companies to which it disclosed the information or data.[131]

The GDPR also includes robust individual rights allowing: "the right to restriction of processing (e.g. if the accuracy of the personal data is contested by the individual)[ ] and the right not to be subject to automated decision-making," which are not present in PIPEDA.[132] Lastly, PIPEDA also falls short of complete protection over the personal information gathered by the majority of businesses for their employees. PIPEDA only regulates the collection, use, and disclosure of employee information from federally regulated employers such as airlines, banks, and shipping companies, while the majority of employers in the Canadian economy remain regulated only by legislation in their provinces.[133] Alternatively, the GDPR regulates employee data and allows the EU member countries to impose even stricter laws addressing employee data.[134]

Until recently, one of the most significant differences between the PIPEDA and the GDPR was the mandatory data breach reporting. The GDPR contains strict provisions which prohibit undue delay in reporting data breaches to supervisory authorities when the breach could lead to a risk to the rights and freedoms of natural persons or of the said individual.[135] Canada's PIPEDA, until recently, did not require this mandatory data breach reporting.[136] These provisions recently changed through the Digital Privacy Act of 2015, which sought to improve regulations regarding the management and use of personal data to bring the PIPEDA into closer alignment with the GDPR.[137]

The regulations, passed both under the 2015 Act and updated subsequently in September of 2017, did not come into immediate effect, but instead were set to take effect on November 1, 2018.[138] These updated mandatory reporting regulations require any Canadian company, or any company that does business in Canada, to notify both

---

130.   Banks, *supra* note 124.
131.   *Id.*
132.   Gittens, *supra* note 126.
133.   Banks, *supra* note 124.
134.   *Id.*
135.   Gittens, *supra* note 126.
136.   Banks, *supra* note 124.
137.   *Id.*; *see also* Chris Willsher, *Mandatory Breach Reporting Takes Effect November 2018*, ODX PIPEDA Regulation Updates (Oct. 9, 2018), https://codx.ca/pipeda-regulation-updates/.
138.   Willsher, *supra* note 137.

the Privacy Commissioner and any affected individuals when the company experiences a breach that can reasonably be considered as resulting in significant harm.[139] Significant harm is defined in the Act as "bodily harm, humiliation, damage to reputation or relationships, loss of employment, business or professional opportunities, financial loss, identity theft, negative effects on the credit record and damage to or loss of property."[140]

§ 10:8.4   The Privacy Act

The Canadian Privacy Act is a law that governs the Canadian federal government's interaction with personal information of residents within Canada. The Privacy Act governs all personal information that the federal government collects, stores, and uses and regulates the information that the Canadian government can disclose about individuals or federal employees. The Act covers an individual's right to access their personal information that the federal government has collected in the course of providing services such as retirement pensions, employment insurance, border security, federal public safety and policing, or tax collection. "Personal information" is defined as "information about an identifiable individual that is recorded in any form."[141]

The Privacy Act further assures that personal information shall not be "collected by a government institution unless it relates directly to an operating program or activity of the institution." When the government collects this personal information about an individual, the government must inform the individual about the purpose for collection. Government institutions must take reasonable steps to ensure that personal information is accurate, up-to-date, and complete. Under the Privacy Act, individuals will be given access to any personal information upon request contained in a personal information bank or under the control of a government institution. Individuals may then request the correction of errors in the personal information or notification to whom the information has been disclosed within two years prior to the request.[142]

§ 10:9   Latin America

As Internet accessibility and the development of IoT technologies in Latin America increases, many Latin American countries

---

139.   *Id.*
140.   Digital Privacy Act, S.C. 2015, c 32 (Can.); *see also* Willsher, *supra* note 137.
141.   Privacy Act, R.S.C. 1985, c. P.21 (Can.).
142.   *Id.*

are showing an interest in cybersecurity and technology issues.[143] Approximately 50% of Latin American consumers are now connected to the Internet, placing the IoT industry in a good position for growth in this region.[144] Consumers in Brazil, Argentina, Chile, and Mexico are all beginning to adopt the IoT more widely.[145] Additionally, countries like Mexico and Brazil lead Latin America in the development of financial institutions technology ("Fintech").[146]

As of 2018, both Brazil and Mexico were among the twenty largest economies in the world, with Brazil ranking eighth and Mexico fifteenth largest.[147] Yet, despite the growth of the markets in these countries, there is a general lack of effective data and cybersecurity regulation. Amongst Latin American countries in 2017, Brazil ranked first in cyber attacks against individuals and infrastructure, while Mexico ranked second.[148] In response, most Latin American countries are following the lead of the EU and the GDPR.[149]

§ 10:9.1   Mexico

Although Mexico has begun to take steps to increase data protection, much work is required to keep pace with the increased growth in the Internet and IoT users. Currently, Mexican consumers maintain an average of two connected devices per capita in comparison to the ten connected devices per person in their neighboring North American countries.[150] But, due to increased investment in the IoT and other technologies, this rate of connectivity is expected to grow exponentially and is predicted to reach 100 million connected devices by the year 2022.[151] Mexico's large economy and the increase in consumer connectivity will inevitably make the country a more vulnerable target for cyber attacks and cybercrime in both the private and public sectors of Mexican society.[152]

---

143.   *Third Annual Latin America Privacy & Cybersecurity Symposium*, JONES DAY FIRM (Apr. 25–26, 2018), www.jonesday.com/third-annual-latin-america-privacy-cybersecurity-symposium-04-25-2018/.

144.   Maria Paz Gillet, *Is Latin America Ready for an IoT Boom?*, IOT EVOLUTION (Jan. 19, 2018), www.iotevolutionworld.com/iot/articles/436542-lat-america-ready-an-iot-boom.htm.

145.   *Id.*

146.   *Symposium, supra* note 143.

147.   Prableen Bajpai, *The World's Top 20 Economies*, INVESTOPEDIA (Aug. 16, 2018), www.investopedia.com/insights/worlds-top-economies/.

148.   *See* LUISA PARRAGUEZ KOBEK, THE STATE OF CYBERSECURITY IN MEXICO: AN OVERVIEW 6 (Wilson Ctr.: Mex. Inst. 2017).

149.   *Symposium, supra* note 143.

150.   Gillet, *supra* note 144.

151.   *Id.*

152.   KOBEK, *supra* note 148, at 15.

Although legislation regarding privacy and data protection in both the public and private sectors of Mexico address some of these risks, specific legislation regarding the enforcement of cybercrimes is still lacking in regard to the IoT and other digital platforms.[153] Mexico still needs more specific legislation to protect data collected from IoT devices.[154] The current Mexican regulations that govern privacy and data protection for individuals are addressed separately through legislation specific to private sector entities versus that required of public sector entities, much like the Canadian system.[155]

[A] Private Sector—Data Protection Laws

The protection of personal data information is recognized as a fundamental right under the Mexican Constitution.[156] The right to privacy is specifically enumerated in Article 16 of the Mexican Constitution, which states that "[n]o one shall be molested in his person, family, domicile, papers, or possessions except by virtue of a written order of the competent authority stating the legal grounds and justification for the action taken."[157] Later in 2009, a constitutional amendment was approved to address data protection rights stating:

> All people have the right to enjoy protection on his personal data, and to access, correct and cancel such data. All people have the right to oppose the disclosure of his data, according to the law. The law shall establish exceptions to the criteria that rule the handling of data, due to national security reasons, law and order, public security, public health, or protection of third party's rights.[158]

Soon after the approval of the amendment approving data protection of personal information as a fundamental right under the Constitution, Mexico passed the Federal Law of Protection of Personal Data held by Private Parties ("Private Data Protection Law") of 2010.[159] The Private Data Protection Law is an omnibus data protection law

---

153. *Id.* at 17.
154. *Id.* at 15.
155. Begoña Cancino et al., *Data Protection in Mexico: Overview,* THOMSON REUTERS PRACTICAL LAW: COUNTRY Q&A (July 1, 2018).
156. *Id.*
157. Constitución Política de los Estados Unidos Mexicanos, CPEUM, Diario Oficial de la Federación [DOF] 05-02-1917, últimas reformas DOF 10-02-2014 (Mex.), www.constituteproject.org/constitution/Mexico_2015.pdf?lang=en.
158. *Id.*
159. Cesar G. Cruz Ayala et al., *Mexico,* THE PRIVACY, DATA PROTECTION AND CYBERSECURITY LAW REVIEW (4th ed., Dec. 2017), https://thelawreviews.co.uk/edition/the-privacy-data-protection-and-cybersecurity-law-reveiw-edition-4/1151292/mexico.

governing the principles and minimum standards expected of private entities such as companies and individuals who collect, use, store, protect, or manage personal data of an individual.[160] This law can be supplemented by sectoral laws and self-imposed regulatory schemes as the legislation recognizes that standards may be different depending upon the industry or sector for which they are developed.

The executive branch of the Mexican government subsequently issued the Regulations of the Private Data Protection Law ("Regulations") in 2011 in order to clarify the scope of the principles outlined in the Private Data Protection Law. The Regulations set forth guidelines for data controllers regarding the level of protections required of private information and guidelines regarding the proceedings and notices to be given to individuals in the event of a breach of information.[161] The Private Data Protection Law and its corresponding regulations are modeled after the European Directive 95/46/EC[162] of the European Parliament of 1995, and therefore require data controllers to protect personal data, obtain the proper consent before processing data, and give notice of informational breaches.[163]

A further amendment to the Mexican Constitution in 2014 approved the formation of an autonomous agency to take charge of the enforcement of the Private Data Protection Law. The former agency that originally acted in a semi-autonomous manner to enforce the provisions of data security, the Federal Institute for Access to Information and Protection of Data, controversially amended its internal regulations and assumed the role of the new autonomous entity. In doing so, the agency adopted a new name: The National Institute of Transparency, Access to Information, and Protection of Personal Data (INAI). The INAI promotes individuals' rights to protection of data as well as supervises and enforces the data protection laws in respect to the private sector. The INAI can also resolve claims and impose fines and penalties.[164]

[B]   Public Sector—Government Data Protection Law

Despite broad policy implications afforded to the right of data privacy under Mexico's Constitution, the Mexican government has not

---

160.   *Id.; see also* Cancino, *supra* note 155.

161.   *Id.*

162.   The prior EU Data Protection Directive (EU Directive 95/46/EC) operated in the EU to protect the privacy of personal data collected about EU citizens, especially in regard to the processing, usage, or exchange of personal information. EU Directive 95/46/EC was superseded in April 2016 by the General Data Protection Regulation (GDPR), which strengthens these protections.

163.   Cruz Ayala, *supra* note 159; *see also* Cancino, *supra* note 155.

164.   *Id.*

been held to the same standards of data protection as private entities until relatively recently.[165] The first formal effort to address personal data protection in Mexico was under the Federal Law for Transparency and Access to Public Governmental Information Act of 2002.[166] This law aimed to secure individuals' right to access any personal information that government bodies held and set out standards for the protection of this information. Until the passage of the General Law for the Protection of Personal Data in Possession of Governmental Entities ("Governmental Data Protection Law") in January of 2017, Mexican citizens were not able to assert their rights to personal data gathered by a government organization or any public official or representative of the federal government of Mexico.[167]

This legislation established a legal framework to regulate the policies and procedures pertaining to personal data collection and protection for data controllers or "regulated subjects" under the law. "Regulated subjects" include government agencies or entities in the executive, legislative, and judicial branches of the Mexican government, as well as any political party or institution that operates using public funds at the federal, state, and municipal levels.[168] The Governmental Data Protection Law also allows individuals in Mexico the right to enforce their "ARCO Rights"—the right to access, rectify, cancel, and oppose—the processing of data controlled by these government entities.[169]

In the event that personal data protection has been breached, regulated subjects must investigate the causes of the breach and implement work plans to rectify security issues. The regulated subjects must also provide notification in the case of a significant breach to the moral or financial rights of individuals. Prompt notification must be made to the relevant individuals whose information was compromised, to the INAI, and to any other relevant parties.[170]

[C] National Cybersecurity Program

Mexico has a tremendous impetus to address its cybersecurity regulations due to the growth of its economy and its standing within

---

165. Mauricio F. Paez, Guillermo E. Larrea & Mónica Peña Islas, *Personal Data Held by Government Agencies Now Heavily Protected in Mexico*, Jones Day Firm (May 15, 2017), www.lexology.com/library/detail. aspx?g=1feb4952-5539-4f16-bd15-023f732202df.

166. Cruz Ayala, *supra* note 159.

167. *Id.*

168. *Id.; see also* Paez et al., *supra* note 165.

169. Paez et al., *supra* note 165.

170. *Id.*

Latin America.[171] Additionally, organized criminal groups operating within Mexico are involved in all types of criminal activity from extortion and kidnapping to identity theft, fraud, and human trafficking, and use digital media to manipulate and disseminate information.[172] Furthermore, the U.S. Drug Enforcement Administration (DEA) has identified drug trafficking organizations that "run like companies, with extensive production and distribution networks, intelligence apparatus and security systems, and they use social media to communicate and the Internet to post their activities."[173] Still further, in 2013, Mexican officials acknowledged that Mexico had been named "the world's number one distributor and second largest producer of child pornography" during the 2013 Conference on Combating Child and Adolescent Pornography held by the Mexican Senate.[174] The Conference confirmed that nearly 85,000 children in Mexico were exploited in the production of child pornography and that 1,330 websites were dedicated to dissemination of pornographic material regarding minors.[175] Still, Mexico has not enacted specific cybersecurity legislation to address crimes regarding financial breaches, information security, and technology-related crimes.

Cybersecurity issues remain largely covered only by the Federal Criminal Code.[176] These provisions are then enforced by the Mexican Policia Federal ("Federal Police"), who remain the lead operational authority for investigating cybercrimes in Mexico.[177] Most investigations have been handled by the Federal Police through their Cyber Police and Scientific Division.[178] Mexico's Computer Emergency Response Team (CERT-MX) is also housed in the Scientific Division of the Federal Police.[179] CERT-MX helps to protect critical infrastructure, manage cyber-attack responses, investigate cybercrimes, and

---

171.   *See* LUISA PARRAGUEZ KOBEK, THE STATE OF CYBERSECURITY IN MEXICO: AN OVERVIEW 15 (Wilson Ctr.: Mex. Inst. 2017).

172.   *Id.* at 16.

173.   *Id.*

174.   *Id.* at 17 (citing senators during the Mexican "Foro Combate a la Pornografía de niñas, niños y adolescents" [Conference on Combating Child and Adolescent Pornography]); *see also* Marguerite Cawley, *Mexico Is World Leader in Child Pornography: Officials*, INSIGHT CRIME (Sept. 27, 2013), www.insightcrime.org/news/brief/mexico-is-world-leader-in-child-pornography/.

175.   *Id.*

176.   KOBEK, *supra* note 171, at 17.

177.   *Id.; see also Mexico*, in Organization of American States, *Latin America and Cybersecurity Trends Inter-American* (2014), www.sites.oas.org/cyber/Documents/2014%20%20OAS%20Symantec%20Cyber%20Security%20Report.pdf.

178.   *Mexico, supra* note 177; *see also* KOBEK, *supra* note 171, at 9.

179.   KOBEK, *supra* note 171, at 6.

respond to other digital threats within Mexico.[180] CERT-MX also gathers ideas from experts in government, commercial, and academic sectors to better implement Mexico's preparation and response protocols in the case of cyber attacks.[181]

In 2012, the Mexican government created the Specialized Information Security Committee (CESI) which was given the task of developing the National Strategy for Information Security.[182] This National Cybersecurity Strategy (ENCS) was released in 2017 and set guiding principles for cybersecurity. The ENCS also identified the private organizations, public organizations, and civil society components needed for collaboration on the implementation, monitoring, and evaluating of cybersecurity threats.[183] Based on the 2014–2018 National Security Program ("Program"), ENCS focuses on multidimensional security by implementing specific policies for cybersecurity to both protect Mexico's national interests and promote peace and stability in the region.[184] The main proponents of the Program include: (1) promoting actions for preventing cyber attacks; (2) strengthening initiatives to prevent attacks on federal executive sites; (3) maintaining compliance and procedures for response teams responding to federal executive cybersecurity attacks; (4) improving technology infrastructure; and (5) establishing opportunities for international cooperation against cyber attacks.[185] The Program also establishes a series of measures that the Mexican government can take to identify potential national security attacks.[186]

Mexican government authorities are trying to develop collaborative relationships with other governments within both the region and the general international community regarding cybersecurity.[187] For example, Mexico is a member of the Forum of Incident Response and Security Teams (FIRST)—a project representing seventy-eight countries—and participates in four teams within FIRST as well as the Organization of American States (OAS).[188] Furthermore, Mexico appears to be coming to terms with the need for increased compliance with international conventions in cybersecurity and data protection.

---

180. *Id.* at 6, 10.
181. *Id.* at 6.
182. INTER-AMERICAN DEVELOPMENT BANK, *Cybersecurity: Are We Ready in Latin America and the Caribbean?*, at 88 (2016), https://publications.iadb.org/en/cybersecurity-are-we-ready-latin-america-and-caribbean.
183. *Mexico, supra* note 177.
184. LUISA PARRAGUEZ KOBEK, THE STATE OF CYBERSECURITY IN MEXICO: AN OVERVIEW 15 (Wilson Ctr.: Mex. Inst. 2017).
185. *Id.* at 10–11.
186. *Id.* at 11.
187. *Mexico, supra* note 177, at 64–66.
188. KOBEK, *supra* note 184, at 6, 11; *see also Mexico, supra* note 177, at 64–66.

The Mexican government recently announced its adoption of the 1981 Strasbourg Convention for the Protection of Individuals with Regard to Automatic Processing of Personal Data ("Strasbourg Convention"). The Strasbourg Convention aims to protect individuals against abuses regarding the collection and processing of personal data.[189] The Strasbourg Convention also regulates supervisory authorities, "outlaw[ing] the processing of 'sensitive' data on a person's race, politics, health, religion, sexual life, criminal record, etc., in the absence of proper legal safeguards" and regulates the electronic movement of data among countries.[190] The signatory nations of the Strasbourg Convention also embrace the right of individuals to request any information stored about themselves and for that information to be corrected.[191]

Also, Mexico was invited in January 2007 to join the Council of Europe's Convention on Cyber-crime ("Budapest Convention"). While the country expressed interest in doing so, it has yet to actually sign on to the Convention due to difficulties in compliance with the Budapest Convention's provisions.[192] The Budapest Convention is the first multilateral treaty that specifically focuses on targeting cybercrime by increasing cooperation among signatory nations. It does this by pursuing more standardized criminal policies, laws, and procedural and investigatory techniques regarding transnational cybercrime.[193] The difficulties in achieving compliance with the Budapest Convention illustrate the substantial challenges Mexico will have in curtailing IoT-related crime.

§ 10:9.2   *Brazil*

[A]   The National Plan of the Internet of Things

Although Latin America has not been thought of as a trendsetter in IoT technology, Brazil has recently emerged as a leader in the region with its introduction of a national plan for IoT advancement and the robust investment made by Brazilian companies in IoT

---

189.   Convention for the Protection of Individuals with Regard to Automatic Processing of Personal Data, C.E.T.S. No. 108 (EU Jan. 28, 1981)8 [hereinafter *Strasbourg Convention*].

190.   *Mexico Acceded to the Convention for the Protection of Individuals with Regard to Automatic Processing of Personal Data (ETS No. 108) and Its Added Protocol (ETS No. 181)*, COUNCIL OF EUROPE NEWSROOM (June 28, 2018).

191.   *Id.*

192.   KOBEK, *supra* note 184, at 8.

193.   *Id.; see also* Convention on Cybercrime, C.E.T.S. No. 185 (EU Nov. 11, 2001) [hereinafter *Budapest Convention*].

development and research.[194] The government has encouraged private sector interest in IoT development through initiatives to support innovators, new partnerships, and institutes of higher learning focusing on these technologies. These strategies were put in place after an important study was launched in 2017, "The Internet of Things: An Action Plan for Brazil," which identified areas of expansion within the digital market.[195]

Following the study in October of 2017, the Brazilian government released a strategic plan called the National Plan of the Internet of Things ("IoT Plan").[196] The goal of this plan is to modernize the public and private sector through IoT innovations while allowing for the growth of new businesses and start-ups.[197] The IoT Plan sets forth strategies and policies to encourage companies, the government, and research institutions to accelerate the usage of IoT devices within Brazilian industries and services.[198]

The four principle areas set as priorities for investment include: agribusiness, the health sector, smart cities, and the industrial sector. These four areas were chosen due to the well-established companies currently operating in the space and the number of opportunities for more IoT development and innovation.[199] Within these four areas, the following improvements have been identified: (1) in healthcare, an increase in the efficiency and cost-optimization of hospital care, (2) in agribusiness, an increase in the efficiency of machinery and effective use of natural resources, (3) in smart cities, a prioritization of mobility, public safety, and utilities, and (4) in manufacturing, the improvement and focus on the development of new IoT products.[200] The IoT Plan stresses cooperation among agencies, companies, and government ministries to help encourage expansion of the IoT market in Brazil.[201] In order to best concentrate efforts in light of constraints on resources and investment, the plan establishes centers of expertise located in institutions that specialize in particular fields within IoT development, such as nanotechnology or connectivity.[202]

---

194. *Brazil Embraces the Digital Age with an Ambitious Internet of Things Strategy*, Urban Hub (Nov. 4, 2018), www.urban-hub.com/technology/brazil-embraces-the-digital-age-with-an-ambitious-internet-of-things-strategy/.

195. *Id.*

196. Fabricio Marques, *Brazil's Internet of Things*, Pesquisa FAPESP (Sept. 2017), https://revistapesquisa.fapesp.br/en/brazils-internet-of-things/.

197. Urban Hub, *supra* note 194.

198. Marques, *supra* note 196.

199. *Id.*

200. Urban Hub, *supra* note 194.

201. *Id.*

202. Marques, *supra* note 196.

[B]   The General Law of Data Protection (LGPD) of 2018

On August 20, 2018, Brazil enacted the General Law of Data Protection (LGPD), which was developed based largely upon the EU's GDPR.[203] This legislation became effective in February 2020 in order to afford any companies or entities that handle personal data time to put systems in place for complying with the regulations.[204] The scope of the LGPD covers the private and public sectors, as well as individuals who process personal data, so long as that information is processed or collected in Brazil or collected in order to offer goods or services in Brazil.[205] This means that the reach of the legislation covers not only all Brazilian companies that operate within its borders, but any company that offers or provides goods or services to individuals in Brazil, even if located outside of the country's borders. The only exceptions to these requirements are when individuals or entities process data only for personal use, artistic or journalistic purposes, academic usage, or for national security reasons.

The LGPD defines the term "data" broadly as: "information regarding an identified or identifiable natural person." This expansive language allows broad regulatory enforcement over any information that could potentially be used to identify an individual, despite a lack of overt or facially recognizable information. Furthermore, the LGPD provides even stronger protections for the subset of "[s]ensitive data [which includes] personal data related to one's racial or ethnic origin, religious and political views, union, religious, philosophical or political affiliations, health, sexual, biometric or genetic data."[206] The LGPD, like the GDPR, includes: "cross-border jurisdiction, . . . [the] right to be forgotten, [ ] the right to access data; requirement[s] to notify data breaches; and the requirement to appoint data protection officers, under certain conditions."[207] The LGPD also uses a similar "risk approach, like GDPR [which] talks about lawfulness, fairness,

---

203.   *The Brazilian Data Protection Law—LGPD*, DEBEVOISE UPDATE (Aug. 20, 2018), www.debevoise.com/insights/publications/2018/08/the-brazilian-data-protection-law-lgpd.

204.   Bruno Bioni et al., *GDPR Matchup: Brazil's General Data Protection Law*, IAPP (Oct. 4, 2018), https://iapp.org/news/a/gdpr-matchup-brazils-general-data-protection-law/; *see also* Michael Baxter, *Brazil's General Data Protection Law Isn't Quite GDPR*, GDPR REPORT (Aug. 21, 2018), https://gdpr.report/news/2018/08/21/brazils-general-data-protection-law-isnt-quite-gdpr/.

205.   Decreto No. 13,709, de 14 de agosto de 2018, Diário Oficial da União [D.O.U.] de 14.8.2018 (Braz.) at art. 5 [hereinafter LGPD].

206.   *Id.*

207.   Baxter, *supra* note 204.

accountability, non-discrimination, purpose limitation, data minimisation [*sic*] and transparency on the use of personal data."[208]

Although the LGPD was inspired by the regulatory structures and purposes of GDPR, and therefore has many similarities, there are also several differences. One difference is that the Brazilian LGPD has potentially lower fines for breaches, due to the fact that the penalties are calculated only on Brazilian revenue, not a data processor's global revenue as required by the GDPR.[209] The LGPD also imposes a nebulous deadline on data controllers, requiring them to inform authorities and individuals about any data breaches within "a reasonable time period." This differs from the GDPR, which specifies the notification must be made within seventy-two hours of discovery of the breach.[210] The LGPD imposes shorter deadlines by which data controllers must comply with requests from individuals, requiring responses within fifteen days of a request, versus thirty days under the GDPR.[211] The Brazilian LGPD also includes a broader, more robust right that individuals may delete personal data under their right to be forgotten.[212]

During the bill's passage, Brazil's President, Michel Temer, exercised his line-item veto power to strike several key sections regarding enforcement of the LGPD.[213] One such veto involved a section of the legislation that would have allowed for sanctions including both partial or full suspension of data processor's permission to collect personal data when in violation of the LGPD.[214] Another of the vetoed sections established an independent agency, the National Data Protection Authority, as well as the National Council for the

---

208. *Id.*
209. DEBEVOISE UPDATE, *supra* note 203.
210. LGPD, art. 48, § 1; *see also* Baxter, *supra* note 204.
211. LGPD, art. 19.
212. *The Brazilian Data Protection Law—LGPD*, DEBEVOISE UPDATE (Aug. 20, 2018), www.debevoise.com/insights/publications/2018/08/the-brazilian-data-protection-law-lgpd.
213. *Id.; see also* Michael Baxter, *Brazil's General Data Protection Law Isn't Quite GDPR*, GDPR REPORT (Aug. 21, 2018), https://gdpr.report/news/2018/08/21/brazils-general-data-protection-law-isnt-quite-gdpr/.
214. DEBEVOISE UPDATE, *supra* note 212. The Brazilian president's veto affected the sanctioning of companies who violate the LGPD through complete or partial suspension of the company's activities related to data processing. These provisions were key enforcement mechanisms for the LGPD. *See Brazilian Personal Data Protection Act: Examining Its Impact on the Subjects of Personal Data, Companies in Charge of Personal Data Processing, and the Public Sector*, MEISTER SCORSIM ADVOCACIA (Apr. 9, 2018), www.meisterscorsim.com/brazilian-personal-data-protection-act-examining-its-impact-on-the-subjects-of-personal-data-companies-in-charge-of-personal-data-processing-and-the-public-sector/.

Protection of Personal Data and Privacy for enforcement of the bill.[215] Brazil's president vetoed this measure, claiming that the Brazilian congress cannot create agencies; instead, he vowed to establish the necessary entity to carry out the LGPD oversight as required through the executive branch.[216]

Until this specific agency is established through the Brazilian executive branch, it is unclear how the LGPD will be enforced.[217] This enforcement will be critical moving forward in order for Brazil to implement security and trust in the IoT field, especially as Brazil pushes to attain regional leadership in the area of technological advances. Although Brazil may not be able to seek a global position of leadership due to its lack of financial and human resources, Brazil could emerge as a model for developing countries, serving as a point of reference in how to improve efficiency, competitiveness, manufacturing capabilities and export of domestic products within the IoT field.[218]

§ 10:10   Conclusion

Two general regimes of data protection have emerged across the globe to address IoT security and privacy concerns. First, there are the countries that ascribe to the philosophy that the best method to achieve security goals is through minimal government regulation over IoT products, through incorporation of the principle of "Security by Design," and by close collaboration between industry, academia, and the government. This model seeks to entrust security concerns to the leadership of private sector companies, encouraging them to self-regulate IoT privacy concerns beginning with the design phase and manufacturing process. This philosophy most resembles the data protection regime embraced by the United States and Japan.

Second, other countries have adopted regulatory schemes more similar to the EU's GDPR. These countries—including EU nations, Canada, Australia, Mexico, and Brazil—opt for robust government regulation of the IoT industry, while still stressing intense collaboration between the private and public sectors in order to rapidly address security and privacy concerns in the IoT technology landscape. The countries following this model have focused on creating legislation, establishing legal frameworks and regulations for private and public

---

215.   Baxter, *supra* note 213; *see also* DEBEVOISE UPDATE, *supra* note 212.
216.   Baxter, *supra* note 213.
217.   DEBEVOISE UPDATE, *supra* note 212.
218.   Fabricio Marques, *Brazil's Internet of Things*, PESQUISA FAPESP (Sept. 2017), https://revistapesquisa.fapesp.br/en/brazils-internet-of-things/.

data controllers regarding the collection of personal data, requirements for notification in the case of data breaches, and the protection of individual rights to privacy, such as the right to be forgotten.

These differing methods to addressing data protection and privacy create great challenges for businesses and organizations operating within the global market. Companies must be aware of the regulations or requirements in the nations in which they do business. Furthermore, as new issues and weaknesses in data security arise, it is likely that the complexity of these different national data protection laws will continue to shift and change. In order to keep companies up-to-date with the constantly shifting landscape of data regulation, companies and organizations operating in the global market would be wise to retain specialized privacy and compliance officers, lawyers, and others who deal exclusively with foreign and international compliance of cybersecurity and data protection laws.

Index

(References are to sections unless otherwise indicated.)

A

B

C

E

F

J

L

R

S

T

Z